To Lady Mohini Kent Noon
from [illegible] Nepal
[illegible]eet
[illegible] UK)

GW01607143

MYSTICS & MIRACLES

SWAMI ANAND ARUN

Published by
Osho Tapoban

Osho Tasspoban is thankful to the following friends for their financial contribution towards the publication of the first edition of this book.

Swami Dhyan Rajesh
California, USA

Swami Bodhi Raghav
Osho Tapoban, KTM

Copyright © 2023 by Swami Anand Arun

First edition : April 14, 2023

Published by:

Osho Tapoban
Kathmandu, Nepal
Ph: +977- 9847807082(Viber/WhatsApp)
+977-1-5112012/13,
tapoban@wlink.com.np
www.tapoban.com

Proofreading - Sampada, Anand Saurav, Yog Pritam, Bodhi Sangeeta

Cover design - Aatmo Neerav

Cover Photo - Bodhi Chaya

Visual recording - Dhyan Sanjukta

Design by Swami Dhyan Yatri

ISBN: 978-9937-758-41-3

All rights reserved. No part of this publication may be reproduced, distributed, or transmitted in any form or by any means, including photocopying, recording, or other electronic or mechanical methods, without the prior written permission of the publisher, except in the case of brief quotations embodied in critical reviews and certain other noncommercial uses permitted by copyright law.

MRP ₹ 450.00 / Nrs 720.00

"DEDICATED AT THE LOTUS FEET OF MY GURU, WHOSE FOOTPRINTS GUIDE ME EVERYDAY."

ACKNOWLEDGEMENT

By the grace of my guru, from my very childhood I came across many mystics and have seen things happening around them which can only be called a miracle. I have shared these stories to my fellow travelers time and again. Neerav, Suvam, Aakash, Arhat, Raghav and Megha have helped me turn it into a form of a book and their dedicated effort has given shape to these stories. I have no words to thank Yatrijee for taking care of the design and publication.

Preface

This book is for seekers, seekers who will not be satisfied with anything but Truth. But what is Truth? After consciously seeking truth for more than five decades in this life, today I have come to an understanding that Truth is not limited to just what we see, what we hear and what we can touch. The expansion of truth is spread far beyond our perception and tangibility. Its vastness is humanly inconceivable, and one can only surrender to it in humility. And that is exactly how I would like you to approach this book, with great humility and an open heart.

Our world functions in a very interesting way. Anything you desire here will be fulfilled someday or the other. From my very childhood I was interested in mystics and aspired for their communion. Life gave me exactly that. Many mystics came into my life and guided me whenever there was a real need. My master Osho has been a shining star amongst this constellation of evolved beings. I call them my light in this stormy journey called life. In this book I write about these mystics and my experience with them. I carry a hope that maybe these stories will work as a steppingstone and inspire and provide strength to that tribe of individuals who, like me, are also seeking the mystical and are geared towards it. I want to tell them that it exists!

Today the human world is ruled by a general concept that for anything to be genuine, it needs to be supported by logic and rationale. To them my stories may seem unreal and false. I am ready for their criticism. But it is not for their approval that I write this book. I write

this book for those who are ready to wander beyond the boundaries of the five senses.

There are animals and birds who can see more than us; some have more hearing capacity than us humans; some can even foretell an upcoming calamity and run to safety before us. Their reality and perception of this world is different from ours but just because it is different and something we can't experience doesn't mean that it does not exist.

Spirituality is an experiential reality and not a debatable one. To experience it you have to take off your glasses of doubt and plunge into this pool of wonder and awe. Some people say that with the leap of science and materialism, the world has changed and mystical incidents have become myths of the past but I disagree with this. My life itself is witness of many such incidents that were beyond the comprehension of my mind.

I have come to know that whenever a seeker is in need and is ready and receptive these incidents still happen regardless of time and space and are happening even today and will keep happening in the future. I pray that may the chapters in this book become an inspiration for trust and pave an opening of boundless possibilities that are waiting for you.

Swami Anand Arun
Osho Tapoban, Kathmandu

TABLE OF CONTENTS

TABLE OF

CONTENTS

TABLE OF CONTENTS

PKG, the Mystic From the North Pole

I have been traveling to North America at least twice a year since 2007 to conduct meditation retreats and spread the word of my master, Osho. On each of these trips, if time permitted, I tried to visit new places to sow the seed of Osho in new ground, and also to quench my thirst to explore this beautiful planet.

In July 2015, on one such trip to America, after our scheduled meditation retreats were over, I and a few of our inmates of the Nirvana ashram in the USA decided to go to Alaska. Just the thought of that secluded land thrilled my heart. Once I was there, I found it pristine, silent and naturally meditative. I felt strongly that if I had the choice to live anywhere on Earth, it would be Alaska. It is more than half the size of India and has a population of just 731,000, and nearly half the people live in just one city, Anchorage. There are even villages where just two to four people live permanently, and there are more than fifty towns with a population of less than 100.

Alaska has vast, open and empty spaces, beautiful seashores, pristine sweet-water lakes, untouched forests and majestic snow-capped mountains. As I was traveling through this wonder of nature, I had a strong recall of PKG, a mystic who had told me he lived at the North Pole. I hadn't been in contact with him since 1980.

Mystics have been my greatest fascination ever since I was a teenager. I have never missed a chance to meet and have spiritual conversations with them. These meetings have not only fed my curious mind, but also helped me overcome difficult hurdles on my own journey. While each meeting has revealed some mysteries of the spiritual world, some of these meetings have been more mysterious than others.

It was 1975, and not even a year had passed since we had opened Asheesh Rajneesh Meditation Centre at my family home in Tahachal, Kathmandu. The meditations were conducted a room of 12ft by 16ft, which also doubled as my bedroom. There were only a few regular visitors to the center. Most of them I had met at the Osho book stall that I used to set up at New Road every evening.

One day, an Indian man in his thirties came to the stall. I don't remember his name, so let's call him Yugal. Yugal was an Osho sannyasin. He said he had come to Kathmandu to have a darshan of the Pashupatinath temple. In those days, it was very rare to meet a sannyasin, and the sweet and simple Yugal won my heart instantly, and we became friends. For the next few evenings, he came to the bookstall and helped me lay out the books, and also helped sell them. On one such evening, I invited him to Asheesh to have dinner with me.

He readily accepted my invitation, and we both left for Asheesh after closing the stall. We had dinner and chatted, and then he returned to his lodge in Sundhara.

After that day, Yugal became a regular at Asheesh, and our friendship deepened. Once he began to know my temperament and felt he could trust me, he revealed his story which was very mystical and thrilled me to my core.

Yugal was from Banaras, and he said that before he met Osho, he was being spiritually guided by PKG who was a professor at the Banaras Hindu University. Unfortunately, PKG had died in a car accident along with his girlfriend, Sarita, a few years earlier. What happened next was most interesting. PKG, after his death, contacted Yugal from the spirit world, and began guiding him on his spiritual path. I found that very surprising. According to Yugal, PKG had guided him to Osho. He had told Yugal that Osho was the greatest guru of this age, and he should go to him and become initiated as soon as possible.

So Yugal went to Pune and was initiated by Osho, just as his guru had instructed him.

I was fascinated by Yugal's story and had a strong desire to speak with PKG as well. I asked Yugal how it was that he contacted PKG, and if I could talk to him as well.

"Tonight, I will ask him whether he wants to talk to you or not. If he agrees, then tomorrow we can invoke him together," said Yugal with a spark in his innocent eyes.

Yugal then went to his lodge and invoked PKG's soul. At that time, a few students had become regulars at Asheesh. Among them were Rameshwor Rai Yadav and Rajendra Mahato who were Osho sannyasins, and both of them later went on to become ministers in the Nepali Cabinet several times. Back then, they were among a small group of sannyasins in Kathmandu. That night, we all were very eager to know whether PKG would agree to talk with us or not.

The next day, Yugal came early to Asheesh and cheerfully informed me, "PKG has said that he would love to talk with you as long as he is invoked at an Osho center, and there are no non-Osho sannyasins around."

The news excited me, and we began preparing for the invocation that evening. Yugal revealed to me the process by which the invocation was done, which was very strange. PKG had given Yugal a mantra which he had to write on a piece of paper. He then had to go outdoors and burn the piece of paper. Once the paper was burnt, PKG would come instantly and enter Yugal's body. Yugal also said he had to remove the Osho mala while performing this ritual, as souls couldn't come close to those wearing the mala, let alone enter their bodies.

That evening, a few of us sat clustered in my room at Asheesh and curiously watched Yugal perform his strange ritual. Yugal removed his mala and placed it on my bed. He then wrote the secret mantra his guru had given to him on a small piece of paper. After that, he went out to the garden, lit a match and burnt the paper, and placed it on the ground. As the fire consumed the paper, the smell of burnt paper wafted in the air. Yugal came back to the room and sat on a chair. Then suddenly he shuddered as if he'd received a minor electric shock. His face brightened and to our surprise, he started speaking in fine English. Yugal was a simple man with a humble background. His Hindi was basic, and he did not speak English at all.

"Hello, this is PKG. I know all of you understand Hindi, but I am speaking in English so that you all know that Yugal is not making this up," PKG said, using Yugal's voice.

"All of you are wearing the Osho mala, so it is very difficult for me to be here. Please go to the other side of the room so that I can be here comfortably," PKG instructed us.

The mala was given to us by Osho so he could work on us, and we had protection against evil souls. To come close to us or enter our bodies, even divine souls had to get permission from Osho himself. Although PKG was a soul of great height, he had difficulty being near us when we were wearing the mala. This increased my gratitude to Osho, who had kept us in such security from the unknown forces of this universe.

We all went to the other side of the small room and huddled together. The conversation that ensued was very interesting and what PKG said intrigued us immensely. I also felt very much in tune with PKG and fell in love with him during our first meeting.

"Is this an Osho ashram? I feel very comfortable here," he said.

I don't remember the detailed dialogue that followed, as forty-five years have passed since then, but I remember the gist perfectly. Among the many things that PKG talked about, what interested me most was what he said about Osho. We invoked PKG for a few evenings. His girlfriend, Sarita, would also come with him, and if he stayed for longer than he should, she would remind him it was time to leave.

PKG and Sarita shared great love, and even after their death, they were together. I had asked him where they lived, and he said, "We live at the North Pole with other high souls who want to continue their sadhana even after death. The North Pole has a lot of empty space, is quiet and nobody disturbs us there, and we can meditate freely."

I asked him how he knew that we were calling him?

"Oh, it's pretty simple," he said, "As soon as Yugal burns the paper with the mantra that I have given him, I can smell the burnt paper from the North Pole."

Perplexed by his answer, we looked at each other in awe, and were hungry for more mysterious information from this friendly soul.

PKG told us we were very privileged to be in the human body because we could attend Osho discourses just by buying a five-rupee ticket. In those days, the entry pass to the Pune ashram was Rs. 5.

"For those of us who are not in the physical body, it is impossible unless we reach the fifth body. I am not in the fifth body, so I don't have access to the Osho ashram, but Sarita is in her fifth body, so she can go there easily," he said honestly.

"Sarita goes into the hall at 8:00 every morning for the discourse, but I have to wait outside with thousands of advanced souls. Once the discourse is over, Sarita comes out and tells me what Osho said in his discourse," said PKG.

He revealed another interesting thing about Osho. "When Osho comes to the hall for his discourse, he does namaste looking towards the ceiling. This is because he is greeting hundreds of self-realized souls who are there to listen to him," he said.

"You must have heard that even Brahma used to come to listen to Buddha talk. Similarly, many divine souls come to listen to Osho."

The next time I was in Pune, I noticed Osho looking at the ceiling while he was doing his namaste, and realized what PKG was talking about.

Another thing that PKG said, which I couldn't believe then, was that the Osho movement would spread most widely in two countries. You have to remember that this was 1975 and the Pune ashram had just opened, and the distribution of Osho's books in the West had just started.

"The Osho movement will spread around the world, and Germany and Nepal will be the two countries in which it will spread the most," he said.

What he said seemed like fantasy to our ears. We could believe that Germany would embrace Osho, but we who were having difficulty selling even a few Osho books on the footpath, couldn't come to believe that Osho's message would spread in Nepal.

But what he said did come true in due course. Germany once had the largest number of Osho establishments. They had ninety-five centers in 1986, but almost all were eventually closed. But in Nepal, things have slowly progressed, and currently there are more than 100 centers.

Another thing PKG said, which is important, is that Osho works on his disciples during their sleep. For a master to work on his disciples, the disciples' minds should not come in between. This happens either during a state of trance, which is very rare, or during deep sleep which happens every night.

"Osho comes to Asheesh every night," said PKG. "I can feel his energy. And he doesn't come alone. Many other enlightened masters come along as well in chariots of light. The light is so strong that we can't handle it and need to run away. He touches your third eye every night to give you energy. So, try to be aware at night, you might feel him."

After this, I became more aware, and a few times I was aware enough to feel a hand touch my forehead. Once when I was half asleep, I felt something and caught a hand while somebody was giving me shaktipat. Along with these esoteric things, we also asked PKG mundane things. For example, Rameshworjee had lost his watch in his hostel. He asked PKG, who had stolen his watch and whether he would find it or not.

"A friend of yours has stolen your watch, and there is very little chance you will get it back. I will not say your friend's name because if you know his name, you guys will fight. And it is not allowed for me to say names in such cases," he said.

By the last day of our meetings, PKG and I had made a very strong bond of trust and friendliness. He was so kind to me that he even gave me the mantra he had given to Yugal and said I could contact him whenever I wanted. But he stressed that I had to take off the mala before invoking him. I still remember the mantra that PKG gave me, but I never invoked him on my own. The only other time I spoke with him was in 1980 when I met Yugal in Pune.

In that meeting, PKG revealed another esoteric secret which astonished me.

"I am happy to share with you that Sarita and I have become Osho sannyasins now, as Osho has started initiating souls in the spirit world as well. The only other master who did this before was Mahavir. No other master has initiated disciples in the astral world," he said.

PKG was delighted that he had also made spiritual progress, and after being initiated, he could now attend Osho discourses. He said that what Osho did was revolutionary because until then, sannyas was only possible in the physical body, but now souls without the body also could pursue their spiritual journey and need not wait to take the physical body to progress in meditation. And there are numerous advanced souls who have been initiated.

PKG also mentioned some very famous people who had left their bodies and become sannyasins in the spirit world. I cannot say their names as some of them are very well known and it would be very controversial.

PKG then said that Osho had instructed him not to talk too much with us, and he quickly left us. That was a short meeting although a very important one as PKG revealed a secret that even Osho had never spoken of. That was the last time I contacted PKG.

In one of my meetings with Osho, I asked him about PKG. He said that PKG was a genuine seeker, and whatever he said was authentic. I also asked him whether I should use the mantra that he had given me to invoke him, as PKG had said I could call him whenever I was in trouble and needed help.

"Why do you want to disturb him?" Osho asked. "I am here to guide you and protect you whenever you are in need. You just need to hold on to your mala and remember me, and I will be there. Don't use this mantra and disturb him unnecessarily. He is doing serious sadhana now."

I never contacted PKG from then on.

I had about six satsangs with PKG, five of them when I had just started my spiritual journey. I was very curious then and asked a lot of questions which he answered indiscriminately. Whatever I asked he answered and attended to my curiosity patiently, just as a wise elder treats the curiosity of little children. His answers not only satisfied my curiosity, but also helped me gain direction in my spiritual life.

While traveling in Alaska, which was the closest I have been to the North Pole, I wondered whether PKG still lived there, or after his initiation by Osho, had moved to another place. But feeling the deep, secluded silence of the northernmost part of the planet, I realized why PKG had chosen to live there.

I dream of visiting Alaska again and again, and while writing these lines, I feel the thrill of that secluded land.

Ghosts in Dowry

My curiosity about the otherworld has taken me to many yogis and saints, but sometimes I have encountered people who were playing with spirits. Although at that time I was taking it just as entertainment, now I know the permanent harms it could have brought me.

I was a twenty-year-old college student studying in Muzaffarpur in Bihar, India. I and my happy-go-lucky Punjabi classmate, Trilochan Singh, were always on the lookout for anyone strange in the area. One day, Trilochan told me about a man with miraculous powers, and he was ecstatic that he had discovered such a baba.

"You won't believe me, but I have come to know of someone who is out of this world!" he exclaimed, his eyes bright with excitement.

"What makes him so special?" I asked, trying to get more information on Trilochan's new discovery.

"Well, no-one knows his real name, but they call him Basuliya Baba. And you won't believe this, but he can get you whatever you want from wherever," he said.

He explained further that if you wanted some sweets or fruits from a particular shop anywhere in India, you just had to give him the money, and your order would appear in his lap within a few minutes.

"That is out of this world!" I said, finding it difficult to believe what he was saying.

I had heard of Tantrikas and black magicians who could make things appear and disappear at will, but I had never had a first-hand experience of such a person. We decided to go to his house the next day. There was no reason to delay meeting such a mysterious man. That night, I could hardly sleep as I was super anxious about meeting Basuliya Baba. The next day, as soon as classes were over, we left for his house. Trilochan had got the directions to his house, which was a little distance away from the bustle of the town, on the bank of the Gandak River.

As we walked towards his house, we were high with excitement and were discussing what we should order from him. After tossing around a few ideas on what we wanted, we settled on peda from Baidyanath Dham. The peda, or sweets made from condensed milk and sugar, were available throughout India, but those from Baidyanath Dham were special and widely known. They had a unique taste that couldn't be replicated by halwais (sweets-makers) from other places.

Once we came close to the bank of the Gandak River, my

excitement only increased. Trilochan pointed to a small but beautiful house on the bank of the river. We rushed towards it.

When we entered the house, we saw a simple but dignified man sitting on a couch. We figured he was Basuliya Baba. Two young boys sat close by.

We introduced ourselves and after some awkward small talk, Basuliya Baba asked us why we were there. We told him we had heard he could materialize things from far away.

"So what do you want?" he said.

As planned, we asked him if he could get us a kilo of peda from Baidyanath Dham. He said, "Of course."

We handed him the amount it cost for a kilo of peda. He held the money in his hand and started talking to us. He made small talk for around ten minutes and suddenly a packet of peda dropped in his lap along with the receipt from the shop where it was bought.

We were shocked out of our wits. It was real after all! Baba handed the packet of peda to us. We held it in disbelief. Our hands were shaking as we opened the packet, the contents still smelling fresh. We shared the peda with Baba and the two boys who were his sons.

As we ate the sweets, Trilochan and I stared at each other in disbelief. The peda tasted divine, exactly like those we had eaten at Baidyanath Dham. But beyond the taste, we were sweating with excitement at what had just happened. We offered a portion of the remaining peda to Baba and his sons, and left their house stunned in disbelief.

After that, we became weekly visitors at Basuliya Baba's. As soon as we had some money we would go to Baba's and ask him to materialize delicacies from distant cities and towns. Sometimes we asked for Madrasi mangoes, and other times, sweets from Mathura. Once I asked for Gillette shaving blades that were only available in Nepal but not in India in those days. They had to be smuggled. Baba said that he could get me a few packets of the blades but he was not allowed to do illegal things, and told us to ask instead for things that were legally available.

As we became friends with Basuliya Baba, I ventured to ask him how he managed to perform such a miracle. Basuliya Baba did no other work; he made his living by materializing people's wishes, and in return they would give him a part of what they ordered as well as a little extra money in gratitude for his service. He would avoid such questions as it was his trade secret, but it is my nature to become close with people I like. Once his heart opened to me, he slowly revealed his secret but told me not to share it with anyone. He was in his forties when I met him, so most probably he has left his body by now. That is why I can tell his story to you now.

He said that as a teenager he couldn't fit in with his family, and was more interested in the mysterious than in worldly affairs, so in the 1940s, he left home and went to Karu which lies in Kamakhya, Assam, as he had heard there were many tantric siddhas in that area. He lived near the famous tantric temple of Kamakhya, and came to see that the tantrikas there indeed lived a very different kind of life. Kamakhya is the place where there are many men and women who have preta siddhi, which means they have acquired psychic powers to control and use spirits for their own purpose.

At Kamakhya, he met an elderly Bengali woman who was adept in preta siddhi. He then lived in her house and fell in love with her daughter. They got married, and as a dowry, his mother-in-law, who had many spirits in her control, gave him four to help him for whatever he needed. The four spirits were now in his domain and had to help him in any way possible.

Basuliya Baba then returned to Muzaffarpur with his wife and four spirit souls.

By the time we met him, he had only two spirits remaining

with him. He told us that two had run away, and one was becoming increasingly undisciplined. Sometimes the spirit would obey him, and other times he would not. Only one out of the four was still reliable, and he was the one that would perform duties such as fetching our peda from Baidyanath Dham. Basuliya Baba told us that he will have to pay a great penance in the coming Dussehra (major religious festival) to tame his unruly preta (spirit).

Control over the pretas was not his only power. He had learnt many other siddhis while he was at Kamakhya. One of those siddhis is what gave him the name Basuliya Baba. The bansuri, or Indian flute, is a very common musical instrument in India, but Baba used it in a very unique way.

Baba's wife was a medical student in Darbhanga Medical College, and to communicate, they used a bansuri and a sankha, a conch shell. Baba would talk to his bansuri and his wife would hear it on her sankha, just like we use mobile phones these days. This was in the 1960s, when even landline phones were very rare in India. As he could use his bansuri as a telephone, people started calling him Basulia Baba.

Baba had a hard time controlling his spirits as they were lower souls and had demands of their own. He had to keep them under control with his own mantra sadhana. But when they would stop obeying him, he would turn to his wife for help, as she seemed to have more control over them. The spirits obeyed his wife more often than they obeyed him, as they previously belonged to her mother.

Tantrikas capture spirits very soon after the bodies die. They live in cremation ghats or in burial grounds, and as soon as somebody dies, the spirits are in a weak and confused state. They get captured, and for years they have to serve their master until they are finally freed. The master can transfer the ownership of the spirit to another person as long as they know the mantra and techniques that control them.

Baba had told me that his spirit could fetch him things that weighed up to 45kg. He said that once they were on a car journey, when they got a flat tire. He told his preta to go and get it fixed. The job was done within half an hour, although there was no tire repair shop in the area.

Me and my friend, Trilochan, were always in the mood to fool around. Trilochan told me he had read in the Filmfare magazine that the famous Bollywood actress, Saira Bano, weighed only 45kg, and that we should ask Baba to fetch her. Just in jest we asked Baba if he could fetch the actress for us. Although he got the joke, Baba told us that we were testing his limits; he scolded us and chased us out of his house.

My friend once asked if he could fetch the question papers of our upcoming exam. But Baba again reminded us that his pretas were bound to perform only legal things, and illegal things would not be delivered.

Apart from his siddhis, Basulia Baba was a simple and good-hearted man. He helped a lot of people acquire things which were otherwise not in their reach.

Being young and curious, we wanted to know exactly how the preta fetched the goods, so we decided to do something in order to know more about the process. Trilochan's family owned a hotel called the Alankar Hotel. They also had a restaurant and a confectionery shop in the hotel. His brother ran the hotel. So we decided to order 1kg 30 grams of laddu (a spherical sweet made from flour, fat and sugar) from his brother's stall. That was an unusual weight, and we were sure nobody else would order laddu by that weight. We told Trilochan's brother to become very aware that day, and if someone asks for 1kg 30 grams of laddu, then grab hold of that person.

We then went to Basulia Baba and told him that we wanted to order 1 kg 30 grams of laddu from Alankar Hotel.

"Why such an odd weight?" he asked.

We lied to him that it was just our wish and there was no particular reason for it.

He took the money in his hand and said, "As you wish."

At Alankar Hotel, there was a big rush and Trilochan's brother had forgotten what we had told him. But when somebody came and asked for 1kg 30 grams of laddu, he suddenly remembered, and in shock, stared at the person who asked, before attempting to catch hold of him. Trilochan's brother later said that a well-built man with a dark complexion had asked for the laddu, but as soon as he looked at him, the man realized something fishy was going on, and suddenly disappeared in the crowd without buying the laddus.

We were waiting very impatiently at Baba's and wanted to know what was going to happen. Suddenly Baba became very angry, and said to Trilochan, "Did you want to kill your brother?"

"What you did was very, very dangerous. You don't play around with pretas. If your brother had touched the preta, he could have killed your brother today. You guys are not playing by the rules. From now on, don't come to my house."

Baba's anger was justified and he made it clear that he would not entertain us anymore.

That was the last time I saw Basulia Baba.

Although adventurous and revealing, the episode with Basulia Baba's preta remains a matter of intrigue to me. Psychic powers can be used for such mundane things as to be a waste of time and energy, and can lead to great dangers. Again, I am grateful to Osho for keeping me away from all siddhis and powers that come as by-products of meditation.

The Talking Statues of the Baul Mystic

In 1978 I visited Calcutta. I had not been there for a considerable period, and in fact, the trip had come about unexpectedly. I used to visit Pune a few times a year to meet my master, Osho, and usually, I took a train via Patna, as that was the cheapest route. But that year, I was traveling with a bunch of friends from Kathmandu, and they insisted we fly to Pune. It wasn't very convenient for me financially to fly as I was short of funds, but eventually, I had to comply because all these friends came from well-to-do families, and they detested the train journey. We decided

we would travel half the journey, to Patna, by plane, and then from Patna take a train. When the tickets arrived, we were taken by surprise because the agent had booked our flights via Calcutta, making them more costly. But since they'd been confirmed, we had no option but to comply. Returning from Pune, I was invited to stay at the house of a sannyasin friend of mine, who was a renowned Calcutta businessman. He had a very luxurious mansion in a posh residential area of Calcutta. Meanwhile, the rest of our group had flown back to Kathmandu.

And so it was that sheer serendipity that brought me to Calcutta, a city that has always been dear and uncannily familiar to me. One winter morning, I was strolling with a friend of mine around Rabindra Sarovar. A few early-morning strollers had gathered around a tea stall and were engaged in a rather lively conversation. As I sat down under a large tree by the lake, relishing the early morning sun and the sound of rustling trees, little did I know that destiny had planned a pleasant surprise for me. Some joggers were stretching nearby. As I was joyfully strolling the park, suddenly, I saw a bizarre scene; a man who was probably in his late forties was pulling out statues and pictures of various Hindu deities and saints from his small sling bag and arranging them in a line. I could see there were pictures of Krishna, Durga, Ramakrishna Paramahamsa, Vivekananda, and a few other saints I did not recognize. After positioning them neatly on parade, he took out some fruits and a piece of peda, an Indian sweet-meat made of condensed milk and sugar, from his bag and started talking to the statues and pictures in Bangla. My Bangla is not that good, but I could make out that in a teasing manner, he was offering sweets to the gods.

"Do you want some peda?" he asked a statue and broke a piece of sweet-meat, offering it to the deity. But suddenly, he changed his mind and ate the sweet himself. Then he leaned towards another statue, asking the same question. As I watched him, he stopped talking and bent closer to the statues, his eyes bulging attentively as if he was listening to them talk. Then spontaneously, he broke into a smile and, turning towards a photo, asked, "Maybe you want some sweets?"

I watched the man for a long time. He continued talking to his statues and photos with an alluring ease as if it was the most natural thing to do. I was captivated. The sun filled the park with crimson light, and a flock of birds came flying by, filling the park with ecstatic clamor. But I couldn't take my eyes off the man. He wore a simple white dhoti and ganji (local attire), like any other Bengali. He had a light brown complexion, and as the early sun gleamed on his skin, his body radiated sensuousness. As he continued his dialogue with his invisible companions, I felt a strong urge to go and meet him. My Swami friend, who was hosting me in the city and was accompanying me on the walk, could see I was greatly intrigued by the man. He tugged gently at my shirt and said, "Don't even think of visiting him. He is infamous for chasing away people with a staff, which he carries with him. It's safe to watch him from a distance."

But the man was magnetic. His madness sparkled with a captivating luminosity. I felt enormously drawn towards him. Although I believed every word my friend said, I couldn't restrain myself. Even before I knew what I was doing, I was standing right in front of the man. He raised his head and eyed me intently.

"What are you doing here?" he asked me in Bangla.

"I do not understand Bangla," I replied, "But I feel drawn towards you."

He looked deeply into my eyes and gestured for me to sit down. Later my friend confessed that he was greatly surprised when I was allowed to sit next to the man because he almost never allowed anybody to come close to him. The man turned towards his statues and asked their permission to talk to me instead. He asked me where I was heading. I told him I was on my way to Kathmandu, my hometown, from Pune, where I had gone to meet my master. When he heard the word 'master' he grew more attentive and enquired about him. So I told him a little bit about Osho, who was known as Bhagwan Shree Rajneesh at that time. He implored me to tell him more. It was a big challenge to sum up Osho's teaching in a few sentences because his teachings are full of paradoxes, and he speaks of ultimate synthesis. Of course, nothing gives me more pleasure than to speak about Osho, but at the same time, because I love him so much, it is equally difficult to know where to begin and when to stop. I was struggling to stitch a few neat sentences together that could at least give this man an idea of who he was when the man asked, "What is his teaching?"

That was easier. I remembered the last discourse I attended at the Pune ashram and started paraphrasing it:

'If you love a flower, don't pick it. Allow it to blossom. Allow it to experience the sun, the storm, and the wind. Allow it to experience life. If you love a flower, don't try to possess it. If you pluck it, it will wither away. When you possess something, you kill its essence. So, enjoy the flower, and relish its beauty, but don't possess it. And it is true with everything else in life. You meet a woman at the seashore. A beautiful woman, full of life, alive, joyous, and you immediately want to draw a marriage out of it. Marriage is like plucking a flower. Then you start destroying the beauty of the other. Enjoy life, enjoy everything that comes your way, but don't get attached to anything.'

"Beautiful! Beautiful!!" the man exclaimed. When I was recounting the discourse, I had closed my eyes and drowned in a blissful trance. When I opened my eyes, I saw he had burst into tears.

"What unparalleled insight! What beauty! Your master must be a Baul," he said.

I had heard about Bauls from my master, but I hadn't met a Baul before. This was my first experience with a Baul mystic. A few years later, I was to participate in a Baul festival at Kenduli, Orissa. It was quite a spectacle. Thousands of Bauls had gathered to celebrate the birthday of the famous twelfth-century Indian poet, Jayadeva, who was born in Kenduli.

The origin of the Baul is debatable. A few believe that the word Baul originates from the Sanskrit word vatul, which means an ecstatic mad person, while others think it is derived from the word vyakula, meaning a restless, agitated person. Regardless of the debate, it is certain that Bauls are ecstatic, nomadic mystics who evoke god through singing, dancing, and celebration. Some people even believe that Bauls' syncretic philosophy and festive approach to God are akin to that of Sufis. However, the Baul approach is very eclectic in nature and resonates not only with the teachings of Sufism but also with those of Tantra, Vaishnavism, and at times Vajrayana Buddhism as well.

The festival had overwhelmed me. The site was quite some distance from the village and was nestled idyllically in a small orchard, around which tents had been erected. A small, clear river flowed nearby. During the day, the Bauls gathered together and celebrated. Bauls carry an ektara, a single-string lyre, all the time. As they dance, they play ektara, dhol (a double-headed drum), cymbals, and other musical instruments. The sound of these instruments, combined with the resonance of ghungroos and nupurs, the anklet bells, was enlivening enough, but with the colorful clothes and the mad, abandoned frenzy in which they dance, I was simply transported to a higher, ecstatic dimension. It was surprising to notice that there was no temple or a particular sacred space; they just celebrated existence itself. The village itself was quite primordial. There were a few thatched huts scattered around the place. It wasn't connected to other villages by sealed road yet. People fetched water from the basin of a river or natural spring and grew their own food. It seemed to fit the mood of the Bauls perfectly. There was no external power to impose authority, and yet there was no crime whatsoever. Even in the Baul gathering, I noticed there was a discipline that wasn't imposed from the outside. It was quite an experience. After this first encounter with the Bauls, I developed a deep reverence towards them. I am also a great admirer of Baul songs. All of Rabindra Sangeet's music is influenced by Baul music. The Indian composers, SD Burman and his son, RD Burman, were great admirers of the Bauls. They incorporated the essence of mysticism and divine romanticism into Hindi songs as well.

"What a beautiful teaching! Your guru is a Baul," he repeated. After hearing the discourse, he had softened towards me and, looking at me lovingly, asked my name. After I told him, he insisted I share a few more words of Osho. I was carrying Osho Times magazine with me, so I just read out a few lines to him. I also showed him a photo of Osho. As I was reading part of Osho's discourse, he broke into sobs again.

"Ah! So beautiful! So beautiful!" he would remark again and again.

While I was busy reading a passage from the magazine, he suddenly nudged me and said, "Arun, your guru is here! You see! You see?!! Under that tree."

Of course, I saw nothing. But the man had started dancing with his ektara. My friend and I were too stunned to say anything. We didn't know what to do. The man was dancing in a frenzy. Then abruptly, he stopped, threw an angry look at us, and yelled in Bangali, "Sala! Tumhara guru khada hai, mei nach raha hun aur tum log baithe ho. Nach Sala!"

(Your master is standing here. I am dancing, and you remain glued to the ground like a fool, you idiot! Dance!)

Here was an unpredictable madman telling us our master was standing under a tree and who had broken into an ecstatic dance while we, quite cluelessly, stared at the space beneath the tree and saw nothing. He picked up his staff, so, rather scared, we joined him in his dance. Of course, we had no idea what was going on, and our dance, too, was forced because we couldn't see Osho.

It was during this awkward dance I fell madly in love with the man.

When he finished, there was a different grace on his face. I asked him how I was to address him. He told me I could simply call him Baba. The sun had grown unbearably hot. It was already midday. We had to take leave. I fished around in my pocket and found a ten-rupee note. Back in those days, ten rupees was a substantial amount. As I offered the note to Baba, I saw my friend cringing. Baba accepted the note and told me to visit him the next morning as well.

On our way back, my friend expressed his surprise that Baba had accepted my offer. "Usually when someone tries to offer him anything, cash in particular, he picks up his staff and beats the hell out of them," my friend said, "And as if the thrashing isn't good enough, he often chases them up to a mile with the staff in his hand." Apparently, my friend had also tried to offer him some money previously, but Baba had become really mad at him, yelling as if he was being taken for a beggar.

The next day, I had my flight booked for Kathmandu. But I was so enchanted by this man Baba; I decided to postpone my flight and spend some more time with him. In those days, it was pretty easy to cancel international flights. There was no extra cancellation charge; one could simply inform the airline and re-book the seat for a date that suited one. I asked my friend if he thought it was a good idea to cancel the flight and spend one more day with Baba. He more than welcomed the idea. He had to go to Bombay in three days, so he suggested I stay there for three more days so he could join me. I called the Royal Nepal Airlines Corporation and postponed my flight.

The whole day I was filled with Baba's presence. He wasn't there continually in my thoughts, but it was as though he had cast a long shadow over my conscious mind. My thoughts intermingled with his presence. I could barely sleep that night, anticipating the meeting the next morning.

It was early morning when I went to meet Baba. He had already set up his deities on display and was busy talking to them when I arrived at the park. I asked him about his past. He was somewhat discreet about it, and yet revealed that many years ago, he had a small electric shop in the city. When he developed detachment from the world and became a Baul saint, he handed over the shop to one of his assistants on the condition that the man supplied rations to Baba for his survival. The man could then keep all surplus profit for himself. Baba had a small shelter in the city.

"You are the first person from whom I have accepted any money," Baba confided. "I don't accept money from people because money carries the karmic impression of the person who gave it to you. If the person has earned money by bad means, I will also have to share his bad karma. And usually, rich people don't earn money the good way, so I don't want to burden myself with anyone else's heavy karma for the sake of a few rupee notes."

He was also very particular about not eating at anybody else's house. He had a simple routine: he would wake up early and come to Rabindra Sarobar to spend the morning there. At midday, he would go back to his hut and cook his only meal for the day. When I asked him what he did for the rest of the day, he replied, "Oh, I have guests to attend to in the evening."

"Who visits you?"

"Oh! All these celestial beings. They come to me in the afternoon and don't leave until I am asleep."

I was surprised to hear about these celestial beings and asked him to tell me about them in detail. He said life has many forms, and there are many saints in non-physical forms - they also need good company. So I have satsang with them every evening. He then asked me to tell him more about Osho's teaching, and as I was relating some of the discourse to him, he suddenly stood up and exclaimed ecstatically," He's come. He's come. Rajneesh is here!" And then he sprung into his mad dance again.

That was my first experience with a Baul, and not being all that mature in meditation, I was stupefied by his spontaneous outbreak of ecstatic dance, and yet my reverence and admiration for him deepened.

On the third day, as usual, I went to see him in the park. I used to skip breakfast to be with him, and on that day, I became unusually thirsty and wanted a cup of tea. A few hundred meters away, I spotted a small tea shop. I told Baba I wanted a cup of tea, and he said to get some but to hurry up. I stood up and was about to leave when he called me back.

"Arun don't go. The guy who is brewing tea had sex last night and hasn't taken a bath or changed his clothes, so if you drink the tea, you will be tormented unnecessarily by sexual thoughts."

I was amazed. From where I was standing, I couldn't even see the guy properly, but Baba could see that much further. I was surprised. He became my teacher and taught me many things. He used to say one must bathe after three acts: getting a haircut, returning from a funeral, and having sex.

Baba had great insight into life. He was a simple man, and yet his vision was penetrating. For instance, at this time, in 1978, I hadn't had my past-life experience yet. During one of our conversations, my friend said light-heartedly, "Baba, Arun loves Bengal very much. He just loves Calcutta."

Baba smiled and said in Bangla, "That's because he was here in his immediate past life. His house is still here in the city." Little did I know, but I was to get a glimpse of my past life soon, confirming what Baba had said.

After the third day, a small problem arose. My friend was leaving for Bombay, and in India, when the male head leaves the house, it is customary for the guest to take leave too. Of course, I wanted to spend more time with Baba, but I wasn't in a position to be able to afford to stay in a hotel. So naturally, I, too, had to prepare to leave. My friend, however, could see that I was really keen to spend more time with Baba, and so was gracious enough to postpone his Bombay visit for three more days. My joy knew no bounds.

My friendship with Baba had been a matter of great surprise for my friend as well. He also had great regard for Baba, but because of Baba's reclusive nature, he wouldn't dare to come close to him. When he saw that Baba had grown very affectionate towards me, he asked me to invite Baba to dinner at his apartment. Baba only agreed because he couldn't say no to me. The moment we entered the elevator, Baba said, "Arun, I feel suffocated. I don't want to go." But we were almost there, just a few floors below, so I insisted that seeing we were so close we might as well accept the invitation. Baba said, "The arrows are piercing me from everywhere."

"But there are no arrows Baba. What do you mean?"

"This apartment is full of greedy people. Their desire, ambition, greed; it all pierces me like arrows."

I didn't know what to do. By the time we reached the 12th floor, where my friend lived, Baba pressed my shoulder urgently and said, "Arun, if you want to kill me, only then take me for lunch." Much to my horror, I saw that he had grown pale and ghostly. I couldn't believe my eyes. He had started shaking feverishly. So I called an auto and dropped him off at Rabindra Sarobar, bidding him farewell.

We departed with great love, and I asked him to visit me in Nepal. He said, "I shall definitely visit you." At that time, we had already opened the Ashish Meditation Centre. "Rajneeshjee has a center there; then I shall definitely come." But unfortunately, he couldn't come to Nepal, and over the years, traveling my usual route via Patna, I didn't go to Calcutta, so I never saw him again. I met my businessman friend a few times in Pune and then for the last time when Osho was in Kathmandu in 1986. I asked him about Baba. He said, "Baba remembers you; he always asks about you. And he wants to come to Kathmandu."

So after spending a week with this mad Baul saint, I had to return home. But that one-week satsang with Baba left a lasting impression on me. I don't know whether he was enlightened or not, and it's not my concern either. Now I have heard that he has left his body. But such is the power of love that even today, the memory of him stands out vividly in my mind, and his divine madness fills me with awe and inspiration.

When I recounted the events of this visit to Osho the next time I saw him, he said that the whole Calcutta trip had come about because existence had willed that Baba and I should meet. Osho also said, "After meeting you, he is very happy, and he has benefitted from the visit. Now that he has fallen in love with me, I can also help him."

Mystical Invitation from Meher Baba

Sufis have their own tradition and style. Sometimes we don't understand them because they are mostly ecstatic in love and devotion. They sing, dance, love, and remain in an ecstatic state. And by this path, they attain enlightenment.

There was a Sufi saint called Baba Jaan. She was originally from Balochistan, on the border of Afghanistan and Pakistan, and belonged to a well-to-do Afghan family. She was named Gulrukh and had been spiritually inclined since she was young. When she came of age, her

parents wanted to get her married. Gulrukh felt she was not ready to get married, so she ran away from home and began spending time with Sufi saints to deepen her spiritual experience.

One fascinating aspect of her life was that once she attained a certain spiritual height, she began working as a courtesan. At a young age, she was physically very attractive. When a man wanted to spend the night with her, she would invite him to her place, and before the night was over, she was able to create a spiritual transformation in the man. So the person who came to her seeking sexual pleasure ended up becoming her devotee.

When she became old and felt that her remaining days on Earth were few, she wanted to give her spiritual energy and understanding to somebody worthy so that the master-disciple tradition remained alive.

You must have heard that Buddha gave his highest truth teaching to Mahakashyap. The tradition remained alive in India for 1200 years until Bodhidharma's time. Bodhidharma did not find anyone in India who was capable of receiving his enlightened wisdom. In his visions, he saw there was someone way over in China who had the potential to receive his teachings. So he traveled all the way to China to deliver them to someone worthy. Osho has said that in the eighth century AD, he also left for the journey with Bodhidharma but parted ways somewhere in the Himalayas after staying with him for three months.

Similarly, Baba Jaan did not find anyone in Afghanistan or Persia with the capacity to receive the transmission. In her visions, she saw that a worthy candidate had been born all the way over in Pune, India. So, in her old age she made the long journey from Afghanistan to the central Indian city of Pune. She stayed, like a beggar, under a neem tree on a busy street in Pune and waited for her spiritual son. Although she was very old, she was determined that she would leave her body only after transmitting her truth to him. If she did not manage to make the transmission, a lineage of Sufis would die along with her.

Although Baba Jaan was enlightened, she lived with great discomfort and pain; her only reason for living was the hope that one day he would arrive. And arrive he did after many years. Baba Jaan recognized the young Meher Baba, who was only nineteen then, as he walked across the street corner that she had made her home. She called him over and gave him shaktipat (transmission of spiritual energy) on his third eye by kissing him on his forehead. The shaktipat was so strong that Meher Baba remained in samadhi for nine months. He had to lie down on his bed, unable to do anything else. His parents were very concerned and blamed Baba Jaan for the state of their son.

"He is not your son; he is an avatar," Baba Jaan told them bluntly. "I came here all the way from Afghanistan to awaken him. Now that he is awake, he will awaken thousands of other souls."

It took a long time for Meher Baba to digest the energy transmission that Baba Jaan had delivered to him. If a heavy energy transmission happens in an instant, it can have adverse effects on the body, as it did with Meher Baba. It took nine months for him just to get out of bed, and another year for him to return to normal consciousness.

Meher Baba would then regularly meet with Baba Jaan so he could fully understand what had happened to him and why he had taken birth on Earth.

Osho has said that for someone to become enlightened, he must get the help of at least three enlightened masters during his or her lifetime. Osho himself was helped by Pagal Baba, Magga Baba, and Masto Baba. In the Sufi tradition, they say that a person can't be enlightened unless he gets constant help from five enlightened masters.

Baba Jaan was Meher Baba's guru who gave him his first

experience of samadhi, but he needed the guidance of four other masters to be fully enlightened. One of those four was Sai Baba of Shirdi, who was also from the Sufi tradition. The others were Narayan Maharaj, Upasani Maharaj and Tajuddin Maharaj. They helped Baba integrate his mystical experiences with ordinary consciousness after his lengthy samadhi.

When Meher Baba first met Shirdi Sai Baba, Sai Baba also told him he was an avatar and that he would help many people on their spiritual path. Indeed, within a few years, seekers from around the world were coming to him seeking spiritual transformation.

Meher Baba was in silence for the last forty-four years of his life. At first, he went into silence for just a year but then kept increasing the time of his silence and ended up not speaking for the rest of his life. When his disciples requested that he speak, he wrote to them, saying that he would speak the following year, but come the following year, he would again extend his silence. After a few years of writing, he made an alphabetical table to indicate the letters with his fingers rather than talking. Although this was easier than talking, he found this difficult as well. Due to his silence, he was having trouble communicating with his disciples. But since they needed teachings and instructions, he began using hand gestures that could be fully understood only by one of his disciples, Eruch Jessawala. He said that Jessawala was totally tuned to him, being able to understand his gestures and speak their meaning to the disciples. After many years, Jessawala didn't need the help of gestures. Meher Baba would look into his eyes, and he would speak what Baba wanted to say. And Baba was pleased with his words. A disciple can be so totally surrendered to the master that he can even speak the master's thoughts.

Baba also wrote many books through Jessawala. Baba would sit beside Jessawala and look into his eyes, and Jessawala would start typing on his typewriter. Baba's popular books such as Much Silence and God Speaks were among the many written that way. This kind of phenomenon is not just possible while the master is in his body, but even after he has left his body. Krishnamurti also channeled the thoughts of his masters into the book, At the Feet of the Master. Although it was Krishnamurti who hand-penned the words of the book, he never claimed authorship.

Years after Meher Baba had left his body, Jessawala had gone to meet Osho in Pune. After the meeting, Osho mentioned him in his discourses and praised him a great deal, saying he was an example of an ideal disciple as he could be his master's perfect medium.

Enlightened masters and their work are intertwined in mysterious ways. A deep connection existed between Osho and Meher Baba as well. Osho said that if Meher Baba had not lived in Pune, he would not have made his ashram there. Meher Baba had prepared the ground for Osho. Once Osho began giving sannyas in 1970, he adopted Meher Baba's saying, "I am not here to teach, but to awaken you." To that famous saying, Osho added, "You surrender, and I will transform you. This is my promise."

Meher Baba traveled the world many times and had disciples from many countries. As he was born into a Parsi family, he had many disciples from Iran. His disciples came to stay with him for twenty-one days in Pune. This special retreat was called Sahavas. When they were leaving, they asked Baba if they could visit Bombay before going back home. He said they could visit Bombay, but first, they would have to go back to their home country and, from there, catch another flight to Bombay. He felt that a spiritual trip should not be infused with sightseeing if spiritual transformation is one's wish.

He used to say that love and total surrender to the master are the way of transformation. During Sahavas, his devotees would sit silently or chant devotional songs, just spending time with him. This was enough to bring about a change in them.

One of the major aspects of his life was that he worked with Mastas. Mastas were people who had had sudden spiritual experiences and lost their mental balance. Meher Baba called them God-intoxicated. He used to search for Mastas around India and take care of them. Although spiritually very high, Mastas could not function in the world, and society called them mad and discarded them. Meher Baba used to bathe them, clothe them, feed them, and then he would touch their feet. In this way, the Mastas gained some respect in society as spiritual people.

Meher Baba had another strange habit. He would regularly visit cinema halls, and although he had no interest in watching films, he would spend the whole duration of the film in the hall. When asked why he went to films of such low quality, he would say that a cinema hall was one of the only places where a large group of people would sit silently with him for hours. During that time, his energy could heal them spiritually. He said he wanted to share his energy, but people would not come to him, so he resorted to going to films in packed halls, not only in India but also in the West.

Meher Baba had two car accidents. The second one was so severe that it left him with difficulty walking for the rest of his life. He explained to his disciples that a great deal of negativity had gathered around the world, and there was the possibility of a big war. By knowingly getting into an accident and taking the suffering on his own body, he neutralized the negativity that could have had very bad effects on the world. Although he was crippled after his second accident and was confined to a wheelchair and carried around in a palanquin, he was very happy that he was able to be of some help to humanity. Such was the compassion of Meher Baba.

As he was always in silence, he used his touch to heal and transform people. He used to touch, hug and kiss his disciples in order to transfer energy to them. His presence itself was very powerful and healing, which is why people from all around the world came to this master who neither uttered a word nor conducted any meditation.

Meher Baba had a consort whose name was Mehera. She was only sixteen when she first came to visit him with her parents, who were disciples of Meher Baba. On that very first visit, Meher Baba said to her, "You were born for me."

She did not understand Baba at that time, but within a year and a half, she was living with him and serving him. Meher Baba used to say that she was the most spiritual woman of their age. Mehera stayed in seclusion until Meher Baba left his body and met only a few devoted female disciples. Meher Baba would say that she was his shakti (female principle of divine energy). And just as Shiva had Parvati, Aurobindo had Mother, Meher Baba couldn't function without Mehera.

When I visited Krishnamurti Ashram in Ojai, California, the receptionist of the ashram told me that her boyfriend was living in a Meher Baba ashram just a forty-five-minute drive from there. I couldn't resist the temptation, so I went there. The ashram was on a huge compound on a hillock and was just a two-roomed house managed by just one person. Meher Baba had lived there, so it had a strong presence, and I felt very rewarded after my visit. The man managing the ashram said that most of the time it was empty, and people gathered there only on special days. It was he who told me about Mehera.

Mehera's first-hand narrative gathered from more than 200 hours of tape recordings has been made into books, a three-volume set titled Mehera-Meher, a Divine Romance – Volumes I, II & III, by David Fenster. After Meher Baba left his body, Mehera looked after the welfare of Baba's disciples, who lived in his ashram.

In 1987, during the Pune-II days, I was working at the Osho ashram, and I started feeling a great call from Meher Baba during my meditations. I knew very little about him but knew he was born in Pune and that his ashram was also there. I asked around to see if anyone knew about his ashram, as I had a strong desire to visit it. But nobody could give me any information about it. I then remembered my friend, Dr. Phadnis, whose sannyas name was Swami Ajit Saraswati. He used to be an intimate of Osho, but after the closure of Rajneeshpuram in the USA, had left Osho and began following Meher Baba. Many intimate disciples of Osho were forced to leave then, as politics had entered the ashram.

During Pune II around 1988, I called Dr. Phadnis, but his wife picked up the phone. She had been very happy that her husband had left Osho, and when I told her I was a sannyasin and a friend of Swami Saraswati, she gave me a big scolding and told me to stay away from her husband and not to call again. For a week, I was seeking, trying hard to find out more about Meher Baba and his ashram, but to no avail.

However, existence had its own way of getting me to Meher Baba Ashram. Before entering the white robe celebration every night, we had to hang our bags of belongings in the locker room. One night, I found that the belongings of the bag hanging above mine had fallen into my bag. I started placing the objects back into the rightful bag, and as I was doing that, I found a very thin booklet in my bag. I took it out, and to my surprise, it was an introductory booklet on Meher Baba. It had all the information I needed to find Meher Baba's Ashram in Pune. I thanked Osho for the gift.

The next day, I went to Meher Baba Ashram and found it completely empty. There was only one person there by the name of Ramkrishna. He was a disciple of Meher Baba's, and he stayed there alone. He showed us around and said that people only gathered there a few times a year for special events. As he was taking us around, I felt greatly in tune with him and received a lot of energy from the ashram.

I bought a few books and paid Ramkrishna for them. When I got back to the Osho commune, I realized that Ramkrishna had given me way too much change. I felt I should not keep it, so I went back the next day to return it to him.

"It was the wish of existence that you come back here again; that's why I made the mistake of giving you extra money yesterday," he said.

I received much love and energy and felt totally in tune with Meher Baba in the two days I went to Meher Baba Ashram.

I was able to visit Maher Baba's house in Pune in 2012, and it was quite a sight. Meher Baba's room was a tiny nook under the stairs. It was preserved just as he had left it. Although very basic, the energy was utterly intense. It engulfed me and I stayed in a trance for a while. The caretaker of the house also showed me the dent on the stone floor of the room and said that Meher Baba had made the dent with his head while praying for emancipation.

Whenever I travel to the West, I feel Baba's energy and feel the need to talk about him. I have spoken about him extensively and introduced him to many spiritual seekers during my meditation camps and satsangs. The grace of a Master such as Meher Baba is forever present, and we become blessed by his blessings whenever we remember him with a pure heart.

Ramtirtha—Death or Enlightenment

Swami Ramtirtha was a lecturer at the Lahore university and a famous mathematician of his times. A mathematics conference was scheduled and when people came to know that Swami Ramatirtha will be presenting in it, mathematicians from all over India and universities in the UK had come to participate in it.

The University administration knew that Ramtirtha was a great devotee of Lord Krishna and used to spend hours in the morning in meditation and devotion. Even though the University opened in

the morning because of Ramtirtha's exceptional genius he was given the privilege to come to the University after 12pm in the afternoon. Before the conference day the Vice Chancellor called Ramtirtha to his office and said, "we know that you spend your mornings in meditation and devotion but tomorrow as we have the conference and you have a presentation at 11am please come to the University by 10am."

On the day of the conference Ramtirtha sat for his regular meditation with the plan to be at the University by 10 am but he became so immersed in his devotion that he lost all sense of time and space and went into a deep trance. By the time he came back from his meditation it was already 12 noon. Ramtirtha did not have a car and the university was at a distance from his home. With great remorse Ramtirtha rushed to the university. When he reached the university by 1pm it was already lunch time and everybody was having lunch. Renowned mathematicians and professors had gathered from all over and Ramtirtha felt great embarrassment for being so late. After entering the University he went into the attendance room and told the clerk that he had been late and asked for the attendance register. "But you already signed the register at 10am in the morning." Replied the surprised clerk and showed him the attendance.

Ramtirtha was shocked when he saw that his signature was already there. For a moment Ramtirtha could not comprehend what he saw. He rushed into the Vice Chancellor's chambers and even before he could apologize the Vice Chancellor hugged him and said, "You did an exceptional presentation. Everyone loved it. Even the professors from the UK have recommended for your felicitation and we are now promoting you as associate professor." The professors from the UK and other famous mathematicians were also in the chamber and were all congratulating him and lauding him for his genius paper.

That is when Ramtirtha realized that only one person could do such a presentation in his form, it was Krishna himself who had come to the rescue of his devotee. Ramtirtha's heart was overwhelmed and his eyes welled up with tears of gratitude. Krishna himself had to take a human form and conduct a Maths presentation for him. Ramtirtha immediately asked the VC for a blank paper and a pen. Everyone got curious what he was going to write. After writing something on the paper and signing it Ramtirtha handed over the letter to the VC who looked at it with great surprise. "We are all gathered here to laud you for your presentation. We are talking about your promotion and you hand me your resignation?" The VC asked.

"I have come to realize that the Krishna statue in my room is not just a statue, it is Krishna Himself. Because of me he had to come here and give a presentation today. I have full trust that the same Krishna who took care of me today will also arrange for my two-time meals," replied Ramtirtha and resigned from his job. After this, Ramtirtha went to Rishikesh and spent his time meditating and doing his sadhana in the hills of Uttarakhand.

THE BIRTH OF RAMSEWAK

During his sadhana period in Tehri in Uttarakhand, the Maharaja of Tehri Garhwal heard of Ramtirtha's repute and came to meet him. The Maharaja was an intelligent man, but due to the influence of the Western way of life, he had no belief whatsoever in Hinduism. He was a confirmed atheist. The countless yogis who had come to Uttarakhand and met him could not rouse a love of God in him. But most of his doubts vanished in his first meeting with Swami Ramtirtha. As he was hugely impressed by Swamijee, he asked him not to leave the state of Tehri so he could receive his satsang and guidance on a regular basis. Thanks to the time that Maharaja Keerti Shah spent in Swamijee's presence, a great love arose in him for the Hindu faith and he became a strong supporter and promoter of Hinduism.

Seeing the change in the king and the respect that he bestowed upon Swami Ramtirtha, a big crowd of locals began gathering around Swamijee. Such a crowd is full of inquisitive folk, and real seekers among them are almost non-existent. It is a matter of great pain for saints and yogis to live among people with no spiritual thirst. As a result, Ramtirtha left Tehri and went to live in a silent barren cave in the Himalayas. The nearest village to his cave was 3 km away.

A happy-go-lucky farmer discovered that a yogi was living in the cave and started taking him a meal every day at noon. Ramtirtha felt that this arrangement was also due to Krishna's grace, and while eating his food and drinking Ganga jal (water of the Ganga), he thanked Krishna countless times. On hearing this, the farmer's ego was hurt, and one day he gathered enough courage to ask, "I bring you lunch every day exactly on time, but you have never thanked me. Why do you only thank Krishna and not me?"

Ramthirtha answered, "Because I am sure this is his arrangement. Wherever I go, he never lets me sleep hungry and never lets things be uncomfortable for me."

This statement hurt the farmer even more, and he said, "I have some important work to do, so I cannot bring your lunch tomorrow." While leaving the cave, he thought to himself, "Let's see who will feed him tomorrow." As he was leaving, Ramtirtha said, "Don't you worry at all. The one who feeds everyone, from an ant to an elephant, will also feed Ram." Not believing a word Ramtirtha said, the farmer decided to see what would happen when nobody brought him lunch the next day.

When it was time for lunch, the farmer hid behind a bush and kept vigil over the cave. To his surprise he saw an old woman walking towards the cave with a clay pot in her hand. When she reached the cave, he heard her say, "Sadhubaba! Sadhubaba!"

When Ramtirtha came out on hearing her, she added, "Our

family bought a new cow which gives a lot of milk. I felt that I should offer the first day's milk to a yogi. That's why I have brought this milk for you. If you could kindly accept it, I would be very grateful to you." Ramtirtha accepted and drank as much milk as he could. Some milk was still left in the pot, so the old woman asked him to keep it for later. Ramtirtha said it was his rule that he did not keep anything for the future.

"Whatever Krishna wishes, whenever he wishes, is what I am satisfied with," he said. Hearing this, the old woman was filled with reverence for Ramtirtha. She said, "I will come with some food for you tomorrow as well, please accept it." For three days the woman came with food and milk for Ramtirtha while the farmer watched from behind the bushes. After the third day, he was extremely ashamed, and came forth, prostrated in front of Ramtirtha and began to cry. "Dear lord of the forest, please forgive me for wanting to test you. I will not leave your feet unless you forgive me. I did not see your Krishna, but I am astonished to see his arrangement for you. Please bless me so that I also have unfaltering faith towards him just as you do," pleaded the farmer.

The farmer's ego melted and he began bringing lunches to Swamijee with great devotion. He now regarded Ramtirtha as his guru and began taking spiritual counsel from him. He also changed his name to Ramsewak, which means Ram's helper.

GOD-REALIZATION

The story of Swami Ramtirtha's self-realization shows his strong connection with the holy river Ganga and the Himalayas. As soon as he had some leisure time, he would run to the serenity of the Ganga River. He traveled many times from the city of Haridwar to the source of the Ganga at Gomukh. He considered the Ganga his own mother and would pray to her for self-realization.

One day he was meditating on her bank at Brahmapuri, a little above Rishikesh, and was aching for the experience of god-realization. Again, he made a vow that if he is not god-realized within twenty-four hours, he will jump into the Ganga and take his life. The twenty-four hours ended, and the next morning came and he was still not enlightened. As he had vowed, he jumped into the Ganga. The Ganga began drowning her son, but when Ramtirtha became unconscious, she threw him onto a rock on her bank. When Ram Tirtha regained consciousness after some time, he had left unconsciousness forever; he was now a god-realized man. The effort of many lifetimes finally came to rest.

A Magical Night in Nagarkot

The synchronicity between a master and a disciple happens on a higher plane and at a far deeper level than any other intimate relationship. There are many ways humans relate to each other and build connections among themselves, but the relationship between a master and a disciple is one that transcends all, and is the most significant one. It is often impossible to give a grounded explanation to the phenomenon called 'Master and Disciple relationship', and maybe this is the reason why it is also called the MAD relationship.

When a person becomes enlightened, he becomes one with existence, and everything he does creates ripples throughout existence for thousands of years. If a disciple has truly surrendered to an enlightened master, and the master has accepted him as a disciple, there exists a strong connection between the two that transcends all boundaries of time and space, and even life and death. This is the reason why everything that a master does influences the disciple, no matter how far away the disciple might be. If he is in tune with the master, he will receive and reflect the ripples of the master's consciousness.

There have been numerous occasions when I have behaved a certain way, or certain events have happened in my life, which at that particular time, did not have any meaning or explanation. Most times, it looked like I was acting erratically, emotionally driven, illogical or even mad. It wouldn't have been a surprise if anybody witnessing me at those times called me crazy or eccentric, and I can totally understand that viewpoint. But as time passed I always came to understand and receive an answer as to why it happened and what was the reason behind it. Most of the time, it was my master. Today when I reminisce about these incidents, I feel grateful to my master for blessing me with those moments, and making me capable enough to experience his mystical dimension. Today, these very incidents have become the salt and spice of my spiritual journey as a disciple.

I am fully assured that many people who read what I am about to share will not believe me, but it is not for them that I write this. I write it for those who understand the mystical dimension of being with a master, and for those who are slowly maturing in their openness in allowing the same magic to take place in their lives. I write for those who are having similar experiences and are looking for gentle assurance and a nudge to head further in that direction. I write for those who know it in their being that everything in this world cannot be proven with logic and explanation, and that there is more to this life than just that which can be analyzed by the human mind.

It was the full moon of November. On the full moon of every month, we used to have some special programme or satsang at Asheesh, after which prasad was served for everyone. The Kartik Purnima, or the full moon of November, is considered very auspicious by Hindus, Jains and Sikhs. The Sikhs celebrate it as Gurupurab or Prakash Parva of Sri Guru Nanak Dev Ji, the first guru of the Sikhs. Similarly, the Jains celebrate it by visiting Palitana, a Jain pilgrimage center. The Purnima night at the Center had multiplied the energy many fold, and we were all moon drunk after our meditations.

As the night advanced, most of the participants had left, but some of us were still hyper, and the conversations seemed like they would never end. It was nearly midnight, but nobody felt sleepy or tired.

As the night ripened, I was suddenly taken over by a strange idea to go to Nagarkot and watch the sunrise. Nagarkot is a countryside hill station 32 km away from the center of Kathmandu and is frequented by tourists who are there for the spectacular views of the Himalayan range and the sun at dawn and dusk. It was already past midnight, and although the idea seemed most impulsive, I felt a certain mysterious pull towards Nagarkot that could not be explained. The temptation was way too strong to resist, and when I expressed my wish to go, four of my friends, Swami Amar, Swami Swarup, Ma Shradda from Germany and Swami Ramesh agreed to come along with me. We decided to take Ramesh's car.

The winter sky was clear and the moon was in its full glory. The night was silent, but heavy with a mystical vibe as we drove through the empty streets of Kathmandu and uphill to the resort town. In those days, there were not many resorts and hotels in Nagarkot, except for a few small lodges and tea shops. Once we reached the top, there was a huge field in which we parked our car and from where we began looking for a place to stay.

It was bone-chillingly cold outside and we were all shivering as we knocked at the door of one lodge after another. Nobody opened any door, except at one small cottage lodge. The guy opened the door angrily, as we had woken him up from his sleep. When we asked for a room, he snapped back, "We only have two rooms and both are occupied." He slammed the door shut in our faces, leaving us shivering in the cold.

The excitement and thrill were now replaced by the harsh reality of the weather, and everyone began saying, "Let's go back! Let's go back!"

We all agreed to go back and went to the place where we had parked the car. We all huddled up in the car, and just as fate would have it, the car wouldn't start. The same car which had brought us all the way from Asheesh, and was in such good condition, would not start at all. Ramesh tried everything, but all in vain. Every time he turned the key, we hoped and prayed with all our might to hear the sound of the engine revving up ... but nothing. The car just would not start, so we couldn't switch on the heater either. It was so cold that even with five people huddled up in the car, we were still shivering. I felt so cold, I was ready to sleep on the dickey seat if it made me warmer. The lodge wouldn't take us, the car wouldn't start, and the temperature kept dropping. What a tragic outcome to our otherwise moonstruck beautiful night!

"There was no point shaking and shivering in the car on such a beautifully-lit night," I thought. "This is not what we came here for." I asked everyone to get out of the car, and we decided to do a meditation. We went into the middle of the field and started doing Nataraj meditation. Kathmandu was not at all polluted in those days, and the whole range of the snow-covered mountains was visible in the moonlight. Doing meditation with this backdrop out in nature beneath the open sky was a beautiful and thrilling experience for us. Our meditation went very deep, and we became even more intoxicated than before. I still remember, it was almost as if a huge umbrella of energy had covered us, and we were stupefied by it. There was a strong presence. One could almost taste the magic of that mystically-pregnant night, and all five of us were in a divine stupor. Then the impossible happened.

As we all sat there meditating in silence, suddenly we heard in a very pure Hindi dialect, "I have come, do you recognize me?" When we opened our eyes, we saw that one of us was immersed in a deep trance and was speaking to us. Apart from me, nobody else in the group could speak proper Hindi - three were Kathmandu Newars, and one was a German lady. We immediately recognized Osho's Hindi, and also felt his strong presence. We were thrilled. Osho spoke again, "I have called you! And I have called you all for a very special purpose." He then turned towards Shraddha and spoke in English, "You have to help Arun. We have a great plan for Nepal, and I am very happy that you are staying at Asheesh. Don't go to the West! I am very happy how you guys are running Asheesh. You stay there and help Arun to spread my message."

Then he turned towards us and told us about our misfortunes that night. He said, "Don't worry, everything will be OK! I know it is a little cold, but you all have to stay here tonight. This is a special place and I have chosen each one of you to come here tonight, and there is a reason behind it. I have called you all for a special purpose." We didn't know what the special purpose was, or the reason that he had called us, but we were thrilled beyond words.

After that, he gave a personal message to each one of us, "Help Arun in my work. Great work will happen in Nepal in the future, and it will all happen through Asheesh. Asheesh is small, but the energy is not small." He then blessed all of us. Ramesh and Shraddha were very sensitive to energy, and Ramesh started wailing loudly. Shraddha even began screaming and crying. There were Army barracks very close by, and we were concerned that people would come from there because of the noise. We somehow pacified Shraddha, but Ramesh would just not stop. We held his hands and put our hands on his heart to comfort him, but to no avail. He kept wailing and crying like a little child for an hour.

The contact lasted for a few minutes, after which Osho left. Slowly we all started to feel cold, so we went into the car. Ramesh was still crying, and the rest of us were also high with emotion. This was how we spent the whole night in the car. Slowly the sky turned crimson and the sun began to rise. A few cars showed up with people who came to see the sunrise, and one of the cheap lodges opened to welcome the customers. We went there and saw that the guy had empty rooms upstairs, although they were not very decent. We told him that if he had opened when we knocked last night, we could have spent the night there. "I am really sorry! You guys came really late, and we thought you were hooligans, so we didn't open," replied the owner. The same guy later became an Osho sannyasin, such are the strange ways of existence.

We ate something at the lodge, and decided to return to Asheesh. Ramesh offered to go to the city by bus, and bring a mechanic for the car. He said meanwhile, we could wander around or wait at the lodge, or we could all go together by bus, and later retrieve the car. We decided to try to run the car one more time. To our great surprise, the engine revved up as soon as Ramesh turned the key, as if nothing had happened at all. Then we understood that everything had been an existential plan and had been arranged in such a way for us to be there in that place at that time of night.

Four of us were Nepalese, but I was worried for Shraddha. She was from Germany, and I was not sure if her Western mind had been able to process what had happened. I was also a little embarrassed because Osho kept asking everybody to help me. At first, I was avoiding conversing with Shraddha, but when the time was opportune, I tried to explain the sequence of events to her. However, she volunteered, "It all happened because we had to be there. We were drawn to Nagarkot, then couldn't find a lodge, and the car broke down; everything happened so we could be there." I was surprised to see her understanding.

During 'Pune I' years, sometimes Osho would suddenly go into silence. This happened mostly between 1977 and 1981. During these silent periods, he wouldn't show up for the morning lecture or the evening darshan. We were told he was in seclusion because of his poor health, but later I realized that whenever he had to do deeper esoteric work on his disciples spread across the world, he would go into seclusion and silence. So the period of silence might have been for his health, but it had an explicable esoteric purpose.

Sometime after the incident with us in Nagarkot happened, I found out that at the same time, Osho had gone into a ten-day silence. I also discovered that the incident was not exclusive to us, as the same phenomenon had happened on the same night in a few other places around the world. What had happened to us in Nagarkot, had also happened in Chambal Valley in India.

When I went to Pune, I befriended a group of rather jovial and robust men in the dormitory. The group had a leader who was always surrounded by the other men, and they followed him around very obediently. Later, they told me that formerly they were a group of notorious bandits from Chambal Valley, and the man they followed around was their leader there. After coming across one of Osho's books in Hindi, the leader, who had a remarkably charismatic personality, had instantly fallen in love with Osho, and he and his group had begun reading Osho and doing Dynamic Meditation. They knew nothing else; they liked Dynamic so much, they were doing it twice a day. They were all village people, and innocent at heart, so in no time they were having beautiful experiences of meditation.

When I asked them how they had come to Pune, what they told me blew my mind. On the same full-moon night of November, the bandits had gathered in Chambal Valley to listen to one of Osho's discourses. As the night matured, everyone felt a presence permeating the place, which slowly overpowered them. They were drunk with energy as if the moon had cast a magic spell over them. Suddenly the leader was possessed by Osho and went into a trance-like state, speaking in Osho's voice. The voice gave a long lecture and then told them to abandon their dangerous profession and do something simpler to earn their livelihood. It also directed them to come to the Pune ashram. When the bandits told Osho they had done many illegal things and the police were after them, Osho said they were not to worry, and to just come.

It was very strange and mysterious how the same incident had happened to people as far apart as Chambal and Kathmandu, and other places around the world on the same night. It was not just in this instance, but every time Osho went into silence, he manifested in myriad different forms to guide and inspire his disciples.

The incident brought a great change to the lives of the bandits. Their whole gang became initiated into Neo-Sannyas and became Osho disciples. They left their notorious profession and adapted to a simpler lifestyle, by farming.

I had grown up reading stories of great enlightened masters and how they guided their disciples even beyond the laws of the physical realm. Life incidents of great disciples such as Swami Yogananda, Swami Vivekananda, Sri Aurobindo, Mira, Swami Rama, Shivapuri Baba's disciple Madhav Baje, and Indira Devi bear profound testimony to this spiritual phenomenon of how a master can contact and guide a surrendered disciple beyond the limitations of the physical body, time and space. I have met some high lamas and rinpoches who are still being guided by Buddha to this day. Osho has spoken about this esoteric phenomenon in his Hindi book, Gahre Pani Paith. He says that even today, on the night of every Buddha Purnima, an esoteric group of 500 lamas gather somewhere around Mount Kailash in Tibet, and Buddha descends in his physical body and guides them. He has also mentioned in his discourses that there are still people in Vrindavan who have daily contact with Krishna, Mira and Indira Devi about whom I have written in my book, Lone Seeker Many Masters.

I always wanted that kind of contact with my master. When I expressed this desire to Osho many years ago during the early days of my sannyas, he chuckled and said, "It will happen."

And as he said, it did happen. The contact with Osho first happened to me in the early days of Asheesh after I had the vision of Naag Raj, the serpent king, at Asheesh. I have written about this incident in the chapter, Asheesh – The Mystical Ashram, in this book. A while after this vision of Naag Raj, Osho spoke through someone's body and gave me a message, showing me that this kind of contact was possible. The first time it happened, it was very brief. After coming, he asked the same question, but in Hindi, "Do you recognize me?" After a few words of inspiration and blessings, he left. One thing I realized was that in every contact he would always say, "You all work together and remain united." At that time, many other masters also came and gave their message and blessings.

The second time it happened was in Nagarkot.

The third time it happened was after my mother left her body. The incident of how my mother left her body with great ease because of the master's grace is included in the last chapter of my book, In Wonder with Osho.

We had finished the funeral and the death celebration, and had come back from the ghats. I was in shock after losing her, and was grieving. Osho came to console me that very night. As I was in great pain from the loss, he said, "What can you do now? Her body had become very weak and was of no use to her, so she has left with my permission. Don't grieve, or it will be difficult for your mother to depart. I am looking after her now, so you don't need to worry. She will soon be reborn."

Hindus have many rituals for the grieving family, especially for the sons of the house where someone has passed away. After a parent passes away, the sons must shave their heads in mourning and undertake thirteen days of seclusion while eating a minimal sattvic diet without salt and milk. During the contact, I asked Osho what rituals I should follow, and instantly he replied, "You don't have to follow anything. This is not my path. You can eat salt and all your normal food and live normally." When I asked him if I had to shave my head, he promptly replied, "No, no, no, you don't have to do anything. You just do what your heart feels is right." I told him that I would send some money to all Osho centers and ask them to make kheer, or milk pudding, in my mother's memory, and serve it during dinner. He said, "That would be the best thing to do."

All my relatives in Kathmandu and back in the village had shaved their heads to mourn my mother's death. Being the only son, when I did not shave my head, it was looked upon as something unacceptable, and this was the last straw for my extended family. Any connection I had with them was finished, and our communication ended forever. They also fully accepted that now I was of no use when it came to familial duties.

Before leaving, Osho said, "It is difficult for me to remain outside the body for too long, so I have to leave now. But as soon as I have dropped my body forever, this contact will become simpler and easier." After saying this, he left us.

Thirty-two years have passed since Osho dropped his physical body, and as he had promised me, the contact between the master and the disciple has really become simpler and easier today. I openly speak of it and write about it here because there is nothing really to hide. It is as true as the sun and the moon and as present as the air we breathe. When a disciple is ready, the master can speak through a thousand mediums. It is as simple as that.

Today, he is my closest companion, guide and beloved with whom I share everything about my life and the work that he has assigned me. I even share with him the secrets and mistakes in my life that I can't share with anybody else in this world. He compassionately guides me through the ups and downs, and patiently makes me understand what I need to understand as I walk along this path towards my own ultimate liberation, towards my nirvana.

Anagarika Dharmapala

There are a few figures in history whose understanding, willpower and sheer perseverance have revived dying spiritual legacies for future generations. The Sri Lankan Buddhist revivalist, Anagarika Dharmapala, is one such figure for whom I have the highest regard, as his selfless life has always been a source of inspiration for me. Whenever I encounter obstacles while doing work for my own master, Osho, I remember Dharmapala who never gave up his work to re-awaken the Buddha dharma in Sri Lanka and India, and serve as the first

Buddhist missionary to the West. The highlight of his work was that he got the Mahabodhi Temple of Bodhgaya back under Buddhist control, and out of the hands of Hindu priests.

Dharmapala was born on September 17, 1864, to parents who were among the richest merchants in Ceylon, now Sri Lanka. They christened him David Hewavitharane, and gave him a Catholic schooling, but Buddhism attracted him from a young age.

'Dharmapala' means 'protector of the dharma', and 'Anagarika' is a title given to a Buddhist who is neither a full-time bhikkhu nor a householder. Dharmapala took this title instead of becoming a bhikkhu so he did not need to comply with the discipline of monkhood and could devote himself full time to his work.

Colonel Olcott and Madam Blavatsky went to Ceylon in 1880 after forming the Theosophical Society in 1875 in New York. There they declared themselves Buddhists and led the Buddhist Revivalist Movement. Colonel Olcott kept returning to Ceylon where he set up more than 300 Buddhist schools. This is when the young David Hewavitharane met Colonel Olcott, changed his name to Anagarika Dharmapala and devoted himself full time to work for Buddhism. He began his work primarily as a translator to Colonel Olcott. He then traveled the world with Olcott, helping him in his work.

Dharmapala went to India to pay his respects to the ancient Buddhist sites in 1891. First, he went to Sarnath. He found that Sarnath, one of the four most important places for Buddhists, and where Buddha had begun giving his sermons and began the Dharma Chakra Pravartana, was a rubbish dump where locals raised pigs. The old chaityas (Buddhist Shrines) were dilapidated, and people used the bricks from the ruins to make their own huts. On January 22, 1891, he arrived in Bodhgaya for the first time. He found the temple at Bodhgaya, the place where Buddha attained enlightenment, to be desolate; the only beings that roamed there were wild animals. People were afraid to spend the night there. The temple was under the control of mahants (religious superiors) of the Hindu Shaivite sect. All the mahants were against Buddhism, and did not allow Buddhists to enter the temple.

Dharmapala also went to Lumbini, the birthplace of Gautam Buddha, and there the situation was the same as in Bodhgaya: Mayadevi Temple was in the hands of Hindu priests. The locals were worshiping it as the temple of Bandevi, the goddess of the forest, and were conducting animal sacrifice and other shamanistic practices. Dharmapala opposed this, and here, too, he was beaten up by the priests. As the then autocratic Hindu Rana regime of Nepal did not allow Buddhists in their country, he was threatened by the authorities and was forced to return to India.

In 1892, Dharmapala became the editor of the Mahabodhi Journal, and held that position for several years.

One of his noteworthy trips to the West was when he went to the United States for the World Parliament of Religions in Chicago in 1893 as a representative of Buddha Dharma. This is where he met Swami Vivekananda, with whom he became good friends. Along with Swami Vivekananda, Dharmapala was also very well received at the Parliament. Together they were able to introduce the philosophical height of the Eastern religions to the West. It was there he read a paper titled The World's Debt to Buddha. He was the first person to speak publicly on Buddhism to a Western audience.

After doing his best to spread the word on Buddhism in the West, he returned to India, and in Bodhgaya he established the Mahabodhi Society and began a movement to reclaim important Buddhist sites that were either in ruin or had been captured by Hindu priests. He met important figures of the time such as Mahatma Gandhi, Rabindranath Tagore and Rajagopalachari, and made them honorary members of the Mahabodhi Society. On November 3, 1922, he laid the foundation piece of the Mulagandha Kuti Vihara, where Buddha used to stay when at Sarnath, and collected funds from around the world to build it again. Even today, the temple stands as a symbol of Dharmapala's efforts.

Throughout his life, Dharmapala tried to get the Bodhgaya temple out of the control of Hindu priests. Although he was not able to succeed, he put up a great fight, and was beaten up and thrown into jail many times. He fought court cases from the Gaya Court to the Supreme Court, but lost everywhere. He was, however, able to get the entry of Buddhist monks into the Bodhgaya Temple. Today, the management of the Bodhgaya temple is run by a committee comprising four Buddhist monks and four Hindu mahants, and the president of the committee is the Chief District Officer of Gaya, but he has to be a Hindu. Still today, the fight of the Buddhists to get control of one of their most important places goes on, from the Indian Parliament to the Indian Supreme Court.

Dharmapala's struggle lasted a lifetime, and he died in Sarnath in December 1933, aged sixty-eight. It was because of his efforts that Buddhists could practice their ways of penance in Sravasti, Bodhgaya, Kushinagar and other important places. His last words were, "I don't want liberation and nirvana. I will think that I am blessed even if I have to take hundreds of lives to revive and establish Buddhism again in this world."

Dharmapala is an example of what one man can do to revive a religion that had almost vanished from the Indian subcontinent. He began the movement, and was later followed by Dr Ambedkar. The Buddhist revival and the reclamation of important Buddhist sites in India and Nepal was of utmost importance. And for me personally, when I find all kinds of forces trying to crush the Osho movement, Dharmapala's lifetime of struggle gives me the inspiration and strength to resist these forces, and spread Osho around the world.

Rescued by Two Mystics

After my sannyas I used to visit my master in Pune at least two times in a year, sometimes even more. In those days the most economical means of transport for me was taking a bus till Patna and then taking a train to Pune from there. There were flights available but traveling by air was expensive for me. After crossing the Nepal-India border in Birgunj I had to change buses and board an Indian bus in Raxaul. Near the old bus station in Raxaul there was a small tea stall and I used to have tea there while frequenting through this route.

During one of my trips I befriended the owner of the tea stall who was an innocent man. When he came to know about my sannyas life he opened up to me and shared with me about some significant incidents of his life. He was a receptive soul and used to be guided by higher souls and celestial beings. He had a special connection with Devi and she used to protect and guide him. He was a poor man with a very small tea stall and except for tea there was nothing at his shop. But his life was full of significant esoteric incidents and this drew me closer to him. I started visiting him every time I passed through that route and would listen to his different stories with great interest. I called him to Kathmandu and later he also ended up taking Osho's sannyas through me.

Once time it happened so that I was visiting Pune and had already boarded the bus in Raxaul, I took my seat and settled my luggage. When I came to know that the bus was leaving at 3 o'clock and there was still half an hour left I decided to have tea and meet my friend at the tea stall. There was already someone sitting next to my seat so I requested the person to look after my luggage and told him that I will be back in a few minutes to which the person courteously agreed.

As usual my conversation with the Swami at the stall was very interesting as he told me all the otherworldly events of his life. After the tea and our little meeting it was time to leave and the Swami came to the bus stop to see me off. There was still ten minutes left for the bus to leave when we reached the station but to my utter dismay the bus was not there. When I inquired I was told that the bus had already left five minutes earlier.

I couldn't believe what I just heard. All my belongings, my money and some valuables were there in my luggage. It was all I had for my stay in Pune and now everything was gone. I was surprised why my co-passenger had not stopped the bus or told them that I had not arrived. I was extremely sad and didn't know what to do. Just then somebody at the station told us that the bus stopped at the petrol pump a kilometer away and if we were in time I could catch it.

I bid farewell to the Swami and instantly took a tempo and asked the driver to speed me to the petrol Pump. My heart was racing and I had very little hope that we would be able to catch the bus. When we reached the petrol pump sadly there was no sign of the bus. "Had the bus not stopped to refuel? Had it already left? Where was the bus?" My mind and heart were both racing. Someone at the station told me that the bus had already left 15 minutes ago. There was no chance that I could catch a bus that had already left 15 minutes earlier on a tempo.

My heart just sank! How was I going to make it to Pune now? It was more than four decades ago and I was not making much money back then. Every penny was hard earned and had great importance for me to sustain in Pune. I was extremely anxious and worried. I was very angry with the other person who knew that I had gone for tea and had still not stopped the bus. All my excitement to go to my master turned into a sad gloom. In those days there were not many buses and vehicles in that area. I just sat there anxious, worried and with no clue of what I was going to do. I started praying to my master.

Just then a vehicle arrived at the petrol pump. There were two men sitting in the front seat and they had come to refuel. When they saw me so anxious they asked me what my trouble was and I explained everything to them. Instantly the man who was driving the vehicle asked me to jump in the car and offered to drive me to the bus. I was greatly relieved. At least now there was some hope. I asked the men to at least refill the car but they said that then it would be too late to catch the bus. We were already 30 minutes behind. These men were like godsend to me and as soon as I jumped in the car the man sped it.

We were back on road again and I already felt immensely grateful to these men who had appeared from nowhere. The car had very little petrol and I didn't know where these men were headed to but they abandoned everything and were now on this mission to catch my bus. The roads in Bihar are very straight and the bus must have been at a high speed so no matter how much we sped behind we couldn't catch the bus. We had already crossed many kilometers and were in Sugauli and still there was no sign of the bus. I slowly started to lose hope and felt a little awkward as these men had gone way beyond to help me. The two men were so insistent in helping me that they were still hopeful that they would catch the bus. They kept speeding the vehicle.

Finally, when we were midway between Sugauli and Motihari we saw the bus at a halt at a train crossing. My joy knew no bounds, the men were also very happy that they were finally able to catch the bus. I instantly came out of the car and told my friends that I would just check my luggage and come back. When I entered the bus, the man in whose care I had left my luggage looked startled. I figured that he had the wrong intentions and was planning to steal my luggage which was why he had not stopped the bus when it left me.

I scolded the conductor who then told me that he had asked my co-passenger if everything was okay, and he had said it was fine. Bihar in those days was full of thieves, dacoits and criminals and the man on whom I had trusted turned out to be one of them. He was planning to take both my bags which had my money and luggage in it. If I had not been able to catch the bus or if the bag had been stolen I would have been left in the middle of nowhere, couldn't go to Pune or come back to Kathmandu and would have had to face great trouble.

It took me hardly a minute to check the bus after which I came out. I wanted to thank my rescuers and at least pay for the fuel as a gesture of my gratitude. When I came out I was shocked!

The vehicle and the two men were nowhere to be found. It was a straight road and one could see far into the distance and I had only been a minute away, they at least needed some time even to turn the car but there was no sight of it. It was almost like they had vanished into thin air. Even if they sped at a maximum speed I would still see them in a close distance. I was baffled and couldn't comprehend what had happened. Where did my rescuers go?

I was happy that I had gotten back my luggage but was equally surprised about the disappearance of my rescuers. I took the bus to Patna and then the train to Pune but all along the way I could not stop thinking about my two friends who had just vanished Iike they were some magicians. I couldn't even thank them for helping me.

For many years I couldn't understand what had happened, I tried to gather much logic but all of it seemed futile in this situation. It remained a mystery to me for many years. After some time I forgot about it. But recently I again remembered it and finally decided to ask about it to divine enlightened beings who have been guiding me. Even back then I had contact with my master or other beings but I never asked about the situation. One thing with oracles, higher beings and enlightened beings is that they will not tell you or answer you about something until you question them.

When I asked about what had happened back then I finally got my answer. I was told that I was in great need and seeing my pain and suffering my master himself had taken the form of a human and had come to help me along with another enlightened master. I know who the other enlightened master is but I am not allowed to reveal his identity. I don't know why I have been asked to keep the identity of the other master a secret but it is what it is and that is the instruction.

Astral beings can take human forms for a short time and there are many incidents in the lives of many people who have received help from higher beings when they were in dire need of it. This was not the only time when I witnessed similar incidents in my life. Much was yet to unfold in the future.

The Call of Garhwal Himalayas

When Osho asked me to start traveling worldwide to spread his message, I realized the importance of a place where people had been meditating for a long time. The Himalayas are a popular destination for yogis from the Asian subcontinent who seek to live and die in its spiritual ambiance. Relics in India, Nepal, and Tibet date back thousands of years, revealing these countries' long and rich religious, cultural, and spiritual heritage.

It is now proven that water absorbs and transports energy. Yogis and saints

Kedar Nath Temple

have known this for thousands of years. This is why Hindus have worshiped the river Ganga as their mother, and have imparted an eternity of esoteric and occult information into the water. They've built most of their great temples around it. It is believed that the Ganga originated not in this world but descended from the heavens. Also, it has been proven that the Ganga water's unique qualities are not found in any other water body on Earth.

The Garhwal Himalayas reveal a mystical truth that goes far beyond human understanding and experience. Yogis and sages flock there to discover the true spiritual meaning of life by connecting with the divine. The peaks of Garhwal have inspired not only awe and a sense of eternity but also philosophies and poetry. The Ganga and the Yamuna are both sacred rivers in India and begin their journeys here. The popular Char Dham, or the four Himalayan shrines, Badrinath, Kedarnath, Gangotri, and Yamunotri, nestle here and have attracted pilgrims down the ages.

I've had the pleasure of seeing the Himalayas in all their glory every year since my very first visit. The Garhwal Himalayas are said to have a sanctity of their own. Every single rock is a wonder, every hilltop has a divine aspect, and every stream has profound holiness. Since my first trip there, I have felt an irresistible pull, and every time there, I wish to remain longer. The more time I spend there, the more I want to abandon all I know and go there permanently, vowing never to return.

A few friends planned for us to go on a spontaneous and unstructured month-long trip to the Garhwal Himalayas. They were Swami Yog Chinmayajee, his girlfriend Ma Nirvayashi, Swami Prem Chaitanya, who was the Income Tax Commissioner for Bihar, and another sannyasin from Bihar and myself. It was a very memorable trip, and I will never be able to forget it.

Before the trip, I had just started my new role as a business consultant, and a few projects were going on simultaneously. I had asked for a month off for this trip, but my business partner was unsure if he could manage the work without me. Finally, he gave in after I asked several times and stressed how important it was for me to be in the Himalayas. Getting his consent was no small feat, but I have no doubt that the beneficent forces of God were at work.

Most of us, except Prem Chaitanyajee, didn't have much money, so we planned to travel on a low budget. We decided from the beginning, in Bihar, that Swami Chinmayajee and Nirvayashi would not have to contribute any money towards the trip, as they were our visiting guests. Swami Prem Chaitanyajee was providing his car, driver, and fuel, while the other sannyasin from Bihar and I would take care of the remaining expenses, namely food, and accommodations.

Our trip began in Kushinagar, where Gautam Buddha left his body. The town had a calm atmosphere, and we experienced more clarity just by being there. The city is known for its history, stupas, and temples and was pulsating with energy as it was the last resting place of Buddha. Having read about Buddha, loved him, and known him for many lives, in this life, however, it was the first time I had set foot on the holy ground of Kushinagar. I can't convey how happy I was; I felt completely at ease, especially at the Mahanirvana Stupa, which houses a statue of Buddha reclining. As I began meditating, tears rolled down my cheeks as my body began to feel the spiritual energy. Such was the magnitude of the energy field there. I wished to stay a little longer, but my friends said we had a long trip ahead of us, so we left for Gorakhpur, me with a sad heart.

Gorakhpur is about 55 km from Kushinagar. It is regarded as the land of ancient mysticism and a pilgrimage destination. We visited many shrines and temples and thoroughly enjoyed being there. I wanted to visit Maghar and see Saint Kabir Das' samadhi. Maghar is a small town about an hour's drive from Gorakhpur. But as most of my friends were not in tune with him, we drove directly to Lucknow, where we spent the night. The next day, we headed for Kathgodam, which is in the Himalayas.

Being in the Himalayas is a blessing and an unforgettable experience. We arrived in Kathgodam at 6:00 pm on our way to Nainital. When we enquired with the locals, we were warned that hotel rooms in Nainital would be hard to come by. Because it was mid-summer and there was a significant tourist rush, hotel accommodation was practically impossible to get, especially late at night. We were clueless yet confident we would find a solution.

We were advised to spend the night in Kathgodam rather than risk traveling on to Nainital. But being so close to the highlands, I remained determined not to stay on the plains. We knew our driver was tired, but still, I asked him just to take us toward Nainital. With a prayer on my lips, I was hopeful that the loving Himalayas would provide us with refuge.

I kept my faith throughout the ascension and was not disappointed. We managed to organize a night's stay at the Kumaon Mandal Vikas Nigam Guesthouse, which was just 10-15 km before Nainital. But the guesthouse belonged to the government and was quite empty. There were no guests, and it had almost no facilities or amenities, and no food. The guesthouse workers usually left in the evening. What's more, there were no restaurants nearby.

Although our bodies were exhausted from the long trip, we were delighted to be in the Himalayan wilderness. After a long day of traveling, we were famished and decided to stroll a short distance in the hope of finding somewhere to eat. The area was underdeveloped; we were lucky to find a paan shop open, which we had seen in the distance. We hurriedly approached it, believing that this place could assist us. To our dismay, the paan shop owner informed us there were no eateries nearby. He suggested we drive up to Nainital, as there were many restaurants open there. Then we could return to the guesthouse at night. We didn't like his suggestion, as we were already tired from our long travels, and going back and forth for a meal didn't make any sense. We enquired about his dinner plans out of curiosity and hunger. He replied that he usually cooked khichdi for himself every night.

We asked him to make some for us, as it was our last hope to eat that night. He reluctantly admitted he had no vegetables but could prepare a basic khichdi with the daal and rice he had on hand. We figured that anything was better than nothing and immediately accepted the offer. At the time, a modest khichdi seemed like a maharaja's thali, although the shop owner didn't even have basic plates. Our khichdi was served on saucers. Fortunately, he had ghee, so we all poured it on our khichdi and savored it. Still, as I write this, I can recall the flavor and satisfaction that modest but excellent supper provided for us. It was divine, and the paan shop owner was our savior.

The night passed smoothly, and we awoke early the following day to practice Dynamic meditation before listening to Osho's discourse. Osho's recorded discourses were only available on audio cassettes at the time. Listening to Osho and meditating in the Himalayas was a magical experience that left us in euphoria.

After finishing our morning meditation, we arrived at Nainital around 1:00 pm and began looking for a place to stay. As expected, the city was swarming with tourists, and all the nearby hotels were fully booked.

We then looked for a hotel up the hill, where we discovered a simple, small house with very basic furnishings and minimal amenities. It was such a good deal that we booked three rooms with lake views. During our stay, we went for walks around the lake, soaked up the sun, and inhaled the fresh Himalayan air. We meditated and talked about Osho for hours. Swami Chinmayajee had lived with Osho for ten years, so he had many stories about him and the commune.

In some of the conversations Chinmayajee and I had on that trip, it felt like he was relaying a divine dialogue. I recall one of the lakeside conversations.

After we finished our morning meditations, I related some of my spiritual challenges. Chinmayajee responded intuitively, saying, "Don't worry, Arun, something big spiritually is about to happen to you within the next two years." When he said this, it piqued my interest, and I jotted it down in my notebook. To my surprise, his prediction came true. When Osho was living in Rajneeshpuram, America, in 1984, he published a list in which he declared many of his disciples to be bodhisattvas, mahasattvas, and sambuddhas. I was named one of the twenty-one bodhisattvas.

Swami Chinmayajee gave several other insightful talks, which I recall now. He claimed Osho had sent him to assist me and said he had come solely to help me establish an Osho commune. He had no idea how things would turn out, but he was there to support me.

He also told me to stop being so attached to my parents because blindly following their advice wasn't making them any happier and definitely making me sad. I was very attached to my parents at that time and did everything they said. To please them, I even married the girl they had chosen for me, which resulted in a failed marriage. I frequently returned home early from my commune visits, concerned about leaving my parents alone. Plus, I was eager to introduce my parents to meditation and the spiritual path in the hope that they, too, would experience the same joy that I had with Osho. I imagined that I could help them in the same way that Osho had helped me. Chinmayajee said everyone follows their own path, and expecting them to be on the same page as me, was a waste of time. He continued, "I have a mother who is still alive, but I rarely go to see her." I fulfill my obligations by sending her money every month. Chinmayajee continued, "By visiting my mother, nothing great will come of it, but I will lose much more."

Osho was a compassionate master and was taking care of all of his disciples. He recognized that Chinmayajee was the only son and had to take care of his elderly mother, so he mandated that the ashram pay him a monthly allowance. Chinmayajee supported his mother by sending her the 700 rupees he received monthly from the ashram.

Hearing all this made me realize how caring and kind the guru is and how everything is taken care of as long as you surrender to him. This conversation helped me immensely and is so memorable because it helped me understand where I was spiritually stuck.

After staying for a few days in Nainital, we arrived at Kanchi, a wonderful town 20 km down the hill from Nainital. A tiny stream of pure, clean Himalayan water ran through it. Being in Tapoban, I feel Osho has blessed me with more than I can imagine. We have many places to meditate, including the newly-built indoor samadhi and the outdoor Kabir Smriti Mandir. But one thing I constantly miss is running water. In many of my past lives, I've had a passion for being around a water body, especially the Ganga. It is safe to say the fascination continues in this life, too.

We discovered a little tea stall where the owner informed us that this was the place where Neem Karoli Baba created his ashram, in which he lived for many years. In fact, he had just recently left his body in Vrindavan. I didn't know much about Neem Karoli Baba or his teachings at the time, but I was intrigued to learn that a famous saint had resided there. We decided to pay a visit to Baba's ashram, Kanchi Dham. The ashram is set in an enchanting forest surrounded by hills and trees. The fresh sound of the river flowing could be heard from there. Inside was a lovely temple where one could feel Lord Hanuman's presence because of the mantra's strong energy field. We saw a few sadhus with their musical instruments continuously chanting "Shree Ram, Jai Ram, Jai Jai Ram" throughout the day. The chanting was so powerful that it formed a strong magnetic charge throughout the entire space, and the seekers could feel Babaji's presence.

Our guide was generous and recounted many magical stories about him. He even offered us free basic shared accommodation, where we would get food and a blanket with which to sleep on the floor. I asked the guide if there was any literature available so I could learn more about Babaji, to which he said no. Exposure to this amount of divinity was exhilarating, and I could sense a strong energy vibration there. In truth, the neighboring spring water was inviting, but my companions were in a hurry to get to Almora. Swami Chinmayajee knew about Babaji as he had read about him. Still, he was hesitant to stay the night due to the uncomfortable shared accommodation. I was disappointed by this, and after a few hours with a heavy heart, we decided to leave for Almora.

We arrived in Almora in the evening and found decent lodgings at the UP Guesthouse, which looked out on the Himalayas. Almora is located in the Kumaon highlands, where many taals (lakes) and hill stations exist. The area has experienced many historic spiritual events. Swami Vivekananda traveled through this area as a renunciate monk. There was a period in his life when he felt such a strong vairagya (detachment) that he left everything behind and wandered all around India. Along with his kamandal (water pot), he would sleep in various places, sometimes under a tree or sometimes in a dharmashala (public rest house). Swami Vivekananda was a self-respecting man and couldn't bring himself to beg for food, so he would only eat if someone brought him food. Otherwise, he would go hungry. Once, he hadn't received food for two days. Tired, hungry, and thirsty, climbing up the hills of Almora in the scorching heat, he fell down and became unconscious.

Because I had read Swami Vivekananda's biography, I was drawn to Almora. As I reached the location, I observed a Muslim burial ground. The groundskeeper happened to be the grandson of the same individual who had fed Swami Vivekananda when he had fallen unconscious. That compassionate man didn't have much to feed Swamijee because he wasn't wealthy, but he did manage to supply a watermelon. He cut the watermelon and squeezed the juice into his mouth, then put the remainder of the watermelon down for Swamijee to consume after he recovered consciousness. Swamijee was very grateful for this gesture, and the Ramakrishna Mission has now erected a memorial near the site of the incident. I adore Swami Vivekananda and could feel his subtle divine presence at that place.

Swami Vivekananda was my first guru, and I have admired him since my school days. The fact that he had fallen down out of hunger made me realize how much pain he had to endure. Even a yogi from the Saptarishi Lok, at such a height as Swamijee, has to suffer like anyone else in coming to this planet in a physical form. Still today, the Ramakrishna Mission, out of gratitude for the watchman's gesture, takes care of and gives some compensation to his descendants.

Swami Vivekananda established an ashram in the Himalayas after returning from his Western tour, during which he had accumulated some money and resources. The ashram is still operating and serves as a venue for Vedanta practices. Surprisingly, it has no images or statues of any deities, adhering to the traditional shoonyam (starkness) of Vedanta. The ashram has grown in popularity over the last few years. When the head of the ashram visited Kathmandu thirty years after our visit there, he also came to our Tapoban ashram, and I thoroughly enjoyed his company. Adding to the spiritual attraction for him were the panoramic views of the Himalayan hills.

During our stay in Almora, we continued our routine of doing Osho meditations and sharing many beautiful stories about him. We had a long itinerary to carry out and had planned to spend more time in the Himalayas, but we were low on money and resources. After we thoroughly enjoyed our two days in Almora, we left for Ranikhet, a picturesque hill station famed for its stunning views of the western peaks of the Himalayan ranges. We slept in a homestay facility, and the most significant part was our host, a wonderful and compassionate person. He was thrilled to host Osho sannyasins and delighted to give us exquisite food. I can still taste the aloo paratha he served us. He would ask for our preferences, and we would request several sorts of parathas. Our plan in Ranikhet was that there would be no plan and that we would live spontaneously until we were content to leave.

After living in Pune for a short time with Osho, my desire to live in a buddhafield with other Osho sannyasins continued. I had a lot of faith and trust in Swami Chinmayajee and wanted to create an Osho commune with him. I decided that wherever Swami Chinmayajee attempted to make a commune, I would stay there with him, leaving all behind. I preferred to build it in Nepal, but Swamijee wanted to build it in the Indian Himalayas. Agreeing with this decision, we decided to explore the Indian Himalayas for a location for the commune. I thought of Kaushani, which is a hill station located in the Bageshwar district of Uttarakhand, about 50 km from Almora. The panoramic snow-clad view of the Himalayas from Kaushani is dominated by Trisul, Nanda Devi, and Panchuli peaks. Kaushani is situated at an altitude of 7,000 ft, with alpine hills, Pine tree forests, and a meandering creek adorning the majestic look. It is said that the beauty of Kausani also bewitched some of the eminent personalities of India. When Gandhijee visited this place, he was so allured by its aesthetic beauty that he called Kausani the "Switzerland of India".

Kausani experiences snowfall during the winter months, and Swami Chinmayajee was apprehensive about building the commune in such harsh weather conditions, even though initially he was open to constructing a commune in the Himalayas.

Instead, he proposed Bageshwar, around 4,000 ft lower than

Kausani. Bageshwar is located at the junction of the Saryu and Gomati rivers and is home to various holy sites and temples, including the Bagnath, Chandika, and Sri Hari temples.

Although the land was cheap in both places, I preferred Kausani because of the view of the Himalayas. He chose Bageshwar because of the weather, and as we had different opinions, we didn't build a commune at either place. After Osho left his body in 1990, Swami Chinmayajee moved to Bageshwar, where he built the small Osho ashram of his dreams.

The next development in our journey was the most remarkable and impactful; we left the Kumaon highlands and entered the Garhwal Himalayas. Karnaprayag was the first place we came to in the Garhwal Himalayas. We arrived in the afternoon after a long journey. In Karnaprayag, there is a sangham (confluence of two rivers) connecting the Mandakini and Brahmani (Alaknanda and Pindar) rivers. I'd never been to the Garhwal Himalayas before, so this was my first taste of its enchantment. I recall my delightful experience sitting at the sangham; I couldn't comprehend the deluge of bliss.

I had no knowledge or recollection of my previous life at the time. Still, I had so much joy that, even though the entire day had passed, we only realized what time it was around dusk. The air grew cold as time progressed. I was fairly young at the time, as were the other sannyasins with me, and we all stayed out far longer than anticipated. We only went to the Garhwal Vikas Nigam guest house after it became unbearably cold.

The Rudraprayag district encompasses two locations: Kedarnath and Badrinath, and we were en route to Kedarnath. Call it a perfect coincidence or a divine plan, but the Kedarnath Temple was scheduled to reopen the very next day, as though it desired that we seek its blessings.

Because this was a completely impromptu and unscheduled trip, we would determine our next site based on the preferences of locals, or one of us would decide, and the others would follow suit. Some locals suggested we go to Kedarnath, which was reopening after a six-month hiatus. It rang the bell of a new excursion to the most frequented tourist and sage destination. We arrived at Gauri Kund, about 17 km below the Kedarnath Temple, on the banks of the Mandakini River. Gauri Kund is nestled among lush forests, providing a beautiful environment with great views. It is well-known for its hot spring, which has been turned into a bathing spot. We enjoyed having a warm dip in the kund to wash away our weariness. We spent the night in Gauri Kund, where food was available until late, and we enjoyed hot, fresh gobi parathas with Osho's stories.

The following day, we had to walk a few miles to get to the Kedarnath Temple, so we hired two horses, on which Chinmayajee and his friend, Nirvayashi, rode while the rest of us hiked up the hill. The area was still relatively undeveloped at the time, and it was snowing when we arrived in Rambada. We were able to obtain some sabzi and rice. The sabzi was extremely spicy, and I recall having to request jaggery to help us swallow it.

We kept going uphill, despite the increasing severity of the snowfall. We didn't have the required snow shields, nor were we properly dressed — no raincoats or anything to protect us. Due to the forecast snowstorm, the government was preparing to close the temple again for a few days. We made it to Kedarnath, where the marketplace was closed, as were the hotels. We had never seen this much snow before. We would have had nowhere to stay if we had proceeded uphill, as all the facilities had not reopened, so we were advised to return. Staying the night in such a low temperature might have been life-threatening. Aside from the temple priest, a security guard, and a few others, the place was quite empty. We were very firm about staying, as we had come a long way to reach Kedarnath, and it would feel incomplete without staying the night. Also, we were way too tired to walk back all the way down. The energy of Kedarnath was holding us. We were supposed to stay at another Garhwal Vikas Nigam guest house, and its workers had already come, anticipating our arrival. They said that even though they would be happy to welcome us, all the pipelines had frozen, and there was no running water in the bathroom. On top of that, as the guest house had been closed for six months, all the quilts, pillows, and mattresses were damp. It would be very uncomfortable for us to stay in such conditions. The windows were jammed and soaked in snow, and the door was held shut by the snow. The entire house was half covered in snow from all directions. This was the first time I'd encountered a situation where the snow had to be dug away for us to open the door – and not just dug away, it had to be cut through.

However, we stayed there and slept wearing our shoes, jackets, caps, and mufflers; whatever we could find, we wore. I think it was the first time in my life that I slept with shoes on. Imagine sleeping with your shoes on!

As the night grew colder, we blamed Swami Chinmayajee. Because of him, we were stuck in the middle of the snow, unsure whether we would make it through the night. Even though they let us have any number of quilts we wanted, it wasn't helpful, as they were all damp. The three of us slept in the same bed, hoping the combination of each other and the quilts would give some warmth. We were convinced none of us would make it through the night to wake up in the morning. So, we chose to sit up and talk most of the night, and with every chance, we got, cursed Chinmayajee.

It is typical human nature that we tend to blame others for our own suffering. All that frustration had to be purged during the trying time we were going through. As Chinmayajee was in the other room, unfortunately, he became our target and the reason behind all our discomfort.

We woke up from a hard night of shivering and very little sleep. The ice had broken through at night, but in the morning, we were snowed in again. As soon as we woke, we used a pan to heat some water to use in the toilet, as the entire bucket had frozen overnight. The trick was to quickly warm up some water on the stove and combine it with the frozen bucket water to make it usable. Any delay would cause the water to freeze. So we hurried ourselves up for fear of having only freezing water.

When we got out of the guest house the next morning, it felt like a bone-chilling minus twenty degrees Celsius; all we could see was snow everywhere. It was a white utopia unveiling the seraphic view of Kedarnath Temple, along with a frozen Mandakini Lake where a few local sadhus were bathing. We didn't even dare to think of bathing as we were already stiff from the cold. There were shops open where we saw some sadhus smoking chillums with marijuana and generously offering us the same. The police had given everyone notice to visit the Kedarnath Temple as early as possible, as it was snowing heavily, and they were going to close the temple by noon for the next few days. There was one small shop where we found hot aloo sabzi, jalebi, and chai. It was probably one of the sweetest jalebis I have ever tasted. We were so thrilled to be getting warm food that we kept eating and drinking without keeping track of how much we were consuming. Some of us had three or four cups of tea, one after the other. Even the shopkeeper was laughing at us. Out of sheer joy from watching the awe-inspiring view, our anguish from the biting cold disappeared. We took back our words from the night before and thanked Chinmayajee for pushing us to stay the night.

The entire area was full of energy. The darshan at the Kedarnath Temple and a visit to Shankaracharya's samadhi was just what we needed to elevate our mood and recharge our souls. Chinmayajee said, "I always wanted to live in the Himalayas, and finally, it came true!" We forgot about last night's discomfort, hardships, and weather conditions. Even though the guest house owners and local police asked us to return due to the harsh weather that was forecast, we simply wanted to stay there. Eventually, we were forced to trek down to Gauri Kund.

Gauri Kund is the gateway to spirituality and salvation. It is believed that taking a dip in its hot spring water will make a person pure. We dived again and again in the hope of guaranteed purity. It was just so freezing outside that the hot water and heavenly views made it wise to stay in the water for hours.

In the Himalayas, yogis often have difficulty cooking food because their wood gets wet, and they cannot get a fire going. So instead, they put their rice, daal, turmeric, and salt in a cloth pot and use the kund, the hot spring pool, to cook the food - and a hot khichdi will soon be ready. This is what they generally eat to survive in all weather conditions. Observing yogis lounge around the kund to prepare their meals made me realize how the divine assists those who yield to it.

On our way to Badrinath, we came across a Nepali mother who had been livibng full time in the Himalayas and practicing her sadhana.

She is the mother of Pradeep Nepal, one of the leaders in the Communist Party. She considered Mast Ram Baba her guru and lived alone near Badrinath. I met this Nepali ma. She was a simple, kind-hearted lady who was delighted to speak to us in Nepali. I remember asking her in awe how she managed to live there in the freezing winters in a small, thatched hut surrounded by a forest. She lovingly replied, saying that I couldn't understand the pleasure of living there. Every night, she said, the entire area would be covered in snow and serve as a communal place for deities. And living in a place like this, she pointed out, in surrender to existence, existence protected her. She added that no one in the area has ever died from the cold or slept hungry at night. Existence takes care of those who are surrendered to it; all are looked after by existence.

She had left her body soon after I met her son and was telling him these stories. He was amused and delighted that I got to exchange intimate moments with his mother.

We continued our journey, heading for Badrinath, which is located in the Chamoli district of Uttarakhand and known for the much-celebrated Badrinarayana Temple dedicated to Lord Vishnu. However, the road to Badrinath was closed by the government due to heavy snowfall, so we couldn't reach our destination. But we felt courageous, and against all odds, we wanted to push on to Gangotri. This small town in the Uttarkashi district hosted the highest temple dedicated to Goddess Ganga (the holy river Ganges). But when we arrived, even that temple was closed, and the UP government house where we stayed, near the temple, was also surrounded by snow. We then drove on to the next stop, Srinagar.

From Gauri Kund to Srinagar, we stopped at various tiny spots along the way.

Located on the pristine banks of the Alaknanda River, Srinagar is known for the Kamleshwar Mahadev Temple, which is dedicated to Lord Shiva. Swami Chinmayajee liked Srinagar also as a place to build an Osho commune. However, I still preferred Kausani, as Srinagar had no view of the Himalayas, and even the river was very far from the city.

After a few days in Srinagar, we traveled about three hours south to Rishikesh, the world's yoga center and the ultimate spiritual destination for any spiritual seeker. I immediately felt as if I had returned home. It was my first time there, and Rishikesh instantly captured my heart; the purpose of my trip felt fulfilled. There were few hotels around, so we stayed at another Garhwal Vikas Nigam guesthouse. We arrived at the guest house late in the evening. After a quick dinner, we went straight into hibernation for the night.

The next day, we decided to go for a walk along the Ganga. Ram Jhula, the iron suspension bridge, was not yet built, so we had to catch the ferry over. En route, we saw sages, saints, fruit vendors and devotees, temples and shops, all blended into a brilliant canvas. As I sat on the ghat's stairs and closed my eyes, I realized that I'd been wandering around the Garhwal Himalayas for nearly a month. While I'd seen nature's majesty and felt spiritual energy in various places, nothing could compare to this beautiful moment. In an ultimate moment of bliss, in tears, I felt it was the happiest I had ever been, and this place was my final destination.

Rishikesh was a one-of-a-kind experience, both spiritually and materialistically. The holiness of the Ganga, sages, temples, and ashrams all contributed to the peace. There were many shops and enough food to go along with the beautiful mountain views and blue water. I spent most of my time on the ghat, either meditating or roaming around and eating at Chotiwala, one of the most popular and inexpensive eateries. We frequently missed the last ferry, which left at 5:00 pm, to the other side where our guesthouse was. We had to walk about 4 km around the banks and use the Laxman Jhula (pedestrian bridge) to cross the bridge. Swami Chinmayajee would often criticize me, yet I couldn't help but stay in the beautiful ambiance on the ghat. I liked it so much that I proposed he build the Osho ashram in Rishikesh, as it was a lovely site with conveniences and spiritual charm.

In Rishikesh, I discovered that Ma Anand Madhu, Osho's first initiated disciple, who had left the Pune ashram, had settled there for a long silence and penance. I had known her since 1969 and intended to visit her, but Swami Chinmayajee said she was in silence and suggested it would be impolite to disturb her. As a result, I was unable to meet her on this trip.

I had a fantastic time in Rishikesh, but as all good things must end, so must my holiday. Everyone was tired of traveling and wanted to return home from this month-long journey. We were roaming around in Swami Prem Chaitanyajee's car, and he couldn't afford to take any more time off from his income tax job. He wanted to return to work as soon as possible. He also missed his wife and children at home. He was adamant about finishing the trip and going home. I was discouraged and stuck, and all I wanted to do was stay with my spiritual mother, the Ganga, for another month.

I was out of money and couldn't afford to stay alone. Swami Chinmayajee suggested everyone, including his friend, Nirvayashi, go home, and he and I could stay in the Himalayas with the 3,000 rupees he had on him. I was delighted to accept this offer, but there was a catch: he wanted to stay in Srinagar, which fascinated him, but I liked Rishikesh. I hesitantly said we wouldn't be able to find a more comfortable home than this, and I wouldn't be able to see the Ganga in Srinagar. With this disagreement, the idea of staying on was abandoned. In the meantime, I persuaded everyone to stay for a few more days. Soon after, Swami Chinmayajee and Nirvayashi urged me to return to work, as all I did was go around the town like a vagabond carrying a bag of Osho books.

I'd sit by the Ganga, watch the water, read books, and meditate. That was my first affectionate spiritual romance with the Ganga and the most beautiful days of that trip, and in fact, my life.

As humans, we frequently associate our source of life with our parents, who gave us their names and identity to obtain acceptance and approval from the world. As a global traveler seeking the true source of happiness, my search culminated when I discovered my spiritual parents - the glorious Himalayas and Mother Ganga. They showered me with love and divine wisdom as a righteous heir. My mother's holy waters emitted the utmost energy, blessing me with glimpses of samadhi and silence for hours as if time did not exist. I became as light as a feather, like a happy child with his nurturing and loving mother.

It's no surprise that the Garhwal Himalayas and Rishikesh attract me like a magnet every year. I have visited the Himalayas probably twice a year, every year, for the last forty years. Still, the majesty of the ranges, like arms welcoming me home, continues to astound me. I make it a point to take the window seat on every flight. The moment I see the shimmering shadows of the Himalayas, even from afar, the child in me smiles with delight, eager to return to my wonderful homeland.

For many, it may appear to be a mystery, but for me, it is my highest reality.

Mystics in Uniform

My life is a humble example of divine protection. If it was not for the protection, guidance and blessings I have received in my life, I cannot imagine where I would have been or what direction this life would have taken. So many incidents have happened in this life and these guidance and protection have come in all kinds of forms. Whenever I was left confused or wondering about a certain incident in my life I was fortunate enough to always get confirmation and guidance from forces beyond me.

Before taking sannyas, I was very

touchy, emotional and used to get angry easily. If triggered my anger could last for hours. I was going through many mishappenings in my life and was extremely frustrated. I had already met Bhagwan in 1969 but unfortunately had not been initiated. It was 1973 and in those days New Road was the most happening part of Kathmandu city. Every evening everyone in Kathmandu used to go to New Road and you could meet all the who's who of Kathmandu on the same street.

I also used to go to New Road in the evenings and visit the house of an acquaintance in New Road who had a gramophone player in his house. I have always been fond of music and in those days I used to love listening to Hemant Kumar, Manna Dey and Geeta Dutt who were my favorite among Hindi singers while Bacchu Kailash and Aruna Lama were my favorite Nepali singers. My acquaintance was a rich businessman and had many music records in his house. I used to go to his house to listen to music.

One day I was at his house listening to music when the telephone rang. The owner of the house was in another room so I picked up and answered the phone and a drunk voice from the other side questioned me in a very rude way, "Who are you?" I was triggered by the rudeness and I also snapped back at the caller. After a few heated exchanges we both started fighting and started screaming at each other. When the owner came back he realized what had happened and took the receiver from me. Apparently it was his partner who was totally drunk and was not in his senses. He was sitting and drinking with a minister and was showing off to the politician. My acquaintance used to share his house with his business partner, they were both bachelors and used to live there. The partner knew me from before and I also knew him but we couldn't recognize each other on the phone. My acquaintance finally calmed us down and explained the situation.

I was so angered that I could not let go of my rage. I felt insulted and belittled. I thought the partner misbehaved with me out of his pride of money and he wanted to show his power. That provoked me even more. When I came back home my anger had only multiplied. I couldn't bear the insult. When I reached home, I told my friend Arjun jee who used to stay with us at my home at that time about the whole incident and he also got enraged. Arjun Jee was even more hot headed than me and he instantly jumped to the conclusion that we had to teach the guy a lesson.

We dashed to the businessman's house and Arjun jee started screaming and calling out the guy to come out. The partner was not at home but my businessman friend came out. Arjun jee was very angry and started screaming, "How can he misbehave like that with Bhaisahab?" Arjun jee used to call me Bhai Sahab meaning brother. The businessman again tried to console and asked us to let it go and told us that it was just a drunken mistake and not intentional. He was actually right and he had no fault in it but we were blinded by anger. Arjun jee kept screaming for sometime and even banged the door. After our little showdown we came back home.

That evening we again went to New Road for our evening stroll when something unusual happened to us. Four local hooligans pushed us for no reason while walking on the street. We just ignored them and went along our way. We used to go every evening to drink tea and the same thing repeated again when those hooligans again disturbed us. This happened continuously for a few days. We thought that maybe it was unintentional as there was a heavy crowd in New Road and that it must be an accident. We didn't know at first but they were trying to instigate us so that we would also say or do something and they could beat us.

On the fourth day when we were walking near Indra Chowk in New Road, again the same thing happened but this time it was very obvious and the guy pushed me very hard. I snapped back at the thug, "Don't you know how to walk? How are you waking?" There were four of them and instantly the one who seemed to be the leader raised his fist to beat me and said, "Shall I show you how?" He had only been waiting all these days for us to retort back so that he could beat us.

Then what happened was beyond my comprehension. To my utter surprise in a flash of a moment, two tall and well built uniformed army men appeared out of nowhere and one of the two literally picked the thug by his neck and raised him up in the air and said, "Is there no law in Nepal that you will do whatever you want? Shall I kill you? You will beat anyone on the street? Who do you think you are? Is this country under your rule?" The army man was very powerful and he raised the heavy ruffian like a feather."

The other three thugs instantly ran away and the leader who was hanging up in the air started asking for forgiveness. When the uniformed man put him down, he also ran away like his friends.

The two men looked at us and sternly said, "You two should not roam around like this at night, now go home."

We went back home but I could not accept the fact how the two army men had appeared out of nowhere. I kept thinking about it and couldn't let it go. At that time I was very fortunate that I was in contact with a very powerful medium who could channel higher souls and enlightened masters and give me the needed advice. The medium had kept this as a secret until he was instructed by those guiding him that he could reveal everything to me. I used to consult the medium whenever I needed guidance or any kind of spiritual advice. All his guidance turned out to be on point accurate and helped me and was a guiding force of light in my life.

My intuition kept telling me that there was more to this incident and the arrival of the two army men out of nowhere was very strange. Usually whether it's the police or army, they don't jump to instant reaction like that without hearing the two sides. And it was very strange how they appeared from nowhere. I had to consult the higher forces. I asked the medium to establish a contact and inquired about the situation. The answer came, "Don't go to the house of those ill-minded adulterers in New Road and don't roam around till late."

"But we go to New Road in the evenings, is it safe for us? I also come back alone from my work from the same area everyday." I inquired.

"You don't have to worry, you always have protection." Was the answer.

I have noticed that during such contacts enlightened souls never blame anything on anybody but only denote the problem or give hints towards it. We got the reference that the whole incident was related to our fight with the businessmen.

There was a Police Sub Inspector that used to visit our house and just for safety I had told him about the whole incident. One evening as I was coming back from my office I saw the businessman coming from the other side of the road. He greeted me normally like nothing had happened. I couldn't stand it. To clear my doubts I snapped at him, "How dare you do something like that?"

The businessman shouted back, "What have I done?"

Surprisingly at the same time, the Sub Inspector was also coming from the back dressed in civilian clothes. He held the hands of the businessman from the back and twisted it and gave him a hard blow. "So this is the guy who is giving you trouble. Should I put you in jail?" The policeman yelled at him.

The businessman started crying and asked for forgiveness. He confessed his crime and said that he would never do it again. The policeman was bent on taking him into custody but I asked him to let him go once he had confessed.

The businessmen were very rich and had felt greatly insulted when we had gone to their house. It was revealed that they had hired those paid hooligans to beat us and used to watch from a distance everyday. After waiting for three days they had forced the thugs to beat us after nothing had happened.

So who were these two uniformed men who had protected us?

Later during my contact with Bhagwan I told him everything and he revealed to me who those two were. One was Bhagwan himself and the other was another enlightened master whose identity I am not allowed to reveal here. They had appeared in the form of the two uniformed men to save us. A guru is always watching. He protects and takes care of his disciples wherever they are. I hadn't even taken sannyas and yet Bhagwan was taking care of me and protecting me.

I am reminded of another incident. It was 1983 and I was going to America for the first time to see my master in Rajneeshpuram. Many people had come to see me off and my mother was crying the whole time. She had a doubt that I would stay in the USA and not come back. Whenever I went to Pune to see Bhagwan I used to stay for months and not come back until all my money was finished. My mother thought that I would do the same thing.

She kept crying and said, "I know you won't come back and we have nobody to take care of us." Many sannyasin friends had come to see me off and the airport was crowded with its daily arrivals and departures. Just then suddenly a hindu monk dressed in ochre robes appeared out of nowhere and started asking me for alms. One of my sannyasin friends who was a high brow government officer had also come to see me off. He said to the monk, "Don't you see the crowd here? You have to ask for money now?" He tried to brush off the monk and asked him to leave.

Instantly the monk looked at my friend and I can never forget the way he scolded him, "Am I asking you for anything. Who are you to intervene in the middle? How dare you ask me to leave?" There was a sense of great command and power in the monk and all of us got scared.

I took out some money and gave it to the monk and asked for forgiveness. He blessed me and just like he had come he disappeared in the crowd. I couldn't forget the vigor and command in the monk's eyes. He was just a beggar but the power in his voice and his radiant presence demanded respect. When I later told Bhagwan about the incident, he said to me, "You were traveling a very long distance for the first time and were coming to me with very limited money. The monk had only appeared that day to bless you so that your journey would not have any obstacles and you could easily reach me. The begging was just an excuse, he had a higher purpose."

My humble obeisance to all those higher beings who are always there protecting us and showing us the light despite our limited understanding, ignorance and unawareness and guiding us towards our ultimate goal of liberation.

Prabhupada—A Mad Love Affair

I have made many trips to Russia. One thing each trip had in common was that when I was coming back home, at Moscow airport, while waiting to board, I would meet a few Krishna devotees from ISKCON (International Society for Krishna Consciousness) going to Vrindavan or Mayapur in India. They were in the traditional clothes of a devotee with a unique mark on their forehead, distinguishing them from others. They wore a small bag, which hung in front, containing the chanting beads to engage their minds in chanting the mantra, Hare

Krishna. Their mini world reminded us of the Vaishnava devotees in India. And when at Delhi, on our way to Moscow, we also see many ISKCON devotees returning to their country with harmoniums, mridangams, and other musical or religious paraphernalia in their hands.

I had mixed feelings of joy and surprise. In Russia, communication is a big problem for us; not many Russians speak English. The climate is cold and harsh. Alcohol consumption is one of the biggest problems in the country and is one of the highest in the world. But overall, Russian people are very sensitive towards Eastern religions and spiritual practices. There is a very good following there of ISKCON, Sai Baba, Osho, and yoga traditions.

While I was active in my profession, I had a good connection with the ISKCON people in Nepal. At that time, their city temple was near my office in Kamaladi. I was a regular visitor to the temple in the early 80s. The head of the temple was Hansa Gaddi Das. He was a very friendly, gentle, easy-going person and very helpful. We had a very deep friendship, and in 1983, when I was going to the USA to meet my master in Rajneeshpuram, he gave me a letter that enabled me to stay in any ISKCON temple in the USA as a life member. There were many ISKCON temples in America. Later, I was given the job of designing the architecture of the main temple and the national headquarters of ISKCON, which was to be built in Budhanilkantha, on the foothills of northern Kathmandu.

It was my pleasure to work with them. We designed an office block, a residential block, the main temple, a guest house, and the gaushala (cow shed). We had designed many corporate and government administrative buildings all around Nepal, but this project had a special spiritual significance. The person in charge of ISKCON in this region was from Australia, Prabha Vishnu Swami. Prabha Vishnu Swami was a Karmayogi, and he collected most of the funds for this project mainly from Australia. He often visited Nepal and gave us many brilliant new ideas for the temple. I had been visiting the construction site frequently. The location was very good. It was in the foothills, and the streams on both sides gave the place a serene look and feel and also inspired me to build an Osho commune.

Many times I have traveled to other parts of the world to share Osho's vision. In the West, big cities are barren land without any spiritual vibrations. You become hungry for spaces where spiritual vibrations cheer your soul. The ISKCON temples are places where you can get not only good satvik food but spaces that nourish your soul. When you visit such places, you often hear mantra chanting or some worship in the temple. You can join in with them as well. I really became joyful in those temples, and I felt the same energy when I meditated in Tapoban. In America and Europe, all the big cities have ISKCON temples. And behind this grand spiritual movement, you can find one person, A C Bhaktivedanta Swami Prabhupada, who fulfilled his master's instructions by making 108 temples and preparing hundreds and thousands of disciples of Krishna.

The success of the Hare Krishna movement is phenomenal. I have met many ISKCON members and found their devotion to their master and work unique and total. Despite the context of traditional Russian society, ISKCON has been able to create its own distinct cultural milestones in the country. They have a good following in almost all cities in Russia and Ukraine, backed up by good vegetarian restaurants, travel agencies, astrological services, and numerous other businesses. Food is a human's basic need, and Hare Krishna restaurants have maintained their benchmark with fresh, delicious, quality food to satiate your taste buds.

In 2015, Swami Arhat and I were in Moscow during Krishna Janmashtami. We had an Osho meditation camp in Moscow. Our respected friend, Dr. Upendra Mahato, invited us to join the Krishna

Janmashtami celebration in central Moscow. It was in a big hall with majestic decorations, a big stage for kirtan, and thousands of devotees celebrating and singing. There were around 20,000 devotees attired in Indian traditional clothing: men in kurtas and dhotis and women in saris. The hall was full of radiant faces eager to dance and chant mantras. The live music added an aura of divine presence. The local devotees were singing bhajans and playing Indian musical instruments. This program was full of life, had vibrant energy, and was spectacular and mesmerizing. In a special lounge, we were offered delicious food, including sweets, and were also presented with a gift of a sweets pack known as prasadam. There were small shops where one could buy religious paraphernalia brought from India. I never imagined seeing so many Hare Krishna people in one place with such majestic beauty.

I was asked to share a few words about the significance of this great festival. As I had come from Nepal and was an Osho disciple, it was an exclusive privilege and a special honor. I shared my words of wonder and gratitude and spoke about Prabhupada to the best of my knowledge. I thanked them for inviting me to such a grand festival and shared my view that this celebration in Russia was possible only because of the courage and devotion of one man, Srila Prabhupada. I called Prabhupada, the commander of the Hindu religion who had alone spread the message of Krishna in the West and had also said that a person like Prabhupada should be born in every century and that would avoid the Third World War. This was received by great applause from the audience. It was already an hour past midnight, but still, it felt as if the celebration would continue for eternity — a really unforgettable moment.

The Bengali bhakti tradition, Gaudiya Vaishnavism, was well presented in the West by A C Bhaktivedanta Swami Prabhupada. His life was full of struggle, courage, and time-tested devotion to Lord Krishna.

The spiritual revolution that he brought about established an entirely new culture in the West. He traveled around the globe fourteen times and established those 108 temples in a mere eleven years.

Tracing his tradition back five hundred years, an ecstatic mystic, Shree Chaitanya Mahaprabhu, had founded a grand movement of bhakti, a congregational chanting of the holy names of Lord Hare Krishna. He used to walk the length and breadth of Bengal and sing holy names as kirtans.

Wherever he went, villagers would join his kirtan in ecstatic public chanting, and the vibes of the celebration would transform the hearts of thousands. Chaitanya Mahaprabhu is considered to be an incarnation of Krishna and Radha. Radha was always in a state of absolute devotion to Krishna. Shree Mahaprabhu would sing songs glorifying Krishna and his devotees and had immense compassion for people who suffered from their material existence. It is said that Lord Chaitanya Mahaprabhu had prophesied, "In every town and village on Earth, the holy name will be preached, and millions would come to Mayapur."

Many masters of the Gaudiya bhakti tradition had predicted that the bhakti movement would cross the seas in time.

A C Bhaktivedanta Swami Prabhupada was born on Tuesday, September 1, 1896, at about 4:00 in the afternoon, the day after Krishna Janmashtami, which is the date of Lord Krishna's birth and the great festival of devotional celebration. In accordance with tradition, an astrologer wrote Prabhupada's horoscope when he was a child, predicting that at the age of seventy, he would go across the sea, propagate ancient wisdom, and establish many temples.

His father was a cloth merchant who belonged to the respected trading community of Kolkata. As a child, he was raised according to the family's own Vaishnava faith and practice. Prabhupada considered he was a fortunate child because he was always surrounded by relatives who were Vaishnava devotees. He even remembered that when he was only about one year old, there was a great sankirtana in the house, and he also joined the dancing party.

He studied at Kolkata's Scottish Churches' College and completed a university diploma in philosophy, economics, and English literature, along with compulsory Bible classes. As a strong revolutionary sentiment had developed within him to free India from the clutches of the British, he considered it useless to serve the system, and so he rejected his diploma.

In 1922, at the age of twenty-six, he met his guru, Bhaktisiddhanta Saraswati, for the first time, at the insistence of his close friend. He had met many sadhus and gurus, but none impressed him. Many of them were living like parasites and were a burden on society. But this meeting had a very big impact on him. In the beginning, he had a very heated discussion with his would-be guru about the fate of the country. He was convinced that first, India must be freed and acquire its political independence, and only then would its spiritual message be heard respectfully. Nobody hears anyone who is coming from a dependent nation, so Prabhupada insisted that political independence and freedom be attained for India. He argued, "How can we talk about religious freedom and spread our spiritual values while we are being ruled by foreigners?" But his guru offered him a different, broader, grander vision and explained, "Politics cannot settle any problem because it doesn't address the real problem. The problem lies in the man himself. Political changes will never bring peace because these changes are part of human ignorance. Until he realizes his inner connection with God, all his attempts on Earth will be in vain and will be accompanied by failures and frustrations. Life is futile strife if one does not devote oneself to spiritual transformation and does not purify one's heart. When we realize ourselves as part and parcel of God, we can be free and live in harmony with the divine, which is the highest of all the transformations. You are an educated and spirited man, so why don't you spread the teachings of Shree Chaitanya Mahaprabhu?" Prabhupada was convinced, and his heart accepted that Bhaktisiddhanta would be his spiritual master. Ten years after this meeting, Abhay Charan Bhaktivedanta Swami Prabhupada received spiritual initiation and became Abhay Charanaravinda (A C Bhaktivedanta Swami Prabhupada).

He was married to Radharani Devi and had five children. As Prabhupada's life was turning towards spirituality, many problems emerged in his family, and his relationship with his wife declined. Gradually, it became evident that no family member would support his journey of truth. Strict Vaishnavism practitioners don't smoke or eat meat, don't gamble or drink tea, don't allow garlic and onion in their kitchen, and maintain strict sexual behavior. Whenever he used to chant or invite people for satsang to show her aloofness, Radharani would go upstairs and engage herself in drinking tea. It became so unpleasant that Prabhupada had to give his wife an ultimatum — choose him or tea. She chose tea.

His guru had reminded him to print and spread Vedic knowledge. Prabhupada was very busy publishing spiritual literature related to Vaishnavism. It was the master's instruction to print books, and he was single-handedly compiling, typing, proofreading, printing, publishing, marketing, and selling. It was very arduous to do so many things without much financial support or support from the family. In 1944, he started publishing the magazine, Back to Godhead.

His pharmaceutical business, which had been going well, collapsed suddenly. His servicemen and employees took everything, and he could not revive the business.

It was the year 1959. One day, his wife took his draft copy of the Bhagavatam and sold it for biscuits and tea. When Prabhupada returned home and realized what had happened, the words of Lord Krishna in the Bhagavatam flashed through his mind, "When I feel especially merciful to someone, I gradually take away all his possessions." An unwavering resolution filled his heart, and he left home for good.

He went to Jhansi and created the League of Devotees. An old property, Bharati Bhawan, was given to him by his local admirers to carry on his spiritual mission. Everything went well for a while, and he had great plans to expand his work. He even initiated his first disciple. But the crooked local politicians and some influential businessmen had greedy eyes aimed at taking possession of the property. He could not endure the conspiracy and had to surrender the property. Without support, the attempt to establish a spiritual movement in Jhansi could not succeed. It was a time of utter disappointment. But nothing could dissuade him. He felt a deep inner call, and his heart was drawn to Vrindavan.

Vrindavan is the place where Krishna lived five thousand years ago. Many Indians go to Vrindavan to spend the last part of their lives there so that in the aura of Krishna's land, they can focus their minds on devotion to Krishna and die peacefully. But Prabhupada had a different plan. The spark ignited by his master was aflame. In Vrindavan, living on the premises of temples, he studied, prayed, wrote commentaries on Bhagavatam, gained spiritual maturity, and prepared himself for his mission.

During this time of utter hardship, his master appeared in his dream again and again, asking him to accept sannyas, the stage of renunciation in which he could totally devote himself to the cause of spreading the spiritual message afar. He was given the name A C Bhaktivedanta Swami on taking sannyas. As a sannyasin, he felt more blessed, determined, and focused.

The printing and distribution of books were possible only in

Delhi. After finishing writing the commentaries on the 1st Volume of Srimad Bhagavatam, he printed the book. He walked along one dusty street after another to find a person curious enough to obtain a copy. The streets were burning with the heat. Hungry and thirsty, he had great difficulty finding anyone interested. It was unfortunate that under the influence of Western thinking and the desire for material wealth, Indian people had forgotten their own spiritual and cultural roots. The attempt to inspire even a single person to get a copy of the book was an arduous task, and he was not succeeding.

Devoting himself to producing commentaries on the Srimad Bhagavatam, he presented a copy to the then-prime minister of India, Lal Bahadur Shashtri, who appreciated it and recommended the book be kept in every library in the country. Within two years, he continued his commentary and produced two more volumes.

He felt that if Western people heeded his message, only then would Indians take it seriously. But as a sannyasin, he did not have the financial resources to pay for a trip to the USA, so he had to rely on well-wishers who could sponsor him. He asked many people to sponsor his trip, but everyone rejected him. Once when in Mumbai, he felt that a lady by the name of Sumati Morarjee, who was the chairperson of Scindia Steam Navigation Company, could help him arrange his journey to the USA. She had a pious reputation for helping religious people and monks. After waiting for many hours at the front door of the company's building to meet her, he was finally allowed to see her. After seeing his work, she was impressed and ready to help him. When Prabhupada asked her to arrange his trip to the USA, she was surprised. She felt that he was too old to go there to propagate religious wisdom.

In the meantime, Prabhupada had a sponsorship letter in Delhi signed by Gopal Agrawal. He had asked a businessman in Delhi for sponsorship to the USA, saying he wanted to go there to preach and propagate the philosophy of Vedic wisdom. The businessman had arranged for the paperwork to be processed by his son living in Pennsylvania, USA.

Sumati Morarjee, seeing Prabhupada's firm resolution, arranged for him to travel on her America-bound cargo ship. She reserved the first-class proprietor's cabin for him. The name of the ship was "Jaladut" (the water messenger), which in fact, turned out to be prophetic. The ship was carrying a person who would spread Krishna consciousness in the world and bring thousands to the land of its origin, India.

The day before his departure from Kolkata to America, Prabhupada went to Mayapur to visit the samadhi of his guru, Bhaktisiddhanta Saraswati. He prayed and asked for his blessing to fulfill his vision of spreading Shree Mahaprabhu's teaching.

He took a suitcase with a few volumes of the Bhagavatam in it and had only forty rupees in his pocket. The journey took thirty-seven days, during which time he suffered two heart attacks without medical support, and he lost all hope of reaching the USA. But he had a mystical vision in which Krishna was steering the ship and smiling at him. It was a clear message that everything would be alright.

After a brief stopover in Boston, Prabhupada stayed in Pennsylvania, then in a yoga teacher's house in New York. He saw the great material prosperity of America but also noticed a great spiritual void and bankruptcy in the culture. He settled in the Lower East Side of New York, where a large number of hippies had gathered experimenting with drugs and sex. They were revolting against the traditional values of society, rejecting morality and creating a new counterculture based on drugs, sex, and music. They were seeking freedom but were destroying themselves. He did not know how to approach this group. He wanted to show them the right path to inner freedom. There were a few violent attacks on him as well, and his books and typewriter were stolen.

In utter desperation, he started kirtan satsang regularly, and a few young people turned up. Seeing positive responses from these youths, he took kirtan to nearby Tompkins Square Park. It created an unusual scene — an Indian Swami chanting some Sanskrit mantra and a few of his followers dancing and singing in ecstasy. It slowly began attracting people until hundreds of people joined in, chanting and dancing. On October 10, 1966, the New York Times published an article titled "Swami's Flock Chants in Park to Find Ecstasy," with a photograph of Swami chanting and others dancing in the park. It created waves across America. Suddenly, Swamijee and his followers were in the spotlight. It was a great success. It heralded the dawn of a new culture arising in a Western land.

The elm tree under which Prabhupada conducted the kirtan still exists and is named the "Hare Krishna Tree." It bears a plaque as a tribute to this historical activity. Prabhupada later reminisced, "When I came to your country, my primary strength was chanting the Maha-mantra while sustaining myself on public contributions and distributing my Srimad Bhagavatam commentaries."

At the beginning of the movement in New York, Prabhupada used to serve food to two hundred people every Sunday. He was a very skillful cook and could make tasty vegetarian prasadam, which attracted many people. He insisted that whoever came to visit the temple should receive prasadam. He remarked, "I made this movement successful simply by a love feast. They did not come to hear "Hare Krishna"; they came for the love feast." People's taste buds got the best vegetarian food around, and their minds got the mantra to chant. This combination worked magically.

On August 8, 1966, he founded ISKCON in New York to spread the vision and carry on the work, both in America and all around the world. Many youths who felt their lives transformed took initiation and became full-time devotees. Rules for neophyte practitioners were developed to safeguard their spiritual journey: chanting sixteen rounds of Maha-mantra and regulated principles that meant no intoxication, no illicit sex, and no gambling.

Prabhupada suffered another heart attack in San Francisco. The cold climate of the northern hemisphere did not suit him, and he immediately returned to India. He instructed and guided his followers through letters. He addressed all issues of devotees minutely and gave practical suggestions to carry out the work and their personal spiritual growth.

One year later, in good health and with vigor, he returned to America and then began traveling to major cities around the world to expand the movement. People gathered, from small groups of devotees to large gatherings of followers, and temples, ashrams, and communities were created. The first Radha Krishna temple was built in LA, becoming a place of solace for millions.

There was a court case in NY blaming the organization for brainwashing. Local churches and others with vested interests were not happy and had a difficult time watching the popularity of the Hare Krishna movement. Prabhupada admitted that he washes people's minds of drugs, negativity, and wars. Later the court declared that this movement which came from India was not a manipulative cult but a bona fide religious way practiced in India for a thousand years. This decision of the court brought the movement into the spotlight in American society with a very healthy message. It was a great victory.

In 1971, Prabhupada created the first temple for ISKCON in Kolkata despite resistance from religious zealots. He visited Africa, Australia, and Moscow in the same year. The KGB of the Soviet Union declared that the Russian regime's greatest threat was "pop music, Western culture, and Hare Krishna." Prabhupada had started the whole project with a vibrant community of devotees and the ISKCON headquarters in Mayapur, where Chaitanya Mahaprabhu was born.

The last part of his life was very hard because of his failing health. He suffered three heart attacks, was a diabetic, and was confined to his room in Vrindavan. Nonetheless, he engaged himself in commenting on the Bhagavatam. He was constantly surrounded by devotees chanting holy names. He breathed his last on November 14, 1977, to be part of the leela of his beloved Lord Krishna.

Prabhupada produced many commentaries on the Gita and the Bhagavatam. A few weeks before he left the body, he made a statement, "Whatever I have wanted to say, I have said in my books. If I live, I will say something more. If you want to know me, read my books". He has fifty volumes of translations and commentary, sixty volumes of lectures, thirty-seven volumes of conversation, and five volumes of correspondence, each approximately four hundred pages in length, in both printed and electronic form. To survey all his work is a project for a lifetime.

To one question from a journalist, he briefly summarized his life, "My life is simple. I was a householder. I still have my wife, my children, and my grandsons. My guru maharaja gave me the order, "Go and preach this wisdom in the Western countries." So I left everything on the order of my guru maharaja, and I am trying to execute the order. That's all."

Maharishi: Guru of The Beatles

During my college days, I used to go and visit every saint that came to town. When I heard that Maharishi Mahesh Yogi was in Patna, the city where I was studying engineering, I just had to go and attend his satsang. This was in 1968 when Maharishi was only fifty-seven, but he was already world-famous, and the crowd that had gathered to hear him talk was fairly large. I had made it a point to sit in the front row whenever I went to hear a guru talk, and this time was no exception. Although it was very difficult to get through the crowd, I made my way to the front row and sat right in the middle to get the best view. When Maharishi arrived, I found him to be very jolly, fresh, and graceful. He spoke in Hindi and said that the purpose of life was to be blissful, and in his presence, there was indeed a blissful aura. I immediately became a part of it.

I used to meet a lot of yogis and saints in those days, but what set Maharishi apart was his contagious joy and happiness. During his talk, he said that he had created thousands of Transcendental Meditation (TM) teachers, but the world was in need of thousands more. He urged young people to learn TM and join the movement, and travel around the world as his messenger. He said he didn't demand much from the TM practitioners, just twenty minutes of TM in the morning and twenty minutes in the evening.

Although I was very much impressed by Maharishi, I did not join his movement because I was connected with the Ramakrishna Mission and had extensively read Ramakrishna and Vivekananda literature. But I have always admired Maharishi's courage and ability to spread meditation around the world to people with no spiritual background whatsoever. Maharishi Mahesh Yogi is a name that is synonymous with twentieth-century spirituality. He was one of the many gurus from India who was inspired to travel to the West and spread the ancient science of yoga and meditation.

Maharishi, born Mahesh Prasad Varma to a well-off business family, went on to get a degree in physics at Allahabad University. After graduating, instead of beginning his profession, he went to the Himalayas on a spiritual quest. He traveled all the way to Badrinath and Kedarnath, looking for a master. He met many monks but finally found his guru when he met Brahmananda Saraswati, the Shankaracharya of the Jyotir Math monastery. Totally devoted to him, he served him as his assistant for eleven years until the guru's death in 1953. Maharishi then went on a two-year silent retreat to an unknown place in the Himalayas. On his return, he introduced the world to Transcendental Meditation, or TM, as it is popularly known. He began teaching TM in India but sensing that it would be better accepted in the West, he seized the opportunity to travel the world. He began a series of world tours in 1958, and by 1965, he had already circumnavigated the world five times, taking TM to as many people as possible. In 1986, he introduced the Siddhi Meditation program, which was for seekers who had already practiced TM and wanted to go deeper. The practitioners of Siddhi Meditation, or yogic flying, as it is popularly known, began their practice by hopping while seated in padmasana, or lotus position, with the ultimate aim of being able to levitate.

TM became famous around the world in the 1960s, and The Beatles, along with other celebrities, met Maharishi and learned TM from him. The film of the Beatles taking part in the TM teacher training program at the Chaurasi Kutia Ashram in Rishikesh in February 1968 gained worldwide attention, and just like The Beatles, Maharishi also became an international superstar. His stardom, brought about by his association with The Beatles, helped make TM a global phenomenon.

Maharishi said that TM, which was devoid of all religious rituals, could be practiced by people of any religion. Most people who tried this simple twenty-minute routine of reciting a mantra silently in their mind felt instant calm and alertness. The mantra was to be different for each person and could only be given by a certified TM teacher for a hefty fee. Countless people had transcendental experiences while practicing TM, which contributed to its worldwide propagation.

In a recent interview, Paul McCartney of The Beatles described his first and most memorable experience while practicing TM when he was in Rishikesh. He said while he was meditating one day, he suddenly felt like a feather floating on hot air. When he reported this to Maharishi, he giggled and said, "That is very good."

In 1982, when I was on a tour of Uttarakhand, I went to Rishikesh and felt as if I had come home. I stayed there for five days just wandering around on the banks of the Ganga River, feeling very blissful and fulfilled. A big part of my mind was telling me to forget everything else and settle down there. One day, I went to visit the Maharishi Ashram of Rishikesh, known as the Chaurasi Kutia, meaning eighty-four huts. It is located on the hill above the Parmarth Niketan Ashram and has a fantastic view of the Ganga. When we were about to enter the main gate, there was quite a commotion going on there. The rule of the ashram in those days was that only men were allowed in. Females of any age were not allowed to enter. This rule had come about because of an alleged scandal that had happened in the ashram. The main reason why The Beatles had suddenly left the ashram was that a friend of theirs had said that Maharishi had sexually assaulted her. Although there was no proof of this, The Beatles hurriedly left the ashram and broke their relationship with their guru. When they left, Maharishi said that he would always have a love for The Beatles, and they were free to do as they wished. For Maharishi, who was a Bal-brahmachari, a celibate since childhood, the allegation brought about instant defamation. No wonder the ashram denied entry to women even decades after this incident.

George Harrison, guitarist of The Beatles, didn't meet Maharishi again until the 1980s. He has said in interviews that during the meeting, he asked for Maharishi's forgiveness for their irrational behavior and to be guided by him again as he was going through a rough time.

By 1982, a long time had passed, but females were still not allowed to enter the Chaurasi Kutia. They were so strict that even infants were not allowed if they were female. When we reached the ashram gate, we saw a man carrying an infant who was barely a year old. The child was his daughter, but as he wanted to take her in, he told the gatekeepers that she was his son. The gatekeepers found the man's behavior suspicious and told him to take off the child's underwear and prove that the child was his son. The man, who couldn't control his humiliation, started sobbing and walked away.

I can never forget that inhuman incident that happened at the ashram gates.

Although I was disturbed by the incident, once I entered the ashram, I found it rather peaceful. Tiny dome-shaped huts were scattered over the property, which was adjacent to a dense forest. When we went to the meditation hall and sat in meditation, I found tremendous peace there. The hall was full of local sadhus from Rishikesh. I was very surprised to see them there. They were not TM practitioners. As soon as the bell rang, signaling the completion of the meditation, they started making a lot of noise. Some of them even began quarreling. I asked what was going on, and a resident said that since the ashram did not have many practitioners, they allowed locals to come and have free food if they attended the half-hour meditation. This created a commotion in the hall, as the hungry sadhus did not want to miss their free meal.

Once I was out of the meditation hall, a man who looked like a resident of the ashram came towards me and greeted me with lots of love as if he had found a long-lost friend. He invited me to his hut, and when we were inside, he locked the door and disclosed that he was an Osho sannyasin.

"I used to live at the Pune ashram, but when Bhagwan left for America, I had to leave. Having no means of earning a living, I wandered around and ended up in Rishikesh. I found out this ashram not only lets you stay for nothing but also gives a stipend of 700 rupees a month if you are a graduate. All I have to do is attend the morning and evening meditations, and the rest of the time, I can do whatever I want. I spend my time reading Osho and doing his meditations. I cannot wear my mala in public and reveal to them that I am an Osho sannyasin, but as I love the Ganga and like the energy of this place, I am very happy here," he said.

Hearing him, I felt that I, too, could do the same. If I was to settle down in Rishikesh, there would be no better deal than this one. I could have accommodation and meals free of charge. The ashram was peaceful, and I could go for a walk on the banks of the Ganga anytime. My newfound friend encouraged this idea as he would have another Osho sannyasin in the ashram. The idea had great appeal, but destiny had other plans for me. I somehow convinced myself that I needed to move on, and so I bid farewell to my new friend.

Although the rules of the Maharishi Ashram were strange, I have visited the place many times in my countless trips to Rishikesh over the years, the main reason being that I found tremendous peace and energy in the meditation hall. Sitting silently there, even for half an hour, would transport me into a world of bliss.

Maharishi's influence in the spiritual sphere of the 20th century is undeniable. Along with countless celebrities, he also nurtured some of the most well-known spiritual figures of the day, two of the most famous being Sri Sri Ravi Shankar and Deepak Chopra.

Ravi Shankar was a Rigveda pundit by training and had become Maharishi's disciple in the mid-1970s. Drenched in the Vedic sciences, Ravi Shankar quickly became one of Maharishi's favorites. Whenever there were functions, Maharishi wanted the four pundits of the four Vedas to be on stage around him, and one of them had to be Ravi Shankar. But in 1981, Ravi Shankar, then also known as Sri Sri, broke away from Maharishi and created the Art of Living Foundation. He took the title of his foundation from Maharishi's famous and only book, The Science of Being and the Art of Living. He then went on to establish a spiritual movement with millions of followers.

Dr. Deepak Chopra, was a practicing endocrinologist in

America when he met Maharishi for the first time in 1984. The personal meeting left a deep impression on the young Deepak Chopra, who had already been practicing TM. Maharishi urged him to leave his medical practice and join him full-time. Deepak soon made up his mind and became apprenticed to Maharishi, who introduced him to Ayurveda, among other things. Although Deepak never became a TM teacher, he helped Maharishi by writing various bestselling books and giving lectures to celebrities, business magnates, and many people from the higher strata of society. Deepak Chopra was a great help to Maharishi, who loved him dearly, but as with Sri Sri, Deepak was not able to fit into the large and complex organization that Maharishi had built around himself. In 1993, they parted ways, and Deepak established the Deepak Chopra Foundation, through which he is still working to uplift human consciousness through meditation, Ayurveda, and yoga.

While Ravi Shankar and Deepak Chopra praised their guru whenever the chance arose, they were not able to continue Maharishi's legacy the way Maharishi had wanted them to. Nonetheless, both are working hard by inspiring millions on the spiritual path and have become two of the most well-known spiritual teachers of our time.

While I have mentioned some of the well-known disciples of Maharishi, I also met one disciple, Swami Sailendra, who is totally unknown to the world and was in seclusion doing one of the toughest sadhanas possible when I met him in 2008. I have written in detail about him in my book, Lone Seeker Many Masters. I met him in the middle of the forest in Amarkantak. He was living in absolute seclusion as per the direct order of his master, Maharishi Mahesh Yogi.

Swami Sailendra had reached the peak of his career, becoming the CEO of some of India's biggest companies. But his success only made him aware of the emptiness of life. This led him to the Himalayas in search of a guru, and he settled only when he met Maharishi in a place called Tapoban, 14,000 feet above sea level. After he learned TM, Maharishi, sensing his great potential with his background in management, took him on a world tour on his private jet. He wanted Swami Sailendra to help him set up the Maharishi University. Swami Sailendra worked for the Maharishi University in Nairobi, Oslo, and the USA but was not happy in the West. He wanted to go back to the Himalayas, but Maharishi told him the best place to continue his meditation would be in the forest of Amarkantak. So, he went there and stayed at the Kalyan Shiva Ashram run by Baba Kalyan Dasji Maharaj. When Maharishi heard that Sailendra was living there, he sent word to him to leave the ashram immediately, go into the dense forest and meditate there alone.

Heeding his guru's command, Swami Sailendra left the ashram with two blankets, two sets of ochre clothes and a bag of wheat flour. In the forest, he made a small canopy with one of his blankets and began his penance.

When I met him, he had been living alone in the forest for years, totally surrendered to existence, and continuing his yogic flying practice. He had given up reading newspapers and even spiritual books.

Although I did not see the spark of God-realization in his eyes, I found an honest seeker in him. He also admitted he wasn't enlightened, but his horoscope predicted he would attain enlightenment in 2017, and he had full faith in the prediction. I don't know if he has attained it or not, but his honesty will surely bear fruit. I felt he must have reached the height of vairagya (detachment) to be able to leave everything and find peace in that abandoned forest. I had a very honest and deep conversation with him, the detail of which is in the chapter, Sadho Sahaj Samadhi Bhali, of my book, Lone Seeker, Many Masters.

A Nepali Osho sannyasin who was living in Japan had gone to

meet Swami Sailendra after reading my book. He came back and told me that he was doing well and had sent his regards.

Meeting Swami Sailendra only increased my respect for Maharishi Mahesh Yogi. Not only had he introduced meditation to complete beginners, but he was also guiding seekers who were aiming to be God-realized in this lifetime.

Maharishi's main wish was to change the collective consciousness of the whole world. After spending a few decades in the USA, he moved to the Netherlands in 1990 and formed the Natural Law Party in 1992. His disciples in many countries, including the USA and England, fought in the general elections of their respective countries. Although they were not successful, they did give the public a chance to vote for a party whose policy was based on natural laws, meditation, and spiritual growth.

One of the most important experiments of Maharishi's organization is popularly known as the Washington effect. This took place when Maharishi invited thousands of meditation practitioners from around the world to come and meditate together in Washington, DC, for a few months. During this time, they measured various indicators in the city and found that the average crime rate, road accidents, blood pressure, hospitalization, and various other adverse things had been greatly reduced.

This experiment scientifically proved the power of meditation on society as a whole and showed that even if a small fraction of the people in a city meditated regularly, many things would change positively. I have read many Gurus say that even if one percent of the population of a city meditates, it will change the psychological and spiritual quality of the whole city. It is also one of my cherished dreams that if 300,000 people of Nepal, which is one percent of the population, regularly practice yoga and meditation and maintain a sattvic vegetarian diet, it will change the consciousness of the whole country.

Just like Osho, Paramahansa Yogananda, Prabhupada, Swami Rama, and many other Indian mystics, Maharishi Mahesh Yogi also tried to establish a large buddha-field in the West to balance the aggressive and negative energy of the world. It is due to the selfless work of saints such as these that the world still functions. Without them, we would have already witnessed the Third World War and self-destruction.

Bhagwan the Healer

With each of his disciples Osho has a unique and individual relation. Every disciple has their own unique story with the master and it is very personal and distinctive to that very disciple. Another such story of surrender and miracle is that of a Swami who was working at the Jeevan Jagriti Kendra run by Ishwar Bhai in Masjid Bundar Road in Bombay during early seventies. The Swami told me about how he witnessed the grace of the Master in an impossible situation after finally choosing the path of surrender and trust during a period of great predicament.

The Swami had an ailing mother at home whose body had been paralyzed for years. After coming to know about Osho's Mt Abu camp the Swami felt a deep calling to attend the camp. He tried to resist the temptation to go as he had an ailing mother at home, and he was the only son attending to her needs. When the calling became too intense, Swami could not stop himself and decided to go for 10-day retreat. He arranged for someone to take care of his mother and left for the meditation camp. His heart felt a little heavy leaving his mother behind but he still took the jump and left.

Mount Abu was one of Osho's favorite places and during the period between April 1971 and January 1974, Osho conducted 10 meditation camps of 9 days before he moved to Pune in March 1974. The meditation camp of January 1974 in Mt Abu happened to be the last meditation camp that Osho himself took before moving to Pune. After that all the camps happened in Pune. Missing the Mt Abu camp even after Osho's precise invitation and instructions will always remain a regret in me as those retreats used to be long residential intensive retreats personally guided by Osho. Many Osho sannyasins were transformed forever through these long intensive camps with Osho.

So, when the Swami arrived in Mt Abu he instantly dived into Osho's energy pool and became intoxicated with bliss. Even though his situation was not favorable, he had taken a risk to be with the master and because he had paid the price for it his meditation also deepened in the camp. He was so happy in meditation that he forgot all about the problems he had left back at home until a telegram arrived bringing the news of his mother's declining health. He was asked to go back immediately as his mother's health was rapidly deteriorating and it seemed that she would not live very long.

The Swami was thrown into a great quandary, and he did not know what to do. He was already feeling guilty for having left his mother behind and the right thing to do now was to go back. However he did not want to leave Bhagwan, he was floating in Bhagwan's waves of bliss and did not want to leave the camp. After churning his mind for hours, he finally decided to ask Bhagwan about what he should do.

The Swami went to Bhagwan and told him everything. He was also very sad that his already paralyzed mother was suffering from more health issues. Bhagwan asked him what he wanted to do, and he told Bhagwan that he was really enjoying the camp and did not want to go back. Like always Bhagwan gave his clear answer, "Then don't go and stay for the camp."

After hearing Bhagwan, the Sannyasin decided not to go and complete the meditation camp. Although his mind and heart constantly bothered him, he still stayed back and remained with Bhagwan. We can only imagine how he must have felt. Nevertheless, he had again taken the jump!

After the meditation camp was over, the Swami returned home with a very fearful mind and a heavy heart. He was already expecting the worst. His mother was already in paralysis and with a further decline in health there was very little chance for her to survive.

When the Swami arrived home what he saw left him flabbergasted. His mother was healthy and was walking around the house. He couldn't believe his eyes. In great amazement he asked his paralyzed mother, "What happened to you? How did you become healthy?"

The mother replied, "One afternoon when there was no one in the hut a Sadhu came outside and started begging for alms. As I was laying down in my bed I shouted from inside and told the Sadhu that I was sick and could not come outside to give him alms and there was nobody else in the house."

"But the Sadhu ignored my words and kept asking for alms. When I told him that I could not move my body the Sadhu said that there is nothing wrong in my body and I should come outside and give him alms."

She told him that the Sadhu was very persistent and kept asking her to try and move the body.

"Just to make the Sadhu happy I moved my body, and I was shocked to see that there was nothing wrong in it and I could move my body. I went outside and gave alms to the Sadhu and thanked him for this miracle. He smiled and gave me blessings and left."

The Swami asked the mother what the Sadhu looked like to which she replied, "He was in white and had a long black beard with a glowing radiant face. It looked like an ancient Rishi had arrived at my doorstep."

The Swami was already in tears of gratitude and showed a picture of Bhagwan to the mother and asked, "Did he look like this?"

Now it was the time for the mother to be surprised. "Yes, this is the same Baba who had come at the door, it is Him! It is Him!" she exclaimed.

The Swami told the mother that the man in the picture was his Guru in whose meditation camp he had gone to and how he was with him in Mt Abu throughout the retreat. It was humanly impossible for him to be there at the house.

The mother and son had both understood how fortunate they had been to have been blessed by the grace of an enlightened master. Their eyes were overwhelmed with tears and their hearts were filled with gratitude for the radiant Sadhu whose immense compassion had graced their lives.

Our heartfelt Naman to HIM!

Swami Anand Arun with Monika Devi

Monika Devi: Disciple of Totapuri Baba

After the completion of our meditation retreat at a beachside resort in Puri, India, in 2004, I went to visit the samadhi of Totapuri Baba, the famous enlightened master who had initiated Ramakrishna Paramahamsa into Advaita Vedanta. The samadhi was on the outskirts of the city on a small hillock surrounded by a forest. Totapuri Baba lived a very long life of 250 years and was known as the Nangta, the naked one, as he was initiated as a Naga Sadhu and wore no clothes, living bare-bodied throughout his life. After leaving Dakshineshwar in Bengal,

Baba traveled to various holy places in North India and, in 1920, arrived in Puri, where he lived until 1961. He left his body in Puri on August 28, 1961. A marble shrine of Baba has been constructed over his samadhi.

The place was charged with Baba's energy, and after meditating there for some time, I wanted to know more about him and his life. As there was no one at the ashram, I waited the whole day for the brahmachari attendant who lived there to come home. He finally arrived in the evening, but as he spoke very little, it was hard to get much information from him. Just as we were leaving, the brahmachari gave me a book written by one of Baba's female Bengali disciples, Monika Mitra. That's how I first came to know about her.

Not much is known about Totapuri Baba, but what I have come to know, I have written in my book, 'Lone Seeker, Many Masters.'

Monika suffered from a chronic headache and had settled in Puri in the hope of recuperating. She had been drawn by a mysterious force to Baba's ashram. Baba spent most of his time in solitude and silence and didn't allow any casual visitors. But after her persistence in visiting him and Baba seeing Monika's good samskaras from past lives, he allowed her to visit him frequently. Monika's memoir is a beautiful collection of her days spent with Baba and the incidents and miracles that happened around him. Today, Monika's memoir is the main source of information available on Baba's life.

Monika's family had brought her to Puri because of her weak health and chronic headache, hoping the tropical weather, the ocean air, and the spiritual energy of Jagannath Puri would heal her. One day, Monika was sitting silently close to where Baba was meditating. He opened his eyes and asked, "What is the matter with you?"

She did not want to bother Baba with mere health problems, so she didn't tell him what was bothering her. But Baba knew what she was suffering from. He called her towards him, put his hands on her forehead, and closed his eyes. Baba was giving an energy transmission, or shaktipat, to her higher chakras. When he opened his eyes after a while, he said, "This disease will not bother you again. You have been cured forever."

By Baba's grace and energy, Monika's ailment was totally healed. When her family came to know of this, they called her back to Calcutta. She did not want to return, but Baba convinced her that now it was time for her to leave. He also told her she would soon be married.

She didn't want to leave Baba's satsang to be married off, but Baba consoled her, saying that sometimes a true and honest householder is more pious than a fraudster hiding in the garb of a monk. He said that for a young woman of her age, it was safer and more enjoyable to live the life of a householder. She told Baba she wanted to travel the world, to which he replied that this desire of hers would be fulfilled through her husband.

As Baba predicted, Monika soon married a decent young man, Sachindra Kumar Mitra, who worked in the United Nations. She lived a happy life, and because of her husband's job, she was able to fulfill her desire to travel around the world with him.

When I first read Monika Devi's book, "Sree Sree Digambar Paramahamsa: History Famed Totapuri Maharaj," I was greatly inspired and moved by her dedication and devotion to Baba, and it helped me come closer to him.

Nowhere has Totapuri Baba ever spoken about his association with Ramakrishna, but in Monika's book, she mentions an incident when she asked Baba if he was Ramakrishna's guru. Baba never entertained casual queries about his age or his association with Ramakrishna. But when Monika questioned him, Baba said to her, "Once I was returning after bathing at Gangasagar, and when I came to Dakshineswar, I saw a young brahmin, Ramakrishna, with great spiritual potential, and because of his love, I stayed there for eleven months."

After reading her book, I really wanted to meet this fortunate lady who had had the privilege of Baba's satsang and to know more about Baba and her life with him. So, the next time I was in Kolkata, I tried to find her with the address I had acquired from the ashram. It was not an easy task to find her house in the crowded city of Kolkata. After an arduous search, we finally arrived at her doorstep. We were invited in, being received by her husband, Sachindra Kumar Mitra, who informed us that Monika was out of Kolkata doing some work. Sachindra also had great respect and adoration for Baba. When I expressed my ardent desire to meet Monika, he said she wouldn't be back for a few days, and so after talking to him for some time, I purchased about 100 copies of her book for distribution and sale at Osho Tapoban and then left.

It was to be fourteen years before I was finally to meet Monikajee. After the meditation retreat at the Ibiza Resort, Kolkata, in 2016, some of our ashramites decided to make a trip to Puri, where they, too, visited Baba's samadhi. There, Swami Neerav met a few Bengali devotees of Baba, who apparently knew the current address of Monika Devi, and gave it to him. The following year, when we were returning to our meditation center, Ramakrishna Meditation Centre, in Bangur, Kolkata, from our meditation retreat at the Ibiza Resort, he told me that he had the address of Monika Devi. I was accompanied by Swami Shashikant, Neerav, and Yogananda. We decided to take a detour and try to find her. After hours of driving through the crowded streets and alleys of Kolkata, we finally arrived at the apartment building where she resided.

It was a multi-story building in a complex of two or three buildings near Kalighat junction. Swami Shashikant, our Center leader in Kolkata, being the local among us, went to find the number of her flat. He talked to the guard; from a distance, we could hear him talking in Bengali, saying, "Puri wale Baba ."As soon as the guard heard those words, he beamed and nodded in affirmation and said he knew exactly where we had to go. This was a positive sign because, after all that driving and searching, we had started to wonder if the address was correct. So, with great relief, the four of us took the lift to the flat, following the guard's instructions. When we arrived at the flat, we were surprised to see that the doors were ajar and there were many people coming and going.

Upon entering the flat, we saw a scene that we had least expected. There were many people sitting there as if in a crowded doctor's clinic, and a bald man with a very fat nearly-bare body, dressed only in a bright dhoti, was cooking something right there in the middle of the room. It was a very noisy atmosphere, and when we asked about Monika Devi, the disciple of Totapuri, everyone just replied that Baba was inside. Now we started to feel that something was missing here, so we inquired about Baba, and they showed us a picture of him that was hanging on the wall. He was huge, with his big belly, bald head, and Hindu attire, and was even larger than his halwai (confectioner) disciple outside. Someone told us they didn't know who Monika Devi was and that they had gathered there to meet this Baba from Puri. He looked exactly like the huge Hindu priests shown in films and seen on television. In the short time we were in the flat, other scantily clad, fat, bald men also kept coming in and out. We were clearly in the wrong place!

We finally realized a great mistake had been made and decided to go. As funny as this incident was, it also left us feeling sad and frustrated. The long trip in the traffic had already made me tired, and I wanted to go back to the Center. But after we came down in the lift, we noticed the small office of the building's manager next to the car park, so we thought we'd make one last effort, although we had very little hope left by now. When we asked the manager there, he said it was very difficult to find a Monika Devi in such a huge building with hundreds of flats. I told him that her husband used to work in the United Nations, and that somehow rang a bell for him. He asked us for her surname, and after thinking for some time, one of us remembered "Mitra." He did find the name in the register and said that she was a very old lady, and he needed to get permission first before passing on the address. After he made a call, he gave us the correct flat number and said we could go up.

Up we went again in the lift but in a different wing of the building. Compared to what we experienced before, this apartment was completely different - calm and quiet. We rang the bell and were welcomed by a young lady who happened to be a distant relative and caretaker of Monika Devi. There was another young woman who was also a caretaker there. Finally, we arrived at the right place!

After seating us in the living room, the women went inside to get Monika Devi. Soon an old lady in her late eighties emerged, supported by the two young women. She looked thin and frail but very sharp. I went close to her and did my pranam (paid my respects), and introduced myself. I was totally surprised when she exclaimed, "Oh! We have met before, also."

I told her that I had come to meet her but had only met her husband and couldn't meet her as she was out of Kolkata at the time, so this was our first meeting. She repeated, in a mysterious way, "No! We have met before, also."

Later, I understood what she meant. I have met many saints and yogis in my life who have also said the same thing to me on our first meeting, even though I had never met them before in this life. Yogis can see into our past lives, so when they say that we have met before, they are referring to our previous lives. It has now become very clear to me that Monika Devi was talking about a previous life in which we had been associated somewhere. I also felt a strong connection and affection towards her on our very first meeting, a communion that is not possible with a stranger. In many of my previous lives, I have been a spiritual adventurer who had many gurus and met many spiritually inclined souls.

It was a small flat, with two bedrooms and a living room, in which she lived with the two young girls. Monika Devi only conversed in Bengali, so Swami Shashikant translated for us. I presented her with my book, "Lone Seeker Many Masters," and told her that I had written about Baba and her story in it. She was very happy to hear that. I had taken some fruits with me and wanted to give her a small amount of money which she was reluctant to take. But the girls accepted it and told her that it was our token of love. When I talked about her book, she told me that now there was a larger edition of it with more stories and pictures. She presented me with the Bengali version and said that the English version was not available yet, so she would give it to us next time. When I asked her about her husband, she said he had already left his body. She showed us some photo albums of her old pictures and talked about her life.

Then a very beautiful thing happened. I asked her about Baba, and she started talking about him. As soon as she began, all of us could feel an immediate change in the energy of the room. A dense presence could be felt, as if Baba was there with us. Monika Devi, who was so weak and frail a few minutes earlier, also seemed to have a new energy in her, which only kept growing the more she spoke about her beloved guru.

I said, "It has already been fifty-seven years since Baba left his body. Does he still guide you?" "Yes, of course!" she replied. "He regularly comes in his physical form into my room and talks to me and guides me even today," she said.

Then she said, "He sometimes comes into this room also, and these girls get scared when he comes."

But the young women, nevertheless, had become accepting of seeing this Baba, with his huge body and matted dreadlocks, talking with Monika.

Although it all sounded out of this world and esoteric, I could understand her and felt the truth in her words. When a disciple is ready, even a master who has left his body can come and guide us. It has been nearly three decades since Osho left his body, but still, he guides me now like he was guiding me before. When he was alive, there were many physical constraints, but now that he is free of his body, he has become more available and active than before. There are still many monks alive today who receive direct guidance from Gautam Buddha himself. There are people who still talk to Krishna. Mystics like Swami Vivekananda, Shivapuri Baba, Neem Karoli Baba, Meera, Ramana Maharshi, Mahavatar Baba, and so many others are still guiding their devoted disciples. All of this is possible with total trust and deep love.

Monika had a simple heart and great love for her master, so it was not a surprise for me to know that Baba still came in the physical form to guide her.

This was not the first time that I had heard about this esoteric mystery of Baba. I had initiated a young man from Orissa into sannyas during one of my Puri meditation retreats. When he heard me speak about Baba, he was so touched that he fell in love with Baba and decided to go and serve Baba's Samadhi temple in Girnar. The last time I met him at the Girnar temple, I was surprised to see a man there wearing an Osho mala. That is when he told me how he had been inspired to come to Baba. I was very happy to see him settle as a volunteer in Baba's ashram. He was a simple, innocent Orissa man with little education. He told me Baba used to come to him in the physical form and talk to him. He also said that sometimes when he'd done too much work and was tired, Baba would come and heal him, or would ask him to eat food if he hadn't eaten or would scold him if he had stayed outside until late.

I have experienced and heard about such incidents throughout my life, so I understand the phenomenon, but it is very hard for those who have not had such experiences to accept their existence. No proof can be given for such incidents, but the simplicity of heart and the innocence of both Monika Devi and the innocent Oria Swami were enough proof of the truth they were speaking.

There were many incidents in Monika's life that illustrated Baba's grace and blessings bestowed upon her. When Monika came to Baba, she was only a teenager. Baba used to reprimand anyone who wanted to stay around him or visit him. Monika fell so much in love with him that she stayed in Puri and would come and serve him every day. She would clean the ashram and cook something for Baba. Baba would scold her and ask her not to come. He would sometimes tell her to go to the Jagannath temple, or go to the beach in Puri, rather than coming to the ashram. He would ask her, "What is there to see here?"

Baba, who was a Naga Swami, used to stay naked in his ashram, and as Monika was just a teenage girl, he did not want her around.

But Monika's love and devotion always brought her to Baba's doorstep. On one such occasion, she was meditating and serving the ashram, and somehow the time slipped by. It had become very late. Even today, not many people frequent Baba's ashram; it's isolated by a forest surrounding it. We can only imagine how it must have been back then. Monika could not stay in the ashram, and neither could she go back home in the dark. She went to Baba and told him the problem.

Baba came down from the temple with her, then just closed his eyes. After a little while, he opened his eyes, and there was a bull standing right behind Monika. She was startled to see such a huge animal which had seemed to come from nowhere; just a few minutes earlier, she and Baba had been alone. Baba looked at Monika and said, "Go with this bull. It will safely escort you back to a rickshaw and protect you."

Monika turned and went with the bull, which quietly escorted her back safely through the forest, along the lonely path away from the temple, until she found a rickshaw. The bull waited until Monika was in the rickshaw, and then it returned to Baba.

Baba rarely spoke to anyone and, most of the time, was immersed in his state of meditation. However, there are many stories from various disciples of how Baba helped them in their difficult times. Baba was a compassionate, enlightened being, but at the same time, he was equally hard on his disciples when they became unaware.

As Monika could not stay at the ashram, she rented a room in Puri. The house where she stayed had a big papaya tree that used to bear delicious fruit. The lady who owned the house was very strict and would not let anybody eat her fruit. One day, Monika decided to steal a ripe papaya. Having plucked it from the tree, she ate the flesh and buried the skin in the sand.

That day, like every other day, she went off to the ashram to be with Baba. As soon as Baba saw her, he became very angry with her. He scolded, "You have been coming to me for such a long time, and still, you steal from others. Either stop stealing or don't come to me."

Monika was shocked to see Baba's powers and realized she could not hide anything from him; he could see right through her. He could read her mind and see into her past lives as well. She felt very guilty and started crying, asking for Baba's forgiveness. Seeing that she had done it out of teenage mischief, Baba forgave her and asked her not to repeat such behavior.

My first meeting with Monika Devi also became my last meeting with her. Swami Shashikant had gone to meet her again after that and told me she was asking about me and asked him to convey her remembrance and affection to me. Two years after our meeting, one day, the memory of her was very intense, and I wanted to meet her but was unable to go. So, I asked Swami Shashikant to go and see her and offer her some fruits and money on my behalf. He went to her apartment but discovered she had already left her body. He later called to inform me. But she had kept her word that she would give me a copy of her revised book, and Shashikantjee brought the treasure back for me.

Monika Devi was a highly elevated soul. It was rare for a Bengali girl in her teenage years to have had so much trust and devotion for a Naga Baba living in a wild-animal-infested forest and to have served him with selfless love and dedication. Today, Monika Devi, her husband, and Totapuri Baba are no longer on this earth, but I am sure that they are together on some higher plane. Just remembering such pure souls is a kind of meditation that purifies the heart and brings a great sense of spiritual tranquility.

My Satoris on the Banks of the Ganga

The Japanese have coined a beautiful word for the instant experience of no mind when one becomes absolutely present in the moment and feels the bliss of stillness and calm in the absence of thoughts - they have called this state 'satori', or time-bound enlightenment. Although it is a temporary state of elevated consciousness, it gives a seeker a glimpse of his ultimate possibility and sows the seeds of samadhi or enlightenment.

The school of Yoga talks about the three nadis, or energy channels, present in us: ida, pingala, and sushumna. The two channels, ida and pingala, are active in a normal person, but when they become harmonious, the sushumna, which is a more subtle channel, becomes activated. Then a person slowly becomes thoughtless, experiences immense bliss, and transcends the concept of time and space. This is what happens during satori. This happens easily to those who go deep into meditation. But people also experience satori at odd moments in life when the mind comes to a sudden stop. In some way or other, we have all experienced the bliss of this experience but are not always able to recognize it.

Osho says, "Satori is a miniature experience of samadhi, but once you get into it, you cannot get out of it. Samadhi is just like the total opening of the lotus, and satori is the beginning of the opening of the petals. Satori is the beginning, and samadhi is the climax."

Before coming to Osho, I did not know anything about satori, but today when I reminisce, I realize that some of the profound experiences I have had in my life were actually experiences of satori. Even before I had taken sannyas or had an active spiritual life, many a time I had experienced this state which I now understand was satori.

I have a strange love affair with the river Ganga, and most of my satoris have happened on her banks. For many people, the Ganga is just a river; for some, it is a holy river that flows next to their holy sites, but for me, she is my mother. I keep saying that the Himalayas is my father, and the Ganga is my loving mother, and wherever there are both, that place is a paradise for me — it is the holiest site on Earth.

The Ganga also flows through the plains in Benaras, Patna, Kolkata, and Gangasagar, but there are no Himalayas there. The Himalayas start from Haridwar, and from Haridwar to Gomukh, there are both the Ganga and the Himalayas, and there is no other place on Earth that enchants me the way this area does.

The last time I experienced satori on the banks of the Ganga was in 2019, before the COVID pandemic had started. Arhatjee and

I had just come back from facilitating a meditation retreat in Moscow, and my soul was thirsty for energy. Every time we go to the West, my eyes long for a glimpse of the Himalayas and the Ganga, and I begin counting the days until we return. Before the pandemic started, I used to visit the Ganga twice a year, but that stopped with the arrival of the pandemic.

We would travel by train, and just arriving at the Haridwar station, I would become ecstatic and feel my soul breathing in delight. For the last few years, we took the flight to Dehradun, and just landing at the Jolly Grant airport, I still got the same feeling.

Swami Sudip and his wife had already arrived the night before at the Delhi airport, and we arrived around 2:00 am from Moscow. The next morning, our flight took off from Delhi at 5:00 am, and we landed at Jolly Grant at around 6:00 am. We were exhausted from our long flight and the wait at the airport, but as soon as we landed in Dehradun, I was exhilarated.

The close proximity of the Ganga, the lap of the great Himalayas, and the air charged with the spiritual vibrations of Uttarakhand, all created a strong milieu, and as soon as we landed, I was mad with ecstasy. I hadn't even seen the Ganga at that stage, but I was thrown into satori, and I have no words to express the bliss I experienced then. I became speechless, unable to utter a word. My associates have seen me in this state before, so they understood and let me be.

Swami Bodhi Vartaman and Swami Prem Chaitanya from Osho Gangadham Ashram in Rishikesh had come with their cars to receive us at the airport, and as we began driving closer to the Ganga, I experienced wave after wave of bliss rolling in. It was like there was an ocean of bliss inside me, and once I caught my first glimpse of the Ganga, it intensified a hundred-fold. I couldn't move my body, I couldn't speak, and all the way to the Gangadham Ashram, I was in this ecstatic state.

Gomukh is 18 km from Gangotri, in the foothills of the greater Himalayan range, and is 4,255 m above sea level.

The Ganga originates as the Bhagirathi at Gomukh, from the Gangotri glaciers in the Himalayas in Uttarakhand, and flows for a total length of about 2,525 km down to sea level to its outfall into the Bay of Bengal at Gangasagar. Most of the important pilgrim sites of Hindus are situated along this 2,500 km stretch along the banks of the Ganga. After Haridwar, the Ganga enters the plains and becomes wider. She passes through many cities, and slowly the waters get polluted with urban and industrial waste. Especially at Kanpur, the waters become immensely polluted due to the industrial waste that is dumped into the river, but even though the quality of the water deteriorates, the purity, essence, and spiritual energy carried by the Ganga remains intact.

I did my engineering studies at Patna Engineering College at Patna University, and it was my great fortune that my college and hostel were located right on the banks of the Ganga. From my very childhood, I was a seeker looking for answers in life and was greatly inclined towards spirituality. In the early stage of my college life, I had not found my guru, and there were times when I was tormented by my spiritual quest and wanted to run away to the Himalayas or follow some hermit or yogi. Even the subject of science and engineering was too dry for my emotionally inclined persona. I used to enjoy music, poetry, literature, and philosophy but was forced to take engineering because of my parents and the social pressure. My personal life was also in great jeopardy, so I used to have bouts of depression and felt suicidal at times. If it wasn't for the solace of the Ganga, I don't think I would have been able to pass my engineering course or even survive those dark times.

Whenever I felt low, I would go to the bank at night and sit there for hours, and the Ganga would pacify me and compensate for all my sorrows. During times of anguish, I always felt a mother's soothing love and solace in the Ganga. Whenever I went to her lap, it always felt like she was saying, "Why are you worried? I am right here for you." It was during these times that I also learned how to swim.

The intensity of Ganga's powerful presence becomes diluted as she descends to the plains. The way she overpowers and influences Gomukh to Gangotri and triggers a spiritual process in a seeker cannot be felt anywhere along her descent to the plains. But I was surprised to see that at Gangasagar, where she arrives at her destination, she regains her glory, and her intensity becomes concentrated, just as it is between Gomukh and Gangotri. She becomes more powerful than she is at Devaprayag, Rishikesh, or Haridwar, which all have strong energy fields. Gangasagar has a strong buddhafield and is a site of pilgrimage for the Hindus. It is also one of my most favorite places. I have conducted a meditation retreat there, and every time I have been to Gangasagar, I have been duly rewarded. During two of my visits there, I experienced intense satoris, which I will never forget for the rest of my life.

However, despite it having a strong energy field and being a place of great importance, it is extremely neglected and not easily accessible. The trip to Gangasagar is not very comfortable. Firstly, one has to travel 90 km along a narrow and highly congested road to Kakdwip from Esplanade in Central Kolkata and on to Harwood Point. The journey takes more than three hours. From there, after crossing the river Muriganga by boat, one reaches Kachuberia. From Kachuberia, one has to take a one-hour bus trip to finally reach Gangasagar. After disembarking, to get to the meeting point, one then has to take a human-pulled rickshaw to arrive finally at the shores of the Bay of Bengal, where the Ganga dissolves into the ocean. There are very few accommodation facilities at Gangasagar, and the ones that exist are of really poor quality. The Indian government needs to turn its attention to developing this place, as it has the same potential for a spiritual tourism center as Haridwar and Rishikesh. Because of these considerable difficulties regarding Gangasagar, difficulties which were even worse in the old days, the Hindus have a very popular saying, "Other pilgrimages many times, but Gangasagar just one time."

The Hooghly (Ganga's name in Kolkata) carries all the waste from the cities and is highly polluted at the place where it meets the ocean. The water is dark and almost untouchable; however, the intensity of Ganga's power is the same as it is at Gomukh from where she originates.

The trek to Gomukh from Gangotri is 18 km and is a difficult one. Sometimes people also suffer from altitude sickness, and the terrain is rough and steep. About twenty years ago, I made this trek and was highly exhilarated when I reached the origin of the river. It is located in the mountains, and Gomukh, which means the cow's mouth, is a hole in the Gangotri glacier from where the Bhagirathi River, which turns into the Ganga further downstream, first emerges.

It is also believed that it was at Gangotri that King Bhagirath meditated and made the Ganga descend from the heavens to Earth. The trek we made was very difficult and exhausting, but once we reached Gomukh, just drinking a spoonful of water nourished and quenched my thirsty soul. Although the water is very cold at Gomukh, it is highly charged with strong spiritual vibrations, and it remains that way until it reaches Gangotri.

Climate change and global warming are rapidly melting the glacier at Gaumukh. Today, when I check the online videos of Gomukh, it is not the same as I knew it twenty years ago. Every year it shifts a few kilometers towards the north, and it has already shifted 18 km from its original spot.

The first time I had the opportunity to experience the Ganga in the Himalayas was in 1982, when I arrived in Haridwar with a group of Osho disciples. We decided to make an unplanned car trip to the Garhwal Himalayas. This group also included Swami Yog Chinmaya, his girlfriend Nirvesh, and two other sannyasins, one of whom was an Income Tax Commissioner of Bihar. The car was provided by the Income Tax Commissioner, and all the other expenses were covered by the rest of us.

The whole purpose of the tour was to roam like nomads and mendicants in the Garhwal Himalayas without any plans or structure. After traveling for one month in the Himalayas, we arrived at Rishikesh. We approached it from Kumaon Hills and finally descended at Haridwar. This was the perfect place for me. The Ganga's glory in Rishikesh left me stupefied. The beauty of the hills of Uttarakhand and the softness of the turquoise Ganga flowing by the foothills of Rishikesh filled me with awe; struck by the beauty, I did not want to go back. We were sitting by the ghats on the eve of our supposed departure, and I started to cry. I pleaded with my group, saying there was no way I could go back, and asked them to leave me behind.

Chinmaya Swami's tuning was more with the Himalayas, and he preferred Srinagar in Garhwal to Rishikesh. My friends could not understand my situation, and they tried to convince me logically in all kinds of ways. "We have already traveled for a month, and also, the money is about to finish. You have responsibilities back home, and there is much spiritual work that we still need to do in Nepal," they said.

I replied, "I can't go back. People provide free food to the yogis and hermits in this area, and no one goes hungry around here. Somehow, I also will be taken care of. I am educated, so I will do some work in an ashram and can sleep on one of their balconies." I was very emotional and kept crying. Although my friends did take me back, they were forced to stay a few more days in Rishikesh because of me.

The water of the Ganga does not spoil even over a prolonged period of time because of its self-cleansing properties. Its water has an oxygen level that is twenty-five times higher than any other river in the world. This is one of its self-purifying attributes, giving it the ability to remain fresh even for years. Slowly, scientists are doing more research to find out about this unique quality of the Ganga, but this is not the only reason why this river is special.

In every religion, the deepest esoteric secrets are stored in or passed onto different objects in nature that keep them alive and transmit them to those who are ready to receive them. The Hindus have passed all their esoteric findings and secrets to the Ganga. This is why the Ganga is not just a river but a flowing temple to the Hindus and to every seeker on the path who can tap into this treasure.

Similarly, the Jains have passed on their secrets to Parasnath, the dry hills in Bihar, where, out of the twenty-four Tirthankaras of the Jains, twenty-two left their bodies. Fifty-five years ago, when I was a young student, I experienced the energy the Buddhists have given in their secrets to the Bodhi Tree. When I was in Bodhgaya for the first time and was meditating under the Bodhi tree, every time a leaf fell and touched my body, I received a strong electric shock.

If we can learn to decode these hidden messages, we can access the deep insights and secrets of soul liberation which they carry. There have been thousands of enlightened masters in the Hindu religion, and most of them have either lived and meditated along the banks of the Ganga or have left their bodies there. Many masters have been cremated on the banks of the Ganga, and many samadhis of enlightened masters can be found near the Ganga. Many yogis have also taken jal-samadhi in the Ganga by submerging in the river until their soul left their bodies. Almost all the important holy sites of the Hindus have been built along her banks, and this has been done intentionally. The Ganga stores some deep messages in her, and a genuine seeker can feel it just by going into her auric field.

I still remember when I was only five years old and was traveling with my parents. We were going to Baidyanath Dham in Deogar in Jharkhand, India. There was no bridge back then, so we had to take a steamer to cross the Ganga on the way to Patna. At Hajipur in Sonpur district, there is a confluence of the rivers Gandaki and Ganga where every year, a huge mela, or religious carnival, is held.

My father's friend had a house just next to the confluence, and we were staying there. It was 1949, and in those days, most of the houses in India did not have private toilets, so we had to go out into the field. In the morning, one of the servants accompanied me to the field for toileting, then took me to the riverbank, and I had a bath in the river. Having finished my bath, the servant put me on the ghats and had his bath. I still have a clear memory of that morning. As I was sitting there looking at the beauty in the meeting of the Ganga and the Gandaki, a huge wave of bliss arose in me, and I went into a trance. I began crying incessantly and couldn't even move my body. I had no reason for the tears; I was simply overwhelmed by the bliss. When the servant came back, I was in a stupor, and because I did not want to leave the ghat, it was very difficult for him to take me back. This was the first satori of my life at the banks of my mother.

Wherever two rivers meet, a strong energy field is created, and the Hindus have given great importance to such places. Many years later, I came to know that at the same spot where I had bathed and experienced my first satori, Ananda, Buddha's intimate disciple, left his body while crossing the Ganga when he was going from Pataliputra to Vaishali.

Ananda was Buddha's cousin and one of his closest enlightened disciples. I also have a very strong connection with him over many lives and have great respect and love for him. Even though I was only five years old, I experienced my first satori because the Ganga had kept intact the vibrations that were able to trigger a strong spiritual experience in me.

My second satori happened when I was around thirteen or fourteen. My mother was a heart patient, and we had gone to Patna for her checkup. We were crossing the Ganga on a steamer, and I was sitting on the deck when I saw a sight that left me spellbound. A man was standing on the deck looking into the far horizon and was wearing a shirt and pants of dark orange. He was not even a monk but just a normal person wearing an ochre shade. Just seeing that sight triggered a strong déjà vu in me. The combination of the backdrop of the Ganga and the color orange felt extremely familiar and provoked a deep memory hidden in my unconscious. I felt a strong nostalgia that churned my emotions, and again I was thrown into a strong satori.

Tears began rolling down my eyes. This intensified, and I started crying loudly. My uncle saw me and became worried. He asked me what was wrong, but I had nothing to tell him. The sight stirred a memory of one of my previous lives where I must have meditated on the bank of the Ganga as a Hindu monk wearing orange garb. My uncle kept asking me why I was crying, and just to give him some explanation, I told him I wanted a similar shirt and pants to those worn by that person. When we got off the steamer, my uncle went to a shop and bought me an orange shirt made of nylon, which had just come onto the market, and orange cotton pants. Those clothes became my favorite outfit, and for a long time, I wouldn't wear anything else.

Another strong satori that I experienced before taking sannyas was during my college days. I had already met Bhagwan Shree Rajneesh (now referred to as Osho) and had been associated with him for some time. A few friends had just returned from the meditation camp at Mount Abu in Gujarat. Unfortunately, in spite of Osho's invitation, I missed this camp and had not been able to take sannyas as my other friends did. They had brought back Osho's audio lectures and proposed a one-day meditation camp across the Ganga.

My college had a boat club, and as I was a member of it, I could take boats from the club. They had nice boats, two of which we took across the Ganga with ten friends. Osho had just introduced Dynamic meditation during this camp, and our friends had brought the audio for it. After learning this new technique from the sannyasins, we did it on the banks of the river. This was the first time I had done Osho's Dynamic Meditation which was later to become one of the most powerful techniques given by Osho to humankind.

After Dynamic Meditation, we all bathed in the Ganga and then listened to Osho's audio lectures. With Ganga's enchanting ambiance and Osho's voice echoing in the background, again, I started going into satori. I fell down, and my body became motionless as I lay there on the sand.

Someone played Guru Nanak's devotional bhajan, Kahe re bann khojan jayi, sung by the Indian singer Geeta Dutt, on the tape recorder. Geeta Dutt's voice has an otherworldly depth to it, and I have always been a great admirer of her singing. As soon as the song began playing, my satori intensified. The lines of the song had a very profound meaning: "Why, O seeker, do you search outside when the immortal resides just inside you?" It was as if she was singing the longing of my soul. Her beautiful singing conveyed the heavy emotions of a seeker's heart, and I was plunged into the great depths within.

I was sailing on waves of bliss and had transcended the physical realm with no sense of time or space. But no sooner had the song ended my satori also came to an end. I felt like a fish thrown out of the water. I cried and asked my friends to play the song again, and as soon as the song began again, I would go into a deep trance. This continued for some time. The sun was becoming strong as I lay there on the sand. My friends tried to bring me back, but I just was motionless, in a divine stupor. I kept asking them to play the song again and again. It was sheer madness, but as soon as the song stopped, I would start wailing, so my friends had no option but to keep repeating the same song. People cooked food and had a picnic while I just lay there motionless in bliss. After a few hours, the tape recorder's battery ran out, and I finally came out of my state. We returned home.

So, these were the three strong satoris I experienced before taking sannyas: one when I was five years old, the second one when I saw the man in orange clothes, and the third one being the one-day meditation on the bank of the Ganga.

After taking sannyas in 1974, I used to visit Pune two to three times a year to see my master. It was around 1977 when I was traveling with a group of twelve sannyasins to Pune. In those days, I did not have much money, so we used to travel by train. To reach Pune, we had to catch the Toofan Mail up to Allahabad, where the bogey would be detached and then reattached to the Bombay Mail engine that took us to Bombay. We reached Allahabad at around 5:00 am, and there was a wait of five hours before the Bombay Mail left for Pune.

Allahabad, also known as Prayagraj, holds great significance for the Hindus. It is one of the sites where the great Kumbha Mela happens every twelve years. The Triveni Sangam, the confluence of the rivers Ganga and Yamuna, and the mythical invisible river, Saraswati, in Allahabad, is considered one of the holiest sites of the Hindus. The Hindus believe that bathing at this confluence can rid them of many past karmas and ease their path toward moksha. During every Kumbh Mela, millions of devotees throng to this site to bathe at the confluence.

As we had five hours to spare, I asked my friends to go with me to the Sangam instead of sitting there in the bogey. We left two friends who were not particularly interested in the Ganga to look after the luggage, and off we went. First, we took a rickshaw and then a boat to reach the Sangam. All of us went into the water and had a bath at this meeting point of the rivers Ganga, Yamuna, and the invisible Saraswati. After bathing, but still in the water, again I had a strong satori. Suddenly my body became like wood, and I couldn't move. It was such a strong satori I immediately went into a thoughtless and blissful state. I couldn't even come out of the water, so somehow, my friends carried me out and put me in the boat. I was enveloped in a divine state of love. My friends managed to take me back to the train, but I remained in that state for around six hours. As I was traveling with sannyasins, they understood my situation and helped me in every way possible.

After this incident, I understood why Hindus have given so much importance to this confluence of the Ganga and the Yamuna and bathing in it and why the huge Kumbha Mela and other melas are organized at such places. Following my experience there, I used to go to the Triveni Sangam every time I was on my way to Pune. Because of my first experience, the second and third times I went, I had great expectations, so nothing happened. Of course, I was ecstatic every time, but I had my next satori there only during the fourth visit because I had stopped expecting it after the third time.

My love affair with the Ganga deepened after my visit to Rishikesh during our first trip to the Garhwal Himalayas. After Osho went to the USA, my destination also changed from Pune to Rishikesh. I used to go there every time I had an opportunity, and I just rejoiced to roam around on the banks of the Ganga like the sadhus and yogis. I would sit on the bank until late at night and go back to the hotel or ashram where I was staying at around 2:00 in the morning to sleep.

During my visits to Rishikesh, I also met Osho's first disciple, Ma Anand Madhu, who had been living in silence and doing her sadhana on the banks of the Ganga. She lived there for forty-six years, from 1974 until she left her body in 2021. It was also because of the love and care I received from her that I began visiting Rishikesh at least twice a year. This continued even after we built Osho Tapoban here in Nepal. Seeing my deep love and association with the Ganga, Ma Madhu used to call me Ganga Putra, or Ganga's Son.

We also began organizing meditation camps, and I used to facilitate meditation retreats at an ashram in Haridwar or the Vanaprastha ashram in Rishikesh. The camps used to be just an expression of my love for the Ganga, and hundreds of friends used to gather for these retreats, where I shared my love story with the great mother. Many a time during these retreats, while speaking on the Ganga, I used to go into a trance and experience sweet satoris.

I have not counted them, but my life's most profound satoris have happened on the banks of the Ganga. Some of them have happened in Pune in the presence of my master, but more than ten strong satoris have happened in the lap of my mother.

The story of my love affair with the Ganga reached its crescendo in Uttarkashi, where I was facilitating a meditation retreat at the Hotel Trishul. Around one hundred friends from Nepal and India had come for this meditation camp. I have a strong connection with this place because, in one of my previous lives, I had meditated in a place called Ujeli, in Uttarkashi, as a Hindu monk on the banks of the Ganga. On the very first day of the camp, I had one of the most powerful satoris of my life. I couldn't facilitate the session and fell down. Somehow my friends took me back to my bedroom and started doing different things to my body to bring me back.

I couldn't speak, my body was immobile, and my hands and feet had turned cold. Friends did not understand what was happening to me, and Ma Sumitra forcefully made me drink some milk and rubbed warm oil on my feet. Although her intention was to help me, it somehow disturbed my satori, but still, I remained in a trance throughout the night. During strong satoris, the body temperature drops immensely and becomes cold, so it is very important for those around to keep the body warm by covering it with a shawl or a blanket.

No one should touch, disturb or force feed when someone is in a satori since the one going through the satori is in a very sensitive state and is in an extremely fragile situation. Even shaking the body of such a person can be fatal. This is the reason why we are very cautious about this at Tapoban.

The next morning, I woke up and went to the meditation hall to conduct Dynamic meditation, but as soon as I looked at the Ganga, I went into a trance and fell down again. I was overpowered by intense bliss and went into a deep satori. Many friends waited for me to start the meditation, but I could not do anything. I was in a thoughtless state, and an unknown source of joy overpowered me. People waited for some time and slowly began leaving for breakfast while I lay there motionless. After some time, when I was able, I opened my eyes and couldn't believe what I saw. I saw myself lying down, my head in the lap of a beautiful lady wearing a white sari. She had a beatific smile and was looking at me with great love as she caressed my head. She looked like she was in her middle age, and the simplicity and purity of her beauty were just like that of Ramakrishna's wife, Ma Sarada.

I immediately recognized her! It was Ma Ganga herself who had appeared in front of me. Love and devotion can open many doors, and I realized that when a seeker really wishes with love and devotion, even the impossible can become possible. I remained in a trance throughout the time we were there, so I was unable to facilitate the camp. Some people became angry with me, and some left the camp to go sightseeing.

Celebrated in myth and legend, in literature and art, the Ganga, in many ways, is a living mystery, but at the same time, as a river, she is a life-giver to the millions who have settled on her basins and to those dependent on her ecosystem.

Spiritually, no seeker has come back empty-handed after surrendering to the Ganga. She has always been a mother to those on the path of meditation, and that is why, for eons, saints and hermits have chosen to live, meditate and leave their bodies on her banks. As with my story, every seeker who is in this love affair has their own experience of her mystical presence.

The Ganga is a living phenomenon of divinity, purity, and love. She is the mother of every seeker on the path of truth and will provide for all those who have a deep love for her and trust in her. But to understand this mystical side of the Ganga, one has to dive deep into this mad love affair with an open heart and a receptive being. I will remain forever grateful to the Ganga for her love, blessings, and the solace she has given me, and if existence permits, I would love to leave this world on her banks, in the lap of my mother.

More than sixty percent of Ganga's water is from Nepali rivers, so if not in India, I would love to end my journey on the bank of one of her tributaries in Nepal. There are many beautiful spots, like Chisapani, Banghat, Chatara, and Devghat, situated on the banks of these rivers, and it would be a blessing to complete my physical journey in one of these places.

Madalasa: The Hermit Princess

It is the year 2023 and after attending the 5 day World Book Fair in Delhi where we also had a book stall by Tapoban, my heart again longed for the hallowed banks of the Ganges. I was immensely delighted as we were able to host 8 book Osho exhibitions in different cities of India within two months which was a great success and helped us immensely in sharing his vision. After a few days in Delhi after the exhibition I was again in Rishikesh, answering the ever beckoning call of my mother.

The recent developments that I have

seen in the area of infrastructure and roads in modern India is highly commendable. Unlike before now it only takes about 4 hours of a smooth drive to reach Haridwar from Delhi. I hear that this duration is also being shortened to 2 hours with the upcoming new expressway.

Rishikesh is my leisure city. Just walking around the alleys by the banks of Ganges, exploring different bookshops, visiting ashrams, drinking local kulhad tea by the roadside or just sitting silently watching the waters of Ganges nourishes my heart and soul like nothing else. It is an incomparable joy and no place in this world can suffice for it.

This time also I visited many ashrams and met many godward souls living in the refuge of the great Himalayas and the holy river originating from its ancient foothills. One of my favorite places to visit while in Rishikesh is the Mastaram Baba ashram where the enlightened mystic Mastaram Baba used to live with a few of his disciples while he was alive. This time when I visited the ashram I got a very pleasant surprise which made my visit immensely worthwhile.

In my book 'Lone Seeker Many Masters' I have written about Babaji, his disciple Nani Ma and Prakash whom I had met in person and many other significant incidents from Babaji's life and his disciples which I had heard directly from Nani Ma and Prakash. I had also written about an Indian princess Madalasa who came from a princely state near Ayodhya and belonged to the Sooryavangshi Rajput lineage and had come to Baba at a very young age.

Madalasa felt jaded and detached with the world at an early age of 15 and had come to Baba's refuge and had lived with him and served him until she was 38 years old. Baba later sent her back and asked her to get married and live a householder's life. He had also told her that after her worldly desires were fulfilled she would again return back to Baba's ashram.

This time to my utter surprise the same princess about whom

I had heard from Nani ma and Prakash and had written in my book was there in the ashram. As Baba had predicted she had left her householder life and had returned and was now living in the ashram. She wore a simple cotton dhoti and was living like any other woman sannyasin in the ashram. Her eyes however betrayed her ordinary attire and still reflected her regal upbringing and background.

I was extremely excited to meet her as she was one of those who had lived with Baba and had experienced his grace directly. She also seemed delighted to see us. When I told her about the incidents I had written about her in my book she confirmed that they were all true and accurate.

She told me more stories from her life which left me in awe of this courageous lady who had left everything behind and had come to Rishikesh at the age of 15 after feeling jaded with the world searching for a deeper meaning in life.

She told me, "I had come in a first-class coach on the train and had arrived at Haridwar Railway station. After taking a bath in the Ganges at the Har Ki Pauri I donated all my money and jewelleries to an old lady beggar on the street and decided to live the life of a mendicant by the Ganga."

"A temple priest saw me and after knowing about my background he told me that it was not safe for a young girl to live alone in Haridwar like that. He took me to his house and gave me shelter for a few days," she said.

After keeping the princess in his house for a few days, the priest felt that it was not appropriate for him to keep a young girl in his house in traditional Haridwar even though he was married and living with his family and took her to the widowed Maharani of Patiala who was also living the life of a renunciate in Rishikesh at the Patiala house after the Maharaja had died. She kept Madalasa with her for a few days and then the Maharani later brought Madalasa to Mastaram

Baba's ashram. At her very first meeting with Baba, Baba welcomed Madalasa and said, "So finally you have arrived." It seemed as if he already knew she was coming and was waiting for her. Madalasa started living in Baba's ashram following his teachings and serving him.

"As it was a hindu monastic ashram, women were not allowed to stay in the ashram and we had to leave after the sunset and could only enter at 3 in the morning. All the women in the ashram used to go to the river bank by the ashram and sleep on the steps on the banks of Ganga. We all used to wait till 3am in the morning and then go in and serve Baba," she said.

I was shocked to hear this and asked her, "What did you do when it rained?"

She simply replied, "We used to get wet."

I was deeply moved by her determination and courage and wondered how a princess who had grown in palatial luxury was able to live in such hardships. Baba's ashram had a very strict rule, and nobody could beg for alms for food and they had to depend on whatever came through charity or donations. When I asked her what they ate? She laughed and replied in Hindi, "Kabhi ghee ghana, kabhi muthi bhar chana aur kabhi wo bhi mana." Meaning "Sometimes we had delicacies fried in ghee, sometimes just a handful of chickpeas and sometimes nothing at all."

When nobody brought food they had to go to sleep just drinking Ganga water. When I think about the austerities and penance in other ashrams and monasteries, my heart fills with immense gratitude for our master Osho who made our lives easier and didn't forbid us from any physical comfort. Osho gave an example to the whole world that it was possible to meditate without renouncing the world and torturing the body.

Madalasa also told me that during Baba's last days he asked

her to go back to the world and marry a young Brahmin who used to come to the ashram and had fallen in love with her. The Brahmin was younger than Madalasa. When Madalasa complained to Baba that he was pushing her away, Baba said to her, "You will come back again. Fulfill your worldly duties and then when the time comes just come back. Don't get lost in the world and just come back."

After Baba left his body Madalasa married the young man and had two children. She used to come to the ashram every year with her whole family for Baba's darshan. Now that both her daughters were married, she had fulfilled all her worldly obligations and had come back to Baba.

During this meeting, the princess told me of a very interesting incident from Baba's life that she had witnessed herself, which left me enthralled and in wonder about the mysteries of Eastern mysticism and Yogic powers.

She said, "One afternoon three men came to Baba and brought along the dead body of a woman. The men had great faith in Baba and prayed to him to bring her back to life. When Baba told them that it was impossible to do so and that they should leave, the men would not listen and kept pleading to Baba saying that she had two children and what would they do without her. When this went on for sometime Baba finally said to them that he couldn't bear to see the children in pain so he would help her and then told everyone present that no one was to ever mention about it ever again and that he didn't want a crowd to gather around him.

"There was a cow grazing close by and Baba asked the cow to be brought to him and took some Ganga Water in his hands and sprinkled it on the cow and the dead woman. Then he took the tail of the cow in his hands and brushed it on the woman's face in circles and sprinkled Ganga water on her. Lo and Behold! The woman started breathing again and came back to life."

I was left speechless. There was a woman in front of me speaking with so much zeal and vigor about witnessing the most impossible feat in the world. Her eyes had truth and trust in them.

Baba had told Madalasa that she would have to take one more life to become fully liberated. She had left her palatial luxury and had dedicated all her youth in the service of a Guru bearing all the austerities and tests that were thrown at her and was back again living a simple life of penance and spiritual pursuit and yet she had no complaints that she would not become enlightened. She was in absolute acceptance with what her guru had said.

She told me, "I don't want anything. I am very happy here and I would be delighted to be born even as the smallest insect or a grain of sand here in this abode of my master."

Madalasa means languid and relaxed with intoxication and that day hearing her stories about Baba and seeing her love and devotion we also left intoxicated with Baba's energy mixed with the whiff of Ganga and her welcoming dunes.

Swami Avadhut Ram and the Blessings of Ma Annapurna

Swami Avadhut Ram was a mystic, yogi, and spiritual master who lived in the city of Varanasi (also known as Banaras) in India. He was born in 1889 in the state of Maharashtra, and his birth name was Raghunath Datta.

At a young age, he left his family and began his spiritual journey, wandering through different parts of India and studying with various gurus and yogis. He eventually settled in Varanasi, where he spent the rest of his life.

Swami Avadhut Ram was known

for his unique teaching style, which emphasized direct experience of the divine rather than religious dogma or ritual. He encouraged his followers to cultivate a deep inner awareness and to see the divine in all beings.

He was also known for his unconventional behavior, which included wearing minimal clothing and sometimes going naked, living in cremation grounds, and engaging in various forms of asceticism.

Despite his unconventional behavior, Swami Avadhut Ram attracted a large following of disciples and devotees, many of whom considered him to be a fully enlightened master.

One of the most popular incidents associated with Swami Avadhut Ram is about his encounter with Ma Annapurna, the goddess of food and nourishment in Hindu mythology. As the story goes, Swami Avadhut Ram was wandering through the streets of Varanasi one day when he came across a woman begging for food. He asked her if she had any food to give him, and she replied that she had nothing to offer except for a small amount of rice.

Swami Avadhut Ram took the rice and began to eat it. However, as he ate, the amount of rice seemed to keep increasing, and he realized that the woman was actually Ma Annapurna herself, testing his devotion and willingness to accept her blessings.

From that day on, Swami Avadhut Ram became known as the "rice mystic," and many of his followers believed that he had attained the grace of Ma Annapurna through his devotion and humility. The incident is often cited as an example of the power of faith and the blessings that can come from showing kindness and generosity to others.

Another popular incident about Swami Avadhut Ram is about the ten rupees that appeared under his pillow every morning.

One night he was wandering in the streets of Varanasi and reached the temple of Ma Annapurna and sat down in deep meditation and prayed. Those days he used to have problems with getting food and was also hesitant in asking for alms. So, he had to sleep hungry many times. That night he prayed to Ma Annapurna and felt her energy in the temple. After darshan he came to the ghat and as sadhus and monks slept in the ghat he also slept keeping his blanket as his pillow. Although he was hungry, he had a very sound sleep.

The mornings at the ghats of Varanasi have a mystical vibe and that is when the devotees come to have a dip in the Ganga. When he woke up, pilgrims were rushing to the ghat. He woke up and was folding his blanket and found a ten rupee note on his pillow. He was greatly surprised and thought that a kind person had left the money under his blanket. He took a bath in the Ganga and ate to his satisfaction as ten rupees had great value in those days.

To his great surprise he found another crisp new ten rupees note under his pillow the next morning. This continued every morning till his last day on earth.

One night he had a vision of Ma Annapurna and she said, "My son, in my city, Varanasi, no monk sleeps hungry. This money will not only take care of your fooding and lodging requirements but also help you in the expansion of your work. And it will continue throughout your life till the date of your death."

Many other Monks of Badrinath, Kedarnath, Uttarkashi, Haridwar and Rishikesh have also shared similar experiences with me. There are places in India that are called the annakshetras. These are places where free food is available for monks and sadhus. There are hundreds of annakshetras in Uttarakhand that are a few hours walk apart. There are also thousands of Gurudwaras in India and around the world that provide free food to anyone who arrives in their kitchens.

I have seen many sannyasins being taken care of around Osho as well. Many of my own friends who came to stay with Osho had little money and didn't feel like going back once their money finished.

I have noticed they faced difficulty with getting food only as long as they had some money left with them. But the day their money finished, existence took care of all their needs. This has also been my own experience. As long as I was counting pennies and saving for tomorrow, I had to survive on very little food but the day I ran out of my reserves, and I surrendered to existence, I started to receive its blessings and that too abundantly. All my needs started to be taken care of.

Maharishi Kartikeya Maharaj

During the Emergency period of India, between 1975 and 1977, imposed by the then Prime Minister, Indira Gandhi, a man rose to utmost power. He became politically influential for a decade, causing much controversy and gaining media attention. He was Swami Dhirendra Brahmachari, the yoga guru of Mrs. Gandhi. He was extremely close to her; he not only helped her form decisions and make appointments, but he also executed some of her orders. He was the owner of Vishwayatan Yogashram in the center of Delhi, now known as the

Morarji Desai National Institute of Yoga. He also owned campuses in Jammu, Katra, and Mantalai on plots of land he had received through his Indira Gandhi association. He flew his own planes and ran luxury air-conditioned and sound-proof yoga ashrams that were frequented by VIPs and socialites. Using his political influence, he also opened a gun factory in Jammu called the Shiva Gun Factory, which became the focus of many scandals, controversies, and attacks on him after the demise of Indira Gandhi. Brahmachari's proximity to Indira, and his influence on her, had earned him the title of "Indian Rasputin."

As famous and infamous as Dhirendra Brahmachari was, his Guru was equally unknown, preferring a solitary life in the Himalayas. His name was Maharshi Kartikeya Maharaj. A young Dhirendra, who was then known as Dhirendra Chaudhary, had met Kartikeya Maharaj somewhere near the Indo-Nepal border when the Master was traveling to Janakpur in Nepal. As Kartikeya Maharaj was said to be the part incarnate of the Hindu god, Hanuman, he had a great affinity with Janakpur. He called it his maternal uncle's home, expressing his love for the land where Sita, the consort of the Hindu god, Ram, was born. The young Dhirendra decided to follow Maharajjee and became his cook for many years. He was a Maithili Brahmin who was a great cook and was famous for cooking delicious meals in those days. Due to his selfless service over the years, he became one of the closest disciples of Kartikeya Maharaj, and it is believed that all his spiritual power and charisma were given to him by Kartikeya Maharaj.

As very few people knew about the yogic life of Maharshi Kartikeya Maharaj, most of his stories remain unknown. Born to a Brahmin family in Awadh, Lucknow, during the 17th century, from his very childhood Maharshi showed extraordinary qualities that surprised everyone. After being childless for many years, Maharshi's father and mother conceived him after devotedly praying and worshiping the Sun god. It was a long pregnancy of eleven months, after which Maharishi Kartikeya was born in the twelfth month, and unlike other children crying at birth, Maharshi was smiling. These two events were similar to the birth of the great Indian hermit, Vyas, who wrote the Mahabharata and was considered an auspicious sign.

Kartikeya Maharaj was not a normal child, and from a very early age, he showed many traits that foretold his future greatness. Some of the incidents that happened in the life of Kartikeya Maharaj may sound too esoteric, mythical, and otherworldly to believe, so we need to approach them with an open heart and a wide perception. This world is made not only of what meets the eye but also of that which does not fit into our normal human perception. The Himalayas have been a storehouse of great spiritual energy, and for ages, seekers have lived and meditated there, creating a conducive space where much can happen. This very possibility where the otherworldly can happen is the very core of Eastern mysticism. Here are some interesting incidents from Kartikeya Maharaj's life which illustrate this state.

WHO DO I SPEAK TO?

Usually, children start babbling after six months and start speaking after fifteen months. But Kartikeya Maharaj did not utter a word even way beyond fifteen months of age. He remained quiet, still not speaking even when he was five years old. This really disturbed the parents, and they thought their child must have been born dumb. In those times, people went to saints and hermits with all their problems. So, the father went to a famous hermit and asked him for help.

The hermit arrived at the house and asked the parents to bring the child. As soon as the hermit saw the child, he realized that Kartikeya was not an ordinary boy. He could see from his aura that he was special and had great spiritual potential. The hermit saw no problem with him but couldn't understand why he did not speak. The hermit asked the parents to give him a little privacy with the child, and after he was alone with the young Kartikeya, he asked, "I don't see any problem with you; why don't you speak, Kartikey?"

The little child looked at the hermit and replied, "I don't see anyone here with whom I can have a conversation. There are animals everywhere; who will understand me?"

The hermit immediately understood Kartikeya's problem and, consoling the parents, said they need not worry. When the time comes, the child will start speaking on his own.

CORRECT PRONUNCIATION OF THE GAYATRI MANTRA

In the Hindu tradition, when a boy comes of age, the Sacred Thread ceremony is performed, where the boy is initiated into Hinduism by a priest. After the ceremony is over, the boy is secretly given the Gayatri Mantra by the priest. Usually, this Upanayana ceremony is performed before the boy turns twelve years of age.

When Kartikey Maharaj came of age, his parents also organized an Upanayana ceremony for him. After all the fire rituals were finished, the priest who was performing the yajna (the rituals done in front of sacred fire) called the boy to come closer to him so that he could pass on the Gayatri Mantra to him. Usually, the mantra is whispered into the ear, and trumpets and conches are blown so that no one else can hear it. But to the surprise of the priest, the young child asked the priest to bring his ear closer instead. The priest was a little taken aback, but nevertheless, he brought his ear closer to the child. The child told him that he did not know the correct pronunciation of the mantra and then taught it to him. The priest was totally shocked to hear such a small child so easily recite the correct pronunciation of the Gayatri Mantra without ever having been taught. Soon the word spread, and Kartikey Maharaj's fame rose as everyone came to know about this extraordinary child.

BRINGING BACK FROM DEATH

As time went by, the fame of the divine child spread far and wide. Soon it became known that the child also had Bani Siddhi, the power to manifest through speech, and people started coming to young Kartikey Maharaj for his blessing and healing powers.

Once, there was a boy who had become very sick in the village, and it seemed that he would not be able to live for too long. The parents had lost all hope, but someone told them of the child with divine powers and advised them to go to him. So, they took the child to Kartikey Maharaj and asked for his help. The little yogi looked at the child and told the parents to do Durga Paath, the chanting of the female form of Shakti, and said he would also pray for the child. For centuries people have resorted to this kind of divine healing, especially in the Eastern world. When people are simple, even trust and faith can do miracles. But today, people have become more complex and mind oriented, and these methods are slowly vanishing.

As Kartikey Maharaj and the family started praying for the child, strangely, a little girl came forward and said, "I am Durga herself, and this boy is destined to die today at 2:30 pm."

To this, Kartikey Maharaj replied, "Many people trust in your power and pray to you. If you do not save this child, in the future, no one will believe in your grace. You have to save him."

The little goddess replied, "Because of your prayers and faith, the boy will live. But from now on, do not use your power to bring people back to life. Existence has its own rules, and everyone has a time span on this earth. Do not try to alter that,"

With the blessings of Durga, the boy woke up at exactly 2:30 pm and asked for food. However, Kartikey Maharaj had received his lesson and, after that, never used his powers to alter the existential rule.

THE DIVINE BLESSINGS

Even as a child, Kartikeya felt deep Vairagya (detachment) with the world and realized he could not live the life of a common householder. His soul constantly longed for the Himalayas, where he wanted to go and meditate. When the beckoning was too strong, at the age of ten, Kartikeya got permission from his mother to become a renunciate, left his home, and traveled to Brindavan. There, he took Sannyas Diksha from a famous Brindavan master. It is believed that the Master was so impressed with the spiritual longing in the young child that he gave all his spiritual siddhis (paranormal and supernatural powers) to the young Kartikeya.

Kartikeya was not an ordinary human; he was, in fact, someone who carried a great legacy of sadhana (spiritual exercise) from his previous lives. So, it is not accidental that so many otherworldly incidents happened in his life. Even as a child, his soul longed for the great Himalayas. His samskaras (mental impressions or recollections) constantly drove him toward a life dedicated to self-exploration and meditation. Although the Master wanted to stop Kartikeya, eventually, he gave in to the boy's determination to go to the mountains and allowed him to leave. Before leaving, the Master told him that the Himalayas were very cold. He gave Kartikeya his pashmina shawl and sent him with his blessings.

On his way to Kedarnath, the ancient Hindu temple dedicated to Shiva, Kartikeya first made his stop at Gauri Kund. Gauri Kund is a Hindu pilgrimage site and base camp for the trek to Kedarnath Temple in Uttarakhand, India. It is situated at an altitude of 6502 feet above mean sea level in the Garhwal Himalayas. At Gauri Kund, Kartikeya had the inspiration to do a twenty-one-day sadhana (daily spiritual practice) to Saraswati, the goddess of wisdom and knowledge. On the twenty-first day, the goddess herself manifested in front of him and, pleased with his sadhana, granted him the blessing that she herself would speak through him (living in his throat). She said that whenever he gave a discourse, even atheists would turn into theists after listening to him.

When the young Kartikeya reached Kedarnath, he decided to visit the Kanti Sarovar (Lake of Grace) and meditate there. The Kanti Sarovar is a glacial lake at an altitude of 12,800 ft above sea level and is about 2 km upstream from the town of Kedarnath. It is part of the Mandakini River system. The legend goes that the Hindu gods, Shiva and his consort, Parvati, lived on the banks of the Kanti Sarovar, and in Kedar, there lived many yogis who Shiva and Parvati would visit. Kartikeya had a great urge to have a darshan with Shiva and Parvati and vowed not to eat anything until it happened. After three days of austerity, without food on the bank of the lake, an old couple came to Kartikeya and asked him not to be so harsh upon himself and advised him to eat food. But Kartikeya was focused on his vow and would not be distracted from his goal. The couple insisted and assured Kartikeya that if he ate food, Shiva would definitely give darshan to him. Finally, after convincing the young boy, the old lady herself cooked the food and fed him.

To Kartikeya's surprise, the couple transformed into Shiva and Parvati, and it was the goddess herself who had cooked food for him. Shiva was so impressed with the boy's austerity he named him Tirthapad (Lord Krishna) Kartikeya. From there, his name went on to become Maharshi Kartikeya Maharaj.

Kartikeya's soul rejoiced in the solitude he had in the mountains, and he did not want to descend to the plains. He felt that the human world was too animalistic, so he decided to live in the snow-capped Himalayas. After Kedarnath, he went to Badrinath and decided to make it his abode.

Badrinath is one of the most popular and religious holy towns of the Hindus located in the Chamoli district of Uttarakhand. The

Badrinath area is referred to as Badari or Badarika Ashram in Hindu scriptures and is a place sacred to Vishnu, with its famous temple located there. After reaching Badrinath, Kartikeya again sat in meditation. It must have been the purity of his intention and the intensity of his sadhana; after three days, Lord Vishnu himself appeared in front of him and blessed him.

The Hindu god said to him, "You have been blessed by Saraswati, Mahadev, and me. Share these blessings with others. People in the world are in great suffering. Go with these blessings and help the people to uplift their consciousness."

THE DISCIPLES GATHER

One day while meditating on the bank of the Ganges in Rishikesh, a long snake came and wrapped itself around the body of Kartikeya Maharaj for three hours. Many people cautiously tried to shoo away the reptile, but it didn't go away. Snakes are believed to be very sensitive to spiritual energies and have always been found in close proximity to meditators or places where meditation happens. For this reason, snakes have always had a place in spiritual mythologies and stories. Many saints and meditators have had snakes come to them or close to their bodies, which is considered an auspicious omen. Soon many onlookers gathered around to see this saint bound by a snake. After three hours, the snake left the body of Kartikeya Maharaj, who seemed oblivious to what was happening on the outside, being deeply immersed in his samadhi (an advanced state of meditation).

After this incident, many people gathered around Kartikeya Maharaj and became his disciples. It was not easy to be his disciple. One had to be ready to give up all the comforts of material life and follow a life of great austerity and sadhana. He had very strict discipline for his disciples. They had to take a bath in the Ganges at 3:00 am and then be ready to sit in meditation with him. To meet this deadline, they had to wake up at 2:00 am. After their bath, they had to sit with him in meditation until 11:00 am. Only then were they allowed their first meal of the day.

The food had to be collected by begging, and for that also, Kartikeya gave special instructions to his disciples: one could not beg more than three times while calling for alms, and one had to beg only to a limited number of houses that is, five to seven houses a day, and come back with whatever was given, and one could not carry any money or savings for the future.

LIFE, WORK AND MAHASAMADHI OF KARTIKEYA MAHARAJ

This great seer and saint, Kartikeya Maharaj, was born into a highly respected and distinguished Brahman family in Uttar Pradesh, a State in Northern India. Many people believed that Kartikeya Maharaj was a part incarnation of Hanuman, like Neem Karoli Baba. He had a charming personality that could inspire his devotees and spiritual disciples. By meditating on him, they used to get their wishes fulfilled and their ideals realized. The very tone of his speech was so melodious and so potent that it would stir the innermost core of the human mind and heart and turn people inward. He possessed matchless capabilities and perfect knowledge of almost everything under the sun.

Apart from his spiritual life, Kartikeya Maharaj had a great love for his nation and was a great patriot. In those days, there were also rumors that Kartikeya Maharaj was actually the Indian freedom fighter and leader, Subhash Chandra Bose, in disguise. Because of his great love for the nation, Kartikeya Maharaj was once asked to take a political lead and head the nation, but he declined.

After completing his sadhana in the Himalayas, Maharishi Kartikeya toured extensively, traveling the length and breadth of

India, where countless people benefitted from him. In his later years, he spent most of his life in Northern India. His latest followers had established two ashrams, one at Guptar Ghat near Ayodhya and one in Gopal Khera near Lucknow. At the ashrams, Kartikeya would give profound lectures to thousands of people, explaining to them the deep secrets of sadhana in the simplest words. He would conduct lectures in which he talked about everything under the sun. In order to help people, he would personally answer their questions which ranged from great spiritual quests of the soul to extremely personal and mundane affairs.

In 1953, he finally reached Ayodhya, the birth-place of Lord Rama, where on the bank of the Sarayu river, during the evening prayer, he entered Mahasamadhi and consciously left his body. It was 8:30 pm on the 23rd of September, 1953. He was sitting in Siddhasana before a large gathering. His body was not burned or buried but submerged in the Sarayu River, as was his wish. Two years before he left his physical body, the great Master had told his disciples that his presence was required in another world.

Yogini from Bandipur

Many obstacles and hindrances present themselves on the path of a spiritual seeker. The higher one ascends on this journey, the more subtle and diverse the complexities become. When one falls while walking on the plains, the injury is not great, but when one slips while climbing the great mountains, the results can be deadly. This is why great masters have described this journey as walking on the razor's edge. Every step must be taken with great awareness and caution. This is why we need a master who has gone through all these difficulties and has overcome them, and, therefore, can guide us rightly.

When we start to meditate and then go deeper into it, many extraordinary and otherworldly experiences can happen. As there is more clarity in our consciousness, our own dormant capacities are released, and we might experience all kinds of yogic superpowers that are not common to a normal human being. The Eastern spiritual scriptures and sources have mentioned eight superpowers and nine treasures available to a person as they go higher in sadhana. They are known respectively as Ashta Siddhi and Nava Niddhi. However, with great power comes great responsibility, and not everyone can handle these powers with greater maturity. Usually, when a seeker experiences these kinds of powers, their ego becomes inflated, and they start thinking of themselves as extraordinary, and this tremendously hinders their spiritual evolution. A tremendous amount of spiritual maturity and guidance is required to be able to handle these powers, and most of the time, sadhakas (those following a particular spiritual practice) have failed and have suffered for lives.

A story of a young sadhika (female meditator), which took place around the great enlightened master, Shivapuri Baba, is a great example of the tragedy that can happen due to overindulgence in siddhis.

Shivapuri Baba came to Nepal at the advanced age of 100 and used to live at the top of the Shivapuri Hills, located on the northeastern side of the Kathmandu valley.

Once he descended into the Kathmandu valley and finally settled in the Dhrubasthali forest adjacent to the airport, more people began visiting him. Baba lived a very private life and was accessible only to a few devotees. He lived with his caretaker, Madhav Baje, whose family still cares for Baba's Samadhi temple in Dhrubasthali.

Baba used to meet his devotees in the afternoon but prohibited people from coming to him at night or staying at the ashram. He used to say, "After you all leave, many celestial beings and elevated souls come to meet me at night. They consult me and share their problems, and I try to help them."

Many otherworldly and esoteric incidents used to happen around Baba, and the story of the female devotee is one of them. This story was told to me by Madhav Baje himself during my many meetings and satsangs with him. Later, Baba's close devotee and disciple, Prof Renulaljee, also confirmed it.

Among the few devotees who used to visit Baba was the woman from Bandipur. Bandipur is a small ancient hilltop settlement over the town of Dumre, 136 kms to the west of Kathmandu. It is a cultural city with houses as old as 200 years and is inhabited by the people of the Newari culture. Perched on a saddle high above the Kathmandu-Pokhara highway, Bandipur has majestic Himalayan views and has now become a famous tourist destination. It has quite a charm, with its single-lane, flagstone streets flanked on both sides by traditional wooden houses dating back to the 18th century. Some of these houses have now been converted into modern cafes and hotels to accommodate the growing number of tourists visiting Bandipur.

Bandipur is now connected to other cities by metal roads, and many buses and vehicles frequently go there. However, in those days, there were no proper roads and transport facilities in Nepal, and one had to walk for days to get from Bandipur to Kathmandu. Despite these difficulties, the yogini used to come frequently to the ashram to visit Baba, and it was surprising to everyone how she could come to Baba often, and from so far away, and then go back again at odd hours. Nobody knew that the woman had esoteric siddhis (spiritual powers) that she had attained through her sadhana and that she was using them to do esoteric travel between Bandipur and Kathmandu. Out of nowhere, she would suddenly appear in front of Baba's ashram gate, and then once out of the gate, after walking a few steps into the forest, she would again suddenly disappear. In yoga, this kind of Siddhi is called Prapti Siddhi, by which one can instantaneously travel or be anywhere at will.

Baba was a charismatic master who drew all kinds of people to him. From kings to monks, and ministers to businessmen, people from all walks of life used to visit Him to be in His presence, receive His blessings, and learn from Him. And the yogini from Bandipur was amongst those who flocked to him. As time passed, the yogini's visits became more frequent, and she became an ardent devotee of Baba. She would come during the quiet hours when nobody else was there, ask Baba her questions, and then as night fell, she would return without anyone noticing.

From the very beginning, the yogini felt a physical attraction toward Baba, which only grew with every visit she made. As her feelings for him developed, she desired to get closer to him. Over time, her emotions became so strong she could no longer restrain herself; the yogini made an effort to get physically intimate with Baba.

Shivapuri Baba was a celibate enlightened yogi who transcended physical desires long ago. Baba immediately stopped her, scolding her for her unconscious misbehavior, and asked her to return to her senses. This provoked her, and she took it as a challenge. She was a proud yogini with many esoteric powers, and Baba's disapproval of her hurt her ego. So she used her powers, turned herself into a tiny germ, and tried to enter Baba's body through his nose. Such a form of act is called the Anima Siddhi. Through the use of this siddhi, one can become smaller than the smallest, reducing one's body to the size of an atom or becoming invisible. Baba immediately knew of her mischief, and through pranayama, he stopped his breath. The yogini waited for some time, thinking that eventually Baba had to breathe, and then she would be able to enter his body.

Baba was an adept yogi who could stop his breath according to his wish. She waited as long as she could, and still, Baba had not breathed. She then realized she could not win over him. This shattered the inflated pride of the yogini, and realizing her mistake, she returned to her normal form. She told him all about herself and her siddhis, everything about the miracles she used to perform and how she had become habituated to using them. She had already realized they had become a problem.

He listened to her story and said that all these siddhis were a hindrance on the path of ultimate realization. He told her to stop using them and gave her instructions on how to free herself from them.

In the beginning, the yogini tried her best to do as instructed by Baba, but soon it became challenging for her. Once we get used to it, it is challenging for us humans to leave even small positions of power, so, understandably, the yogini could not easily give away such precious siddhis, which made her so special. The same distance she could cover instantaneously, now she had to walk for hours. So eventually, she gave up and started using her siddhis again.

Spiritual seekers since ancient times have been caught up in the attraction of using siddhis, either to boost their spiritual ego or to use a siddhi to achieve mundane objectives. But before they realize it, the same power takes over them and stalls their spiritual progress because they are not able to release their self-importance, desires and ego. This is why siddhis have never been seen as a sign of spiritual progress, nor even a goal or milestone along the spiritual path. They are, rather, a big hindrance.

The yogini loved Baba, and she honestly wanted to follow his instructions and evolve spiritually. This tormented her spirit; every time she tried to stop using her siddhis, she would soon break her vow and start using them again. Like a disease, her own powers had infected her soul, and no matter how much she tried, she could not free herself from their clutches.

In great pain, the yogini came to Baba and poured out her woes. She told him that no matter how much she tried, she could not stop using her powers. Baba could understand her sorrow, but he also knew that unless she stopped using her siddhis, there was no way she was going to move forward on her spiritual path. He sternly told her, "Until and unless you stop using your siddhis, you cannot evolve spiritually. It is up to you to make a choice."

The yogini knew she had gone too far, and now there was no way to be rid of the lust for these powers. With great despair in her heavy heart, she bid farewell to Baba's ashram and returned, crying, to Bandipur. We can only imagine how painful it must have been for her to leave communion with Baba whom she loved with all her heart. She had striven to walk on the path of liberation he had shown for her but had failed by slavery to her own powers. In utter hopelessness and despair, she finally came to the decision to free herself from this slavery forever.

"If the siddhis don't leave me, I will leave them, and next time, I will not fall into their trap." The yogini was committed; she went to the highest cliffs of Bandipur and jumped off, committing suicide.

Baba came to know of her tragic ending and said, "She was a courageous woman who gave up her life to give up her siddhis. Everyone cannot do that. In the next life, she will be free of her powers, and because of her good sanskaras, she will continue her sadhana."

This story of the yogini from Bandipur is a great lesson for all those seekers who are attracted to occult powers and siddhis. I have also witnessed these kinds of incidents and experiences in my life, especially in my younger days when I had a lot of interest in this subject and used to indulge in it. Fortunately, I had Osho as a master. He always reprimanded me and kept me from over-indulging in it. He once said to me, "With so many years of meditation, you have also accumulated many spiritual siddhis, but I have kept them all safely with me in my locker. If I give them to you now, chances are that you will misuse them and stray from your spiritual path. Once you are fully liberated, I will give everything back to you. They are your assets stored in a safe deposit box, and you can't open them without my permission."

When Swami Vivekananda had a powerful satori, he also accumulated some occult powers and siddhis. To test his powers, the young and curious Swamijee decided to use them on his friend, Latu, who was also a disciple of Ramakrishna Paramahamsa, and later became Swami Abhdutananda. Latu was an innocent man and an ardent devotee who used to worship many idols, Hindu gods, and goddesses all day. Swami Vivekananda used to ridicule Latu for spending his whole day in worship, and as a true Vedantist, he would ask Latu to meditate instead. Then Swami Vivekananda decided to test his power on him. Just sitting in his room, Swamiji used his concentration power to influence Latu's mind. Latu was in another room. Swamiji ordered him telepathically to pack up all his idols and throw them in the Ganges. Without even a second thought, the poor man packed all his idols in a piece of cloth and headed off to the Ganges to cast them into the river.

Ramakrishna spotted Latu carrying all the deities toward the Ganges. He stopped him and asked where he was going. When Latu said he was going to the river to sink his idols, the master immediately knew that it was Vivekananda's doing and stopped him from going. He asked Latu to put all the deities back in his room. Ramakrishna was very angry and went to Vivekananda, scolding him and saying that from now on, he would not be able to use his siddhis, and he, the master, would keep all Vivekananda's powers locked up with himself. He also told Vivekananda that his powers would be returned to him only three days before he left the body.

Such was the way of Ramakrishna, Osho, and Shivapuri Baba, as this is how all real masters prevent their disciples from falling into the karmic trap of using siddhis and power. I am forever grateful to my master for his vigilance in constantly guiding me on this arduous path of forgiveness.

Swami Dev Teertha Bharati

The last two births of Osho before this life took place in Tibet. Just before this life, Osho left his body in 1230 AD somewhere in Tibet where he was the head of a Buddhist monastery. He was a highly-elevated soul who was in the advanced stage of his practice, and was very close to his ultimate enlightenment. During the last days of his previous life, Osho was 106 years old and doing a special Tibetan meditation practice of silence without food or water for twenty-one days. There was a great chance that on completion of this practice, Osho would

have attained ultimate realization in that life. Unfortunately, on the eighteenth day, a series of incidents took place at the monastery, and during the tragic events, Osho was murdered. He was therefore unable to complete his practice.

This was a blessing in disguise. If Osho had been able to complete his commitment in his previous life, and had become fully liberated, Earth would not have received the great blessing in the form of Rajneesh Chandra Mohan in 1931. Osho had to wait 701 years before finding the appropriate womb to take birth again. When a person dies consciously, he can choose the time and womb of his next birth. It took those seven centuries for Osho to find the right parents. Most of the time, ordinary people take birth again very soon after death, but two levels of consciousness need the appropriate womb to be available for those people to come again: a highly elevated soul or someone with a very low level of consciousness. Cruel people like Hitler, Genghis Khan and Nadir Shah will not be born immediately. Similarly, elevated souls like Rabindranath Tagore, Mahatma Gandhi or Albert Einstein will also have to wait for the appropriate womb.

I also have my own view about Osho's birth. In 1929, Jiddu Krishnamurti dissolved the Order of the Star of the East, and rejected the messianic role of World Teacher, or Maitreya Buddha, for which The Theosophical Society had prepared him for two decades. On August 28, at the Ommen Star Camp, he disbanded the Order in front of 3,000 members, and said, "I maintain that truth is a pathless land, and you cannot approach it by any path whatsoever, by any religion, by any sect. That is my point of view, and I adhere to that absolutely and unconditionally. Truth, being limitless, unconditioned, unapproachable by any path whatsoever, cannot be organized; nor should any organization be formed to lead or to coerce people along any particular path."

It is my personal opinion that Krishnamurti's rejection

of becoming the world teacher, and a medium for the Maitreya consciousness, was also one of the main reasons why Osho's arrival on this planet was rushed and he was born on December 11, 1931. I might be wrong about my calculations, but I believe that if Krishnamurti had accepted the role of World Teacher, Osho would not have taken birth as quickly as he did.

Osho left his body in full consciousness in his previous life, and so was able to choose the time of his birth, the place of his birth, and his parents in this life. Osho's parents were very simple folk and there was nothing obviously special about them. However, many times, Osho spoke about why he chose this couple as his parents, and why they were so special. Osho said his parents were very simple, and the love they had for each other was rare. Osho's mother was just seven years old and his father was ten years old when they were married. Osho said they were so devoted to and in love with each other, they never even thought about another man or woman. "I had chosen this couple for their love, their intimacy, their almost oneness," he said.

I was close to Osho's family, especially his parents. They always showered immense love upon me, and for that I will always be grateful and feel blessed. They always inspired me and supported me for the work I was doing in Nepal. They knew about our Asheesh meditation center in Kathmandu, and whenever I met them, they received me with great love and blessings. Later, I was fortunate enough to spend some time with Osho's father on various occasions, and those times together have left a profound impression upon me, which I will never forget. I first met him in 1974 in Pune when Daddaji, as he was known to us sannyasins, had inaugurated a cow shed at the Pune ashram, and we had participated in the kirtan with him and had all done aarti for the cow and welcomed it into the ashram.

Before sannyas, Osho's father was known as Shri Babulal Jain. He was from Timarni, a small town in the Hoshangabad district of Madhya Pradesh, and was born on Mar 21, 1908, into a family of Digambara Jains of the Taran Panth sect, who worshiped the Jain saint, Taran Swami. Daddaji was a small textile merchant in Gadarwara, and had a shop in front of his house where he used to sell cloth. For a businessman, his honesty was of a rare kind. Whenever a customer came to his shop to buy something and asked for the price, he would tell them the actual cost price he paid for it and leave it to the customer how much profit they wanted to give him. He would say, "I am a businessman and I need profit. This is how much I bought it for, and this much I paid for the transport. It is up to you now, how much more you want to give me as profit." That is how Osho's father used to run his business.

By 1975, almost everyone in Osho's family had already taken sannyas, except his father. The sannyasins included Osho's mother, uncle, aunts, sisters, brothers and their wives and children. Osho and his siblings used to call their father Daddaji, and sannyasins called him that name out of love. Whenever we asked Daddaji when he was going to take sannyas, he would humbly reply, "I am not deserving of it yet. The day I become deserving, I will take sannyas."

That happened in 1975. Osho's father was a sincere meditator; he had been silently meditating every day for a few years. Whether he was in Pune or Gadarwara, every day he would wake up between 3:00 and 4:00 in the morning and sit in meditation until 7:00 am. Sometimes he would even miss Osho's discourses in the morning, and sit in meditation until some time later. I had heard him complain to Osho about how his wife sometimes disturbed him in his meditation by trying to get him to go for the morning discourses.

It is very rare for a father to accept his son as a master. There have been great masters like Krishna, Buddha, Jesus, Mahavir, Guru Nanak and Kabir in the past, but it has never happened that their fathers accepted them as their master and became their disciple. It is very difficult for a father to bow down to his son. Osho's father was a unique man.

About taking sannyas from his son, this is what Daddaji said,

"My wife had invited me many times to take sannyas from him, but I always used to answer that I wasn't mentally ready for it. Sometimes I would go to listen to his discourses, but nothing else! I even participated in some of his meditation camps, but it took me over two years to decide on this adventure, until one day in 1975, I was here in this room, there was a full moon in the sky, and at dawn I was sitting in meditation as usual, when suddenly my body started trembling and shaking on its own, and it went on for a couple of hours. Finally, when I came back to my senses, my sons asked me what was going on, and I told them that what I'd been waiting for years had just started happening to me. Somebody decided to inform Osho, and even though it was only four in the morning, they woke him up to tell him about the latest events. After a few minutes he appeared in my room, and I bowed to him and I touched his feet … and Osho himself bowed and touched my feet, so I bowed again and I touched his feet once more, starting to cry with no control, and at this point he asked Laxmi, his secretary in those years, to give him her mala, and once he had the mala in his hands he placed it around my neck like a garland of love … and this is how I became a sannyasin."

On Oct 30, Osho answered a question about this event, declaring his father to be an exceedingly rare man to be able to bow down to his son like that:

"Just think of bowing down to your own son, coming to the feet of your own son, being initiated. A tremendous humbleness, a tremendous innocence, is needed. That is one of the most difficult things in human relationships. It is not accidental that Jesus's father never came to him."

After taking sannyas, Daddaji became Swami Dev Teertha

Bharati, the father and disciple of an enlightened man. Subsequently, Osho spoke many times about him and his rare quality, and in early 1976, I had the opportunity to experience his quality myself.

It was just a few months after Daddaji had taken sannyas, when I was returning from Pune. I used to travel from Bombay to Patna by train, and from Patna, I would fly back to Kathmandu. The airfare was only a few hundred rupees. Gadarwara lies between Bombay and Patna, so I decided to go there and visit Osho's parents before going on to Kathmandu. I called Daddaji from Bombay and asked him if I could come to visit them. He was very happy, inviting me with great enthusiasm. "Come son, come!" he said. He asked me what time the train arrived and said someone would be there to meet me.

I did not have much money with me but could afford to buy some Indian sweets and a piece of orange cloth for him from which he could make a lungi and kurta, which was our sannyas dress in those days. When the Bombay Mail arrived at Gadarwara station in the late morning, Osho's youngest brother, Amit, was waiting for me. I had met Amit before in Pune. Horse-drawn cart, or tanga, was the only means of transport in Gadarwara back then, so we took one and left for Osho's house which was about 2 km away from the station. When we arrived, Amit took my suitcase inside. I asked the driver how much our fare was, and he said he could not take money from me. He explained that there were strict instructions from Daddaji stating that for whoever came to their house, Daddaji would pay the fare, and so he could not take money from the guest. Daddaji had great respect in the village and everyone knew him there. I insisted, saying that Daddaji was my guru's father and I could not take money from him, but the driver just would not listen to me. After some time, Amit came out and paid the tangewala.

We went inside the house. It was very ordinary with not many rooms. At that time, it was only one storey high. Now it has been turned into a hotel called Yogesh Bhawan, by Osho's uncle, who later bought it. There was a small room that belonged to Osho and it was filled with his books. Daddaji used to sleep in an open verandah-cum-room which had only three walls, the front being open. I was to share this room with him, and my bed was placed on one side of the room, while his was on the other side.

In a Jain household, dinner is served early and nobody eats after sunset. So, our dinner was served at 4:00 pm, and when I seemed a little worried that I would be hungry during the night, Daddaji said there would be a glass of milk for me. Those living in the house were Daddaji, Mataji, Osho's first brother Vijay, his wife and their son, and Osho's youngest brother Amit. Of Osho's other brothers, Shailendra was studying to be a doctor and Niklank was living in his own house close by and ran a small shop, selling clay tiles. Niklank's house was small and very clean.

So I slept that night sharing Daddaji's room, and when my eyes opened at around 5:00 am, I saw that Daddaji had already woken up and was sitting in meditation on his bed. Out of embarrassment, I also sat in meditation. The next day, I found out that he woke up every day at around 4:00 am and sat in meditation until 7:00 am.

During the day, he took me around and showed me all those places that were important in Osho's life. We went to the Shakkar River where Osho used to go every day for a swim, and to all the places where he used to meditate. Daddaji also took me to Osho's school, and later introduced me to Osho's close friends, Kanchedi Lal and Shukaraj Bharati, who were Osho's partners in crime in his mischievous activities during his childhood. Both had already taken sannyas, but I don't know the sannyas name of Kanchedi Lal, as everyone still called him by that name. Daddaji took me to both their houses. Shukaraj was relatively affluent and had a big house. They both shared with me many interesting stories from Osho's childhood and the time they had spent with him. I was received with much love by everyone in the village when they came to know that I had come from so far away.

Daddaji told me he had already distributed his properties among the five brothers, as he did not want any dispute after he left the body. He even showed me the piece of land facing the river that he had kept for Osho. He said he had kept that land because of Osho's love for the river. He used to tell Osho about this land and kept reminding him of it until the last days of his life.

Daddaji and I had been together in many interviews and darshans with Osho in Pune, so Daddaji knew everything about our center in Kathmandu, and Osho's work in Nepal. It was Daddaji's wish to open a center in Gadarwara as well, but he told me there was no one there to run it. He said he had even given money to a few sannyasins to run a meditation center, but somehow it didn't work out and his money wasn't put to the right use. Still, he was willing to put money up if someone was ready to run a meditation center.

Daddaji loved to do kirtan meditation and after dinner everyone would gather at the house, including Daddaji's brother and his family, and everybody would join the kirtan. Osho's two friends also joined in, along with other sannyasins in the village. Everyone was welcome to join these sessions. It was a simple chanting of 'Govinda Bolo Hari Gopala Bolo', and Daddaji would get up and dance a lot and encourage everyone to join in with him. At other times, Daddaji walked with the support of a walking stick, but while dancing, he didn't need it. The kirtans continued wherever he went. Later, when they moved to the Pune ashram, kirtan celebrations took place every noon at his Francis House, and everyone was welcome to join in.

After the kirtan, everyone sat together and talked about Osho and shared stories about him. This went on until late into the night before we finally retired to bed.

I consider it my great fortune that I could spend such beautiful moments with Osho's parents, and I cherish those memories very dearly. After staying there for two nights, I felt a little awkward. I had traveled third class, and Daddaji was aware I did not have any money. He kept the sweets I had given him, but returned the cloth piece, saying it would create a culture in which everyone who comes will start bringing gifts, and this will make it difficult for people. He wouldn't let me pay for anything and I knew that the family's economic situation was not that good. The whole household depended on the money made by Vijay's small hardware shop he had opened in front of the house, on one of the verandahs. Gadarwara was a very small town, and so there weren't many sales. The textile shop had been taken over by one of Osho's uncles and was now being run by him.

Although I was really enjoying my stay there and wanted to stay longer, I told Mataji of my awkwardness and that I should now take leave as I didn't want to be a financial burden on them. To this, Mataji replied, "You are not a burden at all, in fact because of you, Daddaji is eating on time. He cannot eat alone and when it's meal time, every day he goes out to the chowk on his stick and brings someone back to eat with him. With you here, he is eating on time and it's very easy for us."

I was immensely moved by this. Daddaji was a unique individual with a heart of gold, and whoever had the opportunity to come close to him knew this about him. After staying three days and two nights with them I returned to Kathmandu. Osho could have chosen any rich person, or could even have taken birth in a royal household as did Krishna, Buddha and Mahavir, but after staying with Daddaji and Mataji, I understood why this couple was so special and worthy of giving birth to a consciousness like that of Osho's. Daddaji was an emperor of hearts and Mataji was an incarnation of simplicity and innocence.

After coming home, I would communicate with Daddaji by

letter, and he sent me many. Of those letters, I still remember one, in which he had written, "Arun, I feel that I have an old connection with you and that you are a member of my own family." I still have that letter with me. This was the love and kindness that he bestowed upon me, and I can never forget the place he had given me in his heart.

It is always something of great wonder when we think of the relationship Osho shared with his parents. He was their son whom they had given birth, and who they had seen grow up, yet at the same time he was also their master who was doing everything he could to help them transform and be liberated from their unconsciousness. I remember one incident in which Daddaji and Osho were having a conversation and I was witness to it. Osho wanted his parents to move to Pune and had been asking Daddaji to sell the house and come and live with him.

Osho asked Daddaji why he had still not sold the house. To this Daddaji replied, "How can I sell the house to anyone where you have lived and grown? I am looking for the right person."

Osho immediately snapped back, "I know Dadda that these are all excuses! You are attached to that house and don't want to sell it. You are looking for the right person? Sell it to a butcher for all I care! But next time, have the house sold before you come."

Osho was being Osho! And no one could dare say anything to him.

Daddaji didn't say a word but remained quiet.

The next time I went to Gadarwara, Daddaji had sold the house to his brother who had added a few more rooms and was running it as a lodge. I was a little sad that Osho's room was also available for guests, so I asked the uncle to keep that room for meditation, and not to allow guests in there. The uncle told me it was one of his best-selling rooms, as everyone wanted to stay in Osho's room, although it didn't even have an attached bathroom. The room had a lot of energy and was like a temple for us, so I asked Osho's uncle how much he earned from that room. He said he made about Rs 1000 per month. I told him that every year, I would send Rs 12,000 from Asheesh, and asked him not to rent that room. He listened but didn't reply. That was that, and I never had a conversation with him again. My financial proposal never worked out. I don't know if he did what I requested, but later this offer was mentioned in one of the books written by a sannyasin who was present at that meeting. We had gone to the retreat with hundreds of people from Nepal, and some Indian sannyasins had also joined us, and the meeting had taken place in front of everybody. Swami Narendra Bodhisattva was also present at that meeting.

When Daddaji returned to Pune, he was given Francis House in the ashram where he stayed with Mataji, Vijay, his wife and their son. Osho's other brothers stayed elsewhere in the ashram. Osho praised his brother, Vijay, many times for shouldering the responsibility of caring for their parents. When Mataji was growing old, she asked Osho to get married, to find a wife who could take responsibility for the household. When Osho refused and told her he would not get married, Mataji asked him to ask Vijay to get married and bring a wife. As was the tradition in those days, Vijay refused, saying he could not marry while his elder brother was not yet married. However, later Osho convinced Vijay to marry, and that freed Osho from concern about his parents.

The next incident I remember with Daddaji was in late 1978. Ranjan Raj Khanal, who was the principal secretary to King Birendra of Nepal, had come to Pune to see Osho when I was working in the ashram. In those days, he had to ask permission of the King, and the King had granted him permission to go and see Osho. I introduced him to everyone in the ashram, and when I introduced him to Osho's father, Daddaji invited him for lunch at Francis House and asked me to take him and his wife there. I told Daddaji I was catering for them at the Zorba restaurant and he didn't need to take the trouble, but Daddaji insisted and asked me to bring them over in the afternoon. When we went there, Daddaji received us and welcomed us with immense love. There was a small dining table next to the kitchen where me, Ranjan Raj Khanal and his wife sat with Daddaji and Mataji. Mataji had made puris (fried round Indian bread) and served us herself with vegetables in Madhya Pradesh cuisine. While we were eating, Daddaji told Ranjan Raj with great innocence and candor, "You are the principal secretary, so please tell your Maharaja that wherever Rajneesh's work spreads, that country will benefit immeasurably, so if Rajneesh's work spreads in Nepal, it will be very good for the whole country." Ranjan Rajjee was touched by his frankness and simplicity and said he would definitely convey this to the Maharaja. Ranjan Raj Khanal never forgot this meeting, and whenever we met, he would tell me how fortunate and blessed he was to have met Daddaji and Mataji. He said, "Bhagwan's [Osho's] mother herself fed us."

Remembering Daddaji, he would exclaim, "What a simple man! What an honest man!"

During Daddaji's last days, Osho was very worried that he would leave his body without attaining ultimate realization. Daddaji had already attained self-realization, but a little work remained as he was still attached to his body. He had been in hospital for a month, at the beginning of which the doctors had suggested amputating his legs as he had blood clots. Osho refused this request because he did not want to distort the body. Osho went to see him three times: twice off his own bat, and the third time when Daddaji called him to say his last goodbye. When Osho saw him then, there was no struggle, there was no pain, and all his attachments had dropped except his attachment to Osho. Osho knew that Daddaji was going to leave soon and that he was also very close to his ultimate realization, which was the reason Osho had asked the doctors to keep him alive at all costs. Osho said,

"Dadda, you get well soon and when you come back, we will improve Francis House and make a bigger hall for you. I will come tomorrow to see you again."

The next day, Daddaji sent a message to Osho, "Tell Rajneesh that there is no need to take the trouble to come." That made Osho very happy because it showed that Daddaji had dropped his final attachment. On September 8, 1979, Daddaji attained ultimate enlightenment and left his body, never to return to the physical world.

The next day, speaking about his death, Osho said, "It is not a death, but a birth into eternity. He died in time and was born into eternity. Or it is a total death — total in the sense that now he will not be coming any more. And that is the ultimate achievement; there is nothing higher than it. He left the world in utter silence, in joy, in peace. He died enlightened. And that's how I would like each of my sannyasins to die."

At the death celebration in Buddha Hall, Osho placed flowers on his father's body and touched his head. Osho then created an annual festival, Mahaparinirvana Day, on September 8, to celebrate all sannyasins, past and future, who have died and whose deaths are yet to come.

Lama Guru from a Past Life

Tibet is the land of mysticism and meditation. It is the only country in the world where this unique phenomenon happened that the whole country was immersed in the experiment of meditation and inner exploration. For this reason, Tibet can be called the experimental laboratory of inner science.

When Buddhism traveled to Tibet from India, it mixed with the Bon religion, giving birth to a mixture of Bon shamanism and Buddhism, which we know today as Tibetan Buddhism. The concept of reincarnation, clairvoyance, bardo, after-life phenomenon, oracle and mediums, deity worship, and rituals in Buddhism today is a result of this intermingling of the two schools of philosophy. Another important topic that has been greatly explored by Tibetan Buddhism is death. Tibet has tried to find the answers to the questions that surround death and what happens after it, and many esoteric sciences and techniques have been developed to understand this.

In 2010, an incident took place here at Tapoban, which gave us a glimpse into this phenomenon of the after-life.

The story that I am about to relate to today is about an incident that happened in the life of one of Osho's devoted Nepali disciples, Swami Gyan Khalish. Life has blessed him with a unique gift; he is not only a singer, but he also writes his own songs, composing beautiful music for them. I have seen many good singers, but to be able to write your own song and music and then also sing is a rare gift. I have only seen this ability in two other Osho disciples, Swami Yashwant Dev and Swami Gopal Bharti from Bombay, who created and sang beautiful bhajans (devotional songs) and other songs for Osho. Swami Khalish has written beautiful songs whose lines can pull the heartstrings of any Osho lover, and he has sung them in an equally beautiful voice. He also runs our meditation center in Jhapa district in Eastern Nepal.

In 2010, a strange energy began to take over him. Surprisingly, whenever he was taken over by this energy, Swami Khalish would behave very abnormally, acting like a completely different person, and would speak and chant in Tibetan even though he had never known the language. When under the spell of the same energy, even while speaking Nepalese, he would speak with a Tibetan accent. As soon as he became possessed by this energy, he would go into a trance and start saying things that did not make sense to others. This troubled the family members, and so his daughter and son, who both live at Tapoban, decided to bring him to me and asked me to help him.

I have seen many incidents in my life which cannot be explained by the rational mind. Many a time, I have seen people being possessed by energies and spirits that do not belong to them. This phenomenon still needs to be explored, and very little is known about how such things can happen. However, I have seen that there are two kinds of spirits that possess people in reference to their intention and nature. When a person is possessed by an evolved consciousness, the result is always elevating for the one affected by it. But I have also seen people being possessed by lower spirits whose intention is to bring harm to the one they have possessed and to others around them. These kinds of things usually happen to people who are not very mind-oriented, are open, and have a high sensitivity.

So, when I was informed about the situation of Swami Gyan Khalish, I was curious and interested to see what he was going through, and of course, I wanted to help him. I told his children to bring him to my former bedroom, where I also used to meditate. The room has now been transformed into Osho's archive room, where we store things that belong to him and house other important mementos that hold spiritual value.

As soon as he came into my room, the spirit instantly took over him. I could sense this was not a bad spirit. I asked the spirit who he was and why he was disturbing our Swami Khalish. He replied to me in Nepali, heavy with Tibetan pronunciation, "I am a lama and his Guru from a past life, and I have been following him for his last three lives. He was a Buddhist before then and was my disciple. I want him to follow the Buddhist path and respect and worship our main Guru, the Buddha, but he won't listen to me."

Then I asked him, "Are you troubling him because he is following Osho?"

"No, I am happy that he is on the path of meditation and has become a follower of Osho, but I just want him not to forget his previous masters and to pay his respects to the Buddha. He is my spiritual responsibility, and he had promised me in his previous life that he would never forget the Buddha. But today, he has completely forgotten his promise. How can he do that? I know there has been trouble, but I have no intention of troubling him. It's just that I can't leave him, as he is my responsibility. In his previous life, just before this one, he was born a Muslim in India, and I allowed him to fulfill his worldly desires. I am extremely happy that in this life, he is again on the path of meditation and that you are guiding him. But he also needs to pay his respects to his first guru. He just needs to keep a Buddha statue in his room, burn a lamp or incense for the Buddha in the morning, and bow down to him. That would be enough. But that also, he does not follow," the lama replied.

Then he said, "I have been following him for the last three lives so he doesn't go astray from his spiritual sadhana. You are also his teacher; he listens to you. Please advise him."

I understood that he was not an evil soul and was actually a master of Swami Gyan Khalish in a previous life. It was a very interesting phenomenon, and I had some more sittings with the lama, who revealed many mystical things to me. I convinced the family that there was nothing to fear and that it was an elevated soul that had possessed Swami Khalish and who was only there to help him on his spiritual path.

After realizing that he was a lama guru, I would always do my pranam (respectful salutation) before we would start each session. One day the lama did a very unexpected thing. After entering my house, he slowly bowed down with great respect and did his namaste to me. I was surprised to see him do that, so I inquired about it. He replied, "You are also a future Buddha, and that's why I am doing my pranam to you."

I told him that I was an ordinary man and not anyone special to deserve his respect. He again insisted, "You will become a Buddha in the future, and I am paying my respects to your Buddhahood."

Whenever he spoke to me, he would speak in Nepali and then again start speaking in Tibetan, and I had to remind him that I didn't understand the language. He would now and again thank me for guiding his disciple and would start chanting Tibetan mantras and doing namaste to me.

Later, I was able to collect more information when I talked to Puja and Satyakam, his daughter and son, who had witnessed this phenomenon in their father since their childhood. After talking with them, I came to know that, apparently, it had been happening to Gyan Khalishjee since the age of thirteen.

"Our mother was married very young, and when she first saw our father being possessed by the lama, she thought her parents had married her to a shaman," said Puja.

She added, "The lama once said that he had made our father be born in Terhathum, Nepal, in this life so that his soul would not be born far away from the Tibetan belt, and it would be easier for the master to monitor him."

"We were little children, so it was interesting for us whenever our father would get possessed by the lama guru. First, the Guru would come, and then other lamas would follow and would chant all kinds of mantras and beat the drums. The Guru asked us to note down in a diary what he said, and I used to write it down. The diary must still be at our home in Jhapa. The Guru had even made us note down the name of the Tibetan village and the place where our father was born as a Muslim in his previous life," said his son Satyakam.

Remembering other incidents, he said, "Sometimes the Guru would make it very difficult for us. He would need a certain kind of flower, white in color, for his rituals, and we had to get them. They could not have any dirt on them, and no other flower would do. So, when we told the lama that we could not find the flowers, he would tell us the exact house and the exact wall behind which we would find them. And when we went there, the flowers would be there."

"One time, a very funny thing happened which boggled my mind," said Satyakam.

"The lama possessed our father, and in no time, our father was outside on a bicycle. I still remember looking for him and seeing him far away, riding on a bicycle. What shocked me was that his eyes were closed, and his hands were folded while he smoothly pedaled along on a busy highway. I can never forget that scene. My mother's brother had to rush in a car behind him to bring him back."

Over a few days, we had several sittings with the lama, in which we discussed what needed to be done. From his early childhood, Swami Gyan Khalish was spiritually inclined and used to sit alone for hours, but he never believed in idol worship or other rituals. I convinced him to follow what his previous lama guru told him, as it was his promise to his Guru, and he had to fulfill it. Gyan Khalishjee has always respected me, and he did as I told him, and eventually, the lama stopped coming.

Just a few days ago, I talked with Khalishjee on the phone, and he told me that the lama had not come back since our meeting at Tapoban. But now, he still follows the symbolic ritual of paying his respects to his previous gurus.

This whole episode made me realize the compassion of our masters and their difficult task. They have to constantly follow us even after death until we attain our ultimate realization. And we have all been with so many masters and have been disobeying them, falling back into the unconscious circle of life and death.

There is a very beautiful story in Buddhism that denotes the immensity of the compassion of enlightened masters.

The story is that when Buddha reached the doors of Nirvana,

the doors were opened, celestial music was played, golden flowers showered, and angels with garlands were ready to receive him, but he refused to enter. He turned his back to the door. The angels were surprised, and they could not believe it. They asked him again and again,"What are you doing? Your whole life – not only one but many lives – you have been searching for this door. Now you have arrived, and you are turning your back to the door? And we have been waiting for you; the whole of paradise is full of joy – one more person has become a Buddha. Come in! Let us celebrate your Buddhahood together."

But Buddha said, "Unless all those who are in suffering are redeemed, I'm not going to enter. I will have to wait. I am going to be the last; let others move first." And the beautiful story says that he is still waiting at the door.

The Invisible Hermits of Devghat

Hindus have always been fond of rivers and have given great importance to water. They have built almost all their sites of worship next to water, and wherever there was no water, they have created lakes and ponds so one will find all important Hindu temples located next to rivers, lakes and the ocean. Similarly, Hindus have also given great importance to sites where two rivers meet to form a confluence, and have created bathing rituals at such junctions on special dates, considering this practice to be spiritually elevating. Although most meanings behind these rituals have been lost with time, they were all created with the purpose of elevating human consciousness. All the rituals have a scientific reason and were created upon the findings of great seers and adepts who could understand and see beyond what meets the eye.

As modern-day science advances, we have been able to find meanings in a few of these ancient traditions. For instance, the findings of Japanese scientist, Dr Masaru Emoto, has proven the exceptional capacity of water to store information and vibrations for eons, which testifies why Hindus chose their holy sites to be next to water. They wanted the water to record the vibrations of their spiritual practices and attainments so anyone who came close to these water bodies could tune in to them, and benefit.

One of these holy sites is the mystical city of Devghat, in Nepal which is located right next to the confluence of the Seti Gandaki and Kali Gandaki rivers. In Nepali, 'dev' means god and 'ghat' means a flight of wide stairs leading to a river, so Devghat means the stairs of the gods. Considered one of the holiest pilgrimage sites in Nepal, Devghat has been an abode and place of meditation for many seekers, yogis and hermits for hundreds of years. Located about 137 km from Kathmandu city, Devghat in some ways reminds one of Rishikesh, the yoga capital of India.

After crossing the suspension bridge connecting the Tanahun and Chitwan districts, one arrives at the top of a long stretch of hills which are sites for temples, ashrams and caves, all dedicated to Hindu gods, goddesses, and saints. Devghat is bounded by rivers on either side, and on one side is flanked by the ghats that lead to the junction of the Seti Gandaki and Kali Gandaki rivers. It is believed that Sita, the consort of the Hindu god, Ram, spent her last days in Devghat, and died here, which is one of the reasons why Devghat is also home to many elderly people who go and settle there at an advanced age to leave their bodies at this holy site.

During the mid-seventies, I was working as an engineer on a construction project in Hetauda, a city in central Nepal. It was January, and we were going to Hetauda from Kathmandu. We were accompanied by Chinese engineers in a Jeep, while my employer and Osho sannyasin Swami Aatmo Teertha, a German sannyasin Ma Shraddha, the company's accountant and I were traveling in Swami Teertha's brand new German Volkswagen.

It was the first day of the month of Magh of the Bikram Calendar, which is celebrated with a huge religious carnival in Devghat. Every year on this day, there is great fanfare, with local vendors abound, and pilgrims from all over Nepal arriving to have a dip at the confluence on this auspicious day. The celebration continues throughout the night.

On the way to Hetauda, a small diversion from the main highway leads to Devghat, and as we approached it, I felt a very strong pull to visit Devghat. I had been there only once and didn't know much about the little town, but the pull I was feeling was only getting stronger.

I expressed my desire to Swami Teertha to visit the mela (fair) in Devghat, but he instantly refused and called me illogical, as we had a team of Chinese engineers and we were headed towards the factory for work. I even asked him to drop me near Devghat, and said I would see them the next day. He was my employer, and he again insisted that we had no time for detours. I was greatly disheartened, but there was nothing I could do.

As we approached Devghat, a very strange thing happened. The axle of the newly imported car broke, and we couldn't go any further. Swami Teertha was in great dismay and couldn't come to terms with how his brand new, German-built vehicle could break down like that. Somehow, we were able to call the mechanics who spent the whole day trying to repair the car, but in vain. It was to take days before the car could be fixed.

As the evening approached, we had to find a place to spend the night, and that's when I remembered that the house of one of my sannyasin friends was close by in Chitwan, and we could lodge there for the night. He had been staying with me in Kathmandu and was helping me in the running of our Asheesh meditation center in those days. The highway to Mugling was under construction and was not open for public access, but as it was a Chinese project, the Chinese engineers traveling with us were able to get us permission to pass through.

Our engineers stayed in the Chinese camp and the Chinese gave us their Jeep, but they warned us that it could not be driven at night as its headlights were broken. It was already dusk, so we hurried up and went straight to my friend's house in Chitwan.

Secretly my heart longed to go to the mela at Devghat as we were so close, but I didn't dare ask Swami Teertha again, as he had already reprimanded me twice on that suggestion. When we reached Chitwan, the Swami's family welcomed us into their home and gave us dinner. The Swami was not there, and as there were five or six of us, I can only wonder how difficult it must have been for the family to accommodate this group of sudden visitors in their small house. But somehow they managed, and we retired for the night.

Throughout my life I have been very particular about the cleanliness of my bedding. Sleeping is next to meditation and should be treated almost like worship. The cleanliness of our bedsheets and pillows totally affects the quality of our sleep, and especially as meditators, we are more open and sensitive, so we have to take special care about it. This was the reason why Osho, in his early days, used to carry an extra suitcase only for his pillow and bedding.

In the dim light, I could see that our blankets and pillows were a little grubby, but as we settled in, I got a real shock. The blankets were dirty and smelled really bad as if they hadn't been washed for ages. It was almost traumatic. I told Swami Teertha that there was no way I could sleep there, and said that instead of spending the night there, I was going to Devghat, and aksed if he would like to accompany me. He looked at me and said he would rather sleep there than go out in the dark in that cold weather. The distance from Narayanghat to Devghat was 7 km, and as we had to go through the forest, I asked the accountant to come with me, to which he agreed. Shraddha wanted to come too, but as it was already very late, we thought it best that she stayed behind, as it would not have been safe for a young girl from the West to go through the forest in the dark.

Because of the mela, there were buses still running at that time of night. We caught an overly-packed bus heading towards Devghat, and somehow squeezed ourselves in. The bus dropped us at the place where the road construction was going on, and from there we had to walk to Devghat. It was pitch dark in the forest as we passed by Diyalo Bungalow, which was one of the residences of the then royal family. We had been told to be careful as rhinos and tigers roamed the dense Terai forest. At one point, we lost our way, and it took us some time to get back on track again.

It was midnight when we finally reached our destination. Long wooden poles with huge flood lights had been erected, throwing light upon the noisy crowd of pilgrims and locals who had come to the carnival. The air was mixed with the aroma of different kinds of food stalls and the cool breeze coming from the river. Pilgrims and sadhus were scattered along the shore, camping there with their small bonfires to keep them warm through the night. Some local boys were already drunk, and we could hear them talking about the local prostitutes who were providing their services in the darker corners of the carnival. The Maghe Sankranti carnival was a cosmic pot of everything and catered to all kinds of people with all kinds of tastes. One could find the greatest of thugs to the holiest of saints in that crowd.

I didn't know what had pulled me to this place, but even amidst the great noise of that carnival I felt a certain sense of spiritual nourishment. The night was pregnant with mysticism, and I was stupefied and wanted to find a quieter place to sit for meditation. At that time there was no bridge, and the only means of crossing the river was by the wooden boats rowed by the local boatmen. We saw a boat floating against the bank and asked the boatman to take us across. He said they didn't row in the dark.

My companion, the accountant, was already very cold, and boarding the boat was not very safe, so he declined, but something was compelling me. I felt a strange invitation and decided to go and meditate in the empty boat tied to the bank. I left him by a small bonfire next to a tea stall, and went to the boat, climbed in, and sat in for meditation. The cool breeze from the river kept rolling in, and as I sunk deep within, the noise faded away and I was plunged into the bliss of a deep satori. It was a very strong meditation and I lost all sense of time and space. My soul felt immensely nourished as wave after wave of bliss kept rolling in. When I came back from my meditation, I was surprised to know that it was already 4:00 in the morning. Four hours had passed and it felt like a few minutes.

I slowly climbed out of the boat and went over to the accountant who was still waiting for me by the fire. He offered me a cup of tea, and asked, "Where are those hermits that were sitting with you in the boat? Why don't you invite them for tea?"

I had just come out of meditation and couldn't make head or tail of what he was saying. "What hermits are you talking about? I was sitting alone in the boat," I replied in surprise.

"I saw it with my own eyes, Swamijee, and the lights are very bright here. You were sitting in the middle surrounded by six or seven Hindu yogis with long dreadlocks, and you were all meditating together," the accountant replied.

"It's impossible, nobody was sitting with me," I told the accountant who didn't believe me at all.

"Every time I looked at you, they were there and I saw it with my own eyes. Even the tea vendor saw it," replied the accountant.

I was sitting in a very open place that could be seen from everywhere, and no one was even close to the boat. To reassure the accountant, I said, "Let's go and check if there's anyone there." When we went over to the boat, there was nobody anywhere near it. The accountant was also a little surprised now, as he had seen the hermits so many times, and couldn't really comprehend what had happened.

As the sun began to rise and dawn was breaking, the accountant expressed his desire to have the holy dip and invited me along, but I was already shivering from the cold and had no courage to go into the cold water. While he had a dip, I sat there wondering what had really happened.

Afterwards, we went back and joined our group in Chitwan and took the Chinese Jeep to our Hetauda site, as Swami Teertha's car couldn't be repaired for another three days.

I couldn't forget what the accountant had seen. All I could remember was that I was intoxicated by a divine drunkenness for four hours while I was in that boat and had gone beyond time and space in my meditation. I know I had been called, and something had pulled me to Devghat that night, making me disobey my employer and walk through that wild-animal-infested forest in the dark and cold, and then sit in a boat for hours on that cold winter morning, which I would never do normally.

In those days, I was being guided by a high Buddhist lama and mystics from whom I used to seek help or consult when needed. When I contacted them and shared my experience, they told me that I had been called that day, and whatever the accountant saw was real. When I later consulted Osho, he also confirmed it.

The accountant was not expecting to see anything, and in his sheer innocence and spontaneity had been able to catch hold of those higher vibrations which otherwise could not be seen with the naked eye. The mystics hinted that something very auspicious had happened, that I was lucky to have experienced it and should consider it a blessing. They also told me that whatever had happened on that fateful day, happened only so I could be in that boat on that night at that time. All the misfortunes that happened to us that day, the breaking of the axle of a brand-new car, the headlights of the Chinese engineers' Jeep being broken, and us getting unclean bedding at the swami's house had all happened for a reason - so I could be in Devghat that night.

Many such incidents have taken place in my life which cannot fit into the normal understanding of the human mind. I have been left mind-boggled whenever I have tried to understand them. By and by, they have made me realize how mystical and mysterious life can be, and the only way is to live and enjoy it rather than trying to analyze it. This incident and a few others in my life have made me realize that whenever higher beings beckon you for something, no matter what happens, you will have to attend the call, and nothing in this world can stop you.

Paranjothi Omahan—Guru From South India

Hinduism is different from other religions in the world as it has no particular beliefs that everyone must agree with to be considered a Hindu.

It is the most inclusive school of philosophy and comprises many different and sometimes contradictory beliefs. Hinduism is more a lifestyle than a religion and can mean different things to different individuals who practice it. Also, there are many different gods and goddesses that are worshiped in Hinduism, 330 million of them if we count the numbers. It seems that those who developed this religion wanted to make it as inclusive and liberal as possible; '330 million gods' is a metaphor for how Hinduism has tried to cater to the spiritual need of every individual who tried to find solace in this school of beliefs.

So, as we move from the north to the south of India, we can find completely different practices and beliefs in Hinduism. The nature and character of Hinduism followed in the south of India are especially unique as it is believed to have best preserved the Vedic Hindu culture, and the Tamil language spoken in this area is considered to be the oldest language in the world. South India is the birthplace of many Hindu saints and reformers, and even today, many masters live here with their ashrams and followers, all with their own unique practices and sadhanas.

In the year 2000, one fine morning, a group of twenty south Indian people arrived at Tapoban. They were accompanied by their master, Paranjothi Omahan. The Guru was in his mid-forties, clad in a white cotton robe, his smiling face beaming beneath his dark curly hair. The disciples were highly respectful towards him and referred to him as Gurumahan. I was surprised to see these Tamil-speaking pilgrims at Tapoban and curious as to how they had come to know about our Ashram. Later, I learned that they were on their way to Kailash and Manasarovar and were traveling via Kathmandu. I had a very good conversation with the Guru, who only spoke in Tamil. He understood Hindi and English but would speak mainly in Tamil and sometimes in broken English. One of the disciples translated for us.

Back then, we had the old dining hall, where we ate together before going to see the Osho Samadhi. As soon as we entered the samadhi area, the Guru became exhilarated and told all his disciples that they were at a very special place, asking them all to sit in silent meditation. We provided them with cushions, and they all sat in meditation for a long time with their master. The Guru went into deep meditation, and when he came back, I told him about the significance and the history of the spot where the Osho Samadhi had been built. I explained that the forest was called Nagarjuna Hills because the great Buddhist disciple, Nagarjuna, had come to this forest around 2000 years ago and had meditated there for twenty-seven years before attaining enlightenment.

Paranjothi Mahan was a clairvoyant, and he told me of the many mystical dimensions of the spot where the Osho Samadhi is located at Tapoban. He confirmed my statement about Nagarjuna and said the samadhi was in a very sacred spot, advising me to maintain its sanctity by always keeping it clean and pure. He added that when he was in meditation, he could see hundreds of monks in ochre robes, but who were not in their physical bodies, meditating around the samadhi. Then he went on to speak with his disciples in Tamil, telling them about the significance of the samadhi and that Nagarjuna had attained enlightenment at this same spot.

Then the Guru told me that he taught Out of Body Experience to his disciples, and they called it OBE. He had his first experience of OBE at the early age of seven, and since then, had been doing astral traveling. To my surprise, he informed me later that five of his disciples, male and female, had had an OBE that day at Tapoban while meditating at the samadhi and were able to come out of their bodies easily and astral travel. Those disciples had been meditating for many years and had not been able to attain an OBE, but at the samadhi, it was very easy for them as it had a highly charged energy field. He thanked me for creating Tapoban and such a strong buddhafield. He then revealed to me that the spot where the samadhi was located and the area around it was also the burial place of many Nagarjuna disciples who had accompanied Nagarjuna into the forest 2000 years ago. Many of them were highly evolved souls, and some were also enlightened. That explains why the hillock on which the Osho Samadhi is located is in a perfect stupa (hemispherical burial mound) shape.

The Guru told me that in order to witness and experience the different esoteric happenings in that area, the best time to meditate at the Osho Samadhi was at midnight or on full moon nights when the energy is intensified. He also said that during the early hours of the morning before sunrise, a time is known as the Brahma Muhurta, one could experience different mystical happenings at the Osho Samadhi, which was in accord with my previous experiences while meditating there.

I followed his instructions and several times meditated at the samadhi after midnight. I could immediately feel the presence of many evolved souls as if they were sitting right next to me. I couldn't see them, but I kept feeling their presence and their movements around me very strongly. After having had these experiences, I became very curious and decided to sleep there one night, so I took my mattress and blankets down there. As the samadhi is located almost at the base of the valley that cradles Tapoban, there is a deafening silence at night, and as I sat in meditation, I could feel the energy changing. Many mystical events started happening there, and it was almost like a dance of energy around me, which kept on intensifying as the night advanced. This eventually became a little frightening for me, and around 2 o'clock, the energy was so heavy that I couldn't bear it any longer. I went back and slept in my room.

Night-time is a very special time for meditators. During the day, the human world is in full swing. Our energy is very active, and the conscious mind is in constant motion; the atmosphere is filled with so many vibrations of people's thoughts that there is no space for any subtle happenings. At night everything goes to rest. The density of human thoughts also decreases as our conscious mind goes to sleep, and this creates space for subtle forces to come alive. This is also the reason why our masters work upon us during the night.

When we are in a deep sleep, our conscious mind goes into

sleep, making us more receptive and open. At night, the unconscious mind is active, but it is more innocent and less resistant, making it easier for the masters to work upon us. This is the reason why I ask people not to open their sannyas malas before they go to sleep. Osho has said that every night he visits all his disciples and tries to give them energy, and the mala can be very helpful in tracking his disciples. More than its physical function, the mala also has esoteric significance. It connects us with Osho's energy and makes it easier for him to work upon us. However, how much we can receive also depends on our love, trust, and receptivity. The Hindus have emphasized the importance of spending a night visiting a holy place or going on a pilgrimage - they recommend people spend at least one night, or better, three or seven nights at the holy place. It is for the same reason, so people can benefit from the energy that is present in such places.

I call Tapoban a night flower because during the night, the whole buddhafield comes alive, and the energy changes gear. Many people have reported having mystical experiences at Tapoban during the night. People from the villages are more innocent, and their minds are less corrupted than those living in the towns, so the villagers have more otherworldly experiences. On one occasion, we were facilitating a seven-day meditation retreat at Tapoban, and a ma from a village in Dhading, who was sleeping in the dormitory, had come out to go to the washroom. It was late at night, and when she came out, she was surprised to see a big celebration happening in the meditation hall. All the lights were switched on, and the celebration was in full swing with people dancing. She thought to herself, "Swamijee is facilitating a meditation, and no one informed me of it. Why didn't anyone tell me?"

She decided she would join in after coming back from the washroom, but when she returned, she was shocked to see that all the lights were switched off in the meditation hall, and there was nobody around at all. The night was dark and silent. The ma was an innocent village lady who had just woken up from her sleep, and her conscious mind was not very active, so she was able to witness something out of this world that couldn't be explained by logic. Such incidents are not figments of the imagination or hallucinations but just those moments when our vision is more open, and we can see more than meets the eye.

It was not a mere coincidence that five of the Guru's disciples were able to attain something so easily at Tapoban, something which previously they had not been able to experience despite having pursued meditation for many years. The Guru kept telling me how special Tapoban was, and I could tell from his words and gestures that he truly understood the value of this buddhafield. I invited him to treat Tapoban as his own Ashram and asked him to visit whenever he was in Nepal. In those days, we did not have many facilities there, so I could not ask him to stay with us.

This Guru, Swami Paranjothi, was a very interesting man with a deep understanding of mysticism and esoteric knowledge. I realized he also possessed many mystical powers, which I witnessed on many occasions later. After spending the whole day with Paranjothi, I really enjoyed his company and told him that I wanted to meet him again. He invited me to his hotel the next day, saying he would meet us at 11:00 am at the Hotel Marco Polo. After the meeting with us, he and his disciples would be leaving for the airport as they were departing the same day.

The next morning, I got ready to leave, but somehow we were running a little late. When we arrived at the hotel, we realized we had missed Swami Paranjothi; he had already left for the airport. I really wanted to meet him, so I told a fellow sannyasin who was accompanying me at that time that we should go to the airport. He said that we were late, and he must have already passed through immigration, so we wouldn't be able to catch him. I was still insistent on meeting him and told my friend that we should go to the airport anyway and try our luck. My sannyasin friend reluctantly agreed, and off we went to the airport. When we arrived, Swami Paranjothi was still waiting at the check-in with his disciples and was yet to pass through immigration and the security check.

I was very happy that we could meet him and that we hadn't missed him. There was still some time before his flight, and I asked him if we could sit and talk in a restaurant at the airport. He happily accepted my invitation. However, I was aware of his limited time as his flight would soon be announced. Paranjothi was very relaxed and told me not to worry; he said he had ample time.

To my surprise, the disciples informed me that he had already told them at the hotel that our meeting would not happen there, as it would only have been very short. He predicted that I would meet him at the airport instead, and we would have a long meeting. But a long meeting would have delayed his flight, and I was aware of the imminent boarding time. Paranjothi told me again not to worry, just to relax and take my time. I didn't understand this and said, "But Swamijee, your flight is about to be announced."

Again, he said, "Please don't worry. Until you finish what you have to say, the plane won't take off."

I couldn't understand what he meant by this. Then to my amazement, some technical problem was announced, and the plane could not take off at its scheduled time. We sat in the restaurant chatting and eating with his disciples there. We talked about many things, and Swami Paranjothi also disclosed a few things to me that he had seen in his vision. He said that Tapoban is a very pure space, and apart from the inhabitants of the Ashram, there were also many evolved souls who lived there and that it had the support and protection not only of Osho but of many enlightened masters who were not in their physical bodies. He also predicted that Tapoban would grow into a big ashram, become more popular, and attract seekers from all over the world.

At that time, we were in a small ashram in a forest in Kathmandu, and it was difficult for me to believe everything that he was saying. But today, I am slowly seeing all those things manifesting around me. Tapoban has become one of the most active ashrams of Osho and has established itself as an international hub for meditation and soul-seeking. Every year, thousands of seekers from all around the world flock to Tapoban, drawn by the strong energy field there. Tapoban has also established many branches around the globe.

We stayed with Swami Paranjothi at the airport from noon until 4:00 pm, and I chatted my heart out with him. I tried to pay our bill at the restaurant, but he, kindly wouldn't let me. After our long conversation, he then enquired if there was anything else I wanted to ask him. When I said there was nothing left to say, he then said that now the flight would leave. To my astonishment, it was immediately announced over the speakers that the flight was ready to depart. Throughout the meeting, he kept telling me to talk freely and that the plane would only leave after I was finished. And that is exactly what happened. It looked to me as though existence had stopped the plane so I could ask all I wanted to ask him. Before leaving, he invited me to come to his Ashram in Tirumala, saying I could take a flight to Delhi and then another flight to Coimbatore. He said that if I informed him prior to leaving, he would also arrange for a vehicle to pick me up at the airport.

Swami Paranjothi used to go to Kailash and Mansarovar in Tibet every year with his group of disciples, and after we first met, every time he was in Kathmandu, he would come and visit Tapoban. After some years, I also started traveling for our retreats in Russia and the USA and wasn't there at Tapoban when he came. After visiting a few times and not finding me there, he stopped coming.

It so happened that at one time, our company was working for the government, and we were assigned the project of building the IT park here in Kathmandu. It was a joint project of the United Nations, and they sent me to Malaysia to visit the IT park there to learn about the technical side. I was staying at the home of a Tamil Osho lover who was from Sri Lanka. His whole family later took Osho's sannyas from me. One day, he invited some of his Tamil friends to meet me, and among them were a few people who happened to be disciples of Paranjothi. I told them that I knew their master and that we were good friends. Immediately, they phoned him and had me talk with him. Paranjothijee was very happy to talk with me and instructed all his disciplcs to treat me well. He also instructed them to take sannyas from me.

I was later invited to the house of one of the disciples where Swami Paranjothijee's disciples had gathered. They treated me with great respect [illegible] reverence, the way South Indians treat their Guru. I received many gifts, including money and fruits, as Guru Dakshina (gift to a guru for education or guidance). We did one day of satsang and meditation, and nine of Gurumahan's disciples took initiation from me. Paranjothijee was very kind and advised his disciples to help me whenever I was in Malaysia. One of his disciples who had taken initiation from me always came to receive me at the airport whenever I was in Malaysia.

My last meeting with Swami Paranjothi was in Malaysia about seven years ago when I visited Kuala Lumpur to facilitate a meditation retreat. One of his disciples, who was also participating in my retreat, told me that Paranjothijee was also in Malaysia and was staying at a disciple's house. I was very happy to know this, and we went to see him. I was accompanied by Swami Gyan Tanmaya and Ma Bodhi Chaya, who live at Tapoban. The house was a two-hour drive from the city of Kuala Lumpur. He was staying on the outskirts of the city as he preferred solitude and silence. When we arrived, I first met him privately and talked with him for an hour. He was staying in a simple small room. After our meeting was over, I invited Tanmayajee and Bodhi Chaya to come and meet him. Bodhi Chaya was taking our photos when suddenly she started screaming that she was dying and something was leaving her body. Her eyes were closed, and she was in a trance, trying to hold on to her body. I immediately understood that she was experiencing the strong energy field of Swami Paranjothi, and being a sensitive person, she instantly went into a trance. Chaya was half unconscious and was asking for my help, screaming, "Swamijee, help me. I am dying. I am dying."

When we asked her later about the experience that day, she said, "I was just taking the pictures when suddenly I felt that something was leaving my body. I was fully convinced that I was dying. I was not expecting anything and had no idea why we had come to see this man. I felt very trippy and intoxicated. I was immensely scared and was fully convinced that I was going to die in Malaysia. I thought the man must have done something to me, so I started screaming for Swamijee's help, but he just looked at me and did nothing. I kept on thinking, 'Why is Swamijee not doing anything?' The other Guru brought out some small black horn-shaped instrument, and he put it in different places on my body. I felt heavy vibrations everywhere, as if someone was drilling into my bones. He also hit me on my back so many times - but it was not painful - and his disciples were asking me to come back. After some time, I felt fully intoxicated like I was on some drugs. I remember opening my eyes in the car with Swamijee and Tanmaya Swami sitting beside me. I saw the trees outside and felt that I could fly to them. Something inside me felt so loose and free, and I felt I could just fly away. And then again, I would get scared and stop myself. I had to hold onto something so I would not drift away. I was so scared; I was holding the hands of Swamijee and Tanmaya

Swami very hard in order to hold myself back; I must have squeezed their hands badly. Later, when I gained consciousness, I was sitting on the dining chair of the house we were living in, and Swamijee was smiling at me from across the table."

Plant and Animal Disciples of Osho

The presence of an enlightened being is like a rose flower blooming in the spring. Its beauty and fragrance spreads far across and attracts all those who have a receptivity and sensitivity to recognize it. An enlightened master's presence not only moves humans but even trees, plants, animals, birds and other creatures respond to it.

The life of Buddha has many such incidents in which animals have shown exceptional response to his Buddhahood. Once Buddha's jealous cousin Devadutta set loose a mad elephant called Nalagiri in front of the Buddha to hurt him while he was walking on the streets with his monks. As Nalagiri, running wildly and trumpeting, came closer to the Buddha, instead of attacking the Buddha it calmed down and subsequently bowed low and prostrated before the Buddha showing his respect to the enlightened one.

Many times Shivapuri Baba has also mentioned different incidents in which animals used to come to him to sort their problems and conflicts when he was living in the forests of Amarkantak and in Nepal. Shivapuri Baba's closest aide Madhav Baje who also became enlightened mentioned many stories that he had witnessed around Baba. He told me that when Baba was residing in the Shivapuri forest in Nepal, leopards, tigers and other animals used to come to Baba and silently sit next to him and he used to throw them sugar balls as prasad and they would eat it and go away.

The most exceptional case in this regard happened in the life of Ramana Maharshi in which five animals evolved and attained enlightenment directly from the animal kingdom without taking a human form. It is believed that meditation and enlightenment is only possible through the human body but in a very rare case of Raman Maharshi's life, five animals; a cow, a jackal, a crow, a dog and a monkey attained to samadhi through his grace and compassion. The cow whose name was Laxmi was so tuned to Raman's energy that she would not eat until she touched Raman's feet every morning. When she was extremely sick Raman came. He put her head on his lap and blessed her and touched her head with love and compassion, after receiving the grace which she peacefully left her body. Similarly the other four animals also responded very uniquely to Raman's energy and benefited from it. After these animals left their body Raman asked for their samadhis to be built and even today there are five samadhis of these enlightened animals in the Raman ashram.

In Bhagwan's life as well, there are many incidents in which animals, birds and trees have exceptionally responded to his presence.

A SNAKE DISCIPLE

Osho used to work as a lecturer at the Jabalpur university where he was living in a small bungalow in Napier town. He used to ride a bicycle to the University and it was famous as the cleanest bicycle in the whole town. Osho used to maintain and clean the bicycle himself and keep it spick and span. Whether he rode a bicycle or a Rolls Royce his sense for cleanliness and aesthetics was always very high. The bungalow in Napier town had a small garden in front of it and Osho used to work in it himself and tended the flowers there. There were lots of Roses, Royal Jasmine and Night Jasmine in his garden and it was always fragrant with their smell. His garden grew like a forest as he did not like it to be trimmed or pruned.

Every day after coming back from the university he would park the cycle and then walk in the garden. There was a small pathway along the flower rows and he used to relax by slowly walking in his garden. A very strange incident used to happen in that garden. With raised hood a cobra used to patiently wait for Osho every evening during the time of his return from the university. After Osho came back he would look at the snake and give him a loving look after which the snake used to join him for the walk. Osho used to walk to and fro on the path while the snake used to slide along with him on the grass on the other side adjacent to the flower rows. When Osho turned back it would also turn back and stayed with him throughout the walk. It was a very strange incident for others but for Osho it was very normal. He had instructed everyone not to disturb or harm the snake. Later when Osho had to travel to different cities for lectures and programs, the snake would still come and wait for him until the sun went down and then it would quietly slither back into the bushes. This went on until Osho lived in that house.

Throughout my life I have noticed that snakes are very sensitive to energy and are always attracted to enlightened beings and spiritual energy. Wherever meditation happens I have found snakes around those areas. Although the climate in Tapoban is cooler and we are nestled in the hills, there are many kinds of snakes here which are sometimes seen slithering around my house, the meditation hall or the samadhi area. It has been more than three decades since we have been living here but they have never disturbed or harmed anybody, and we have not disturbed them.

When Osho was 14 years old, he was experimenting with death as a renowned astrologer had predicted that he would die at the age of 14. Every day he would go to an old Shiva temple and lie down waiting for his death. There also, a snake used to come and slither over his body while he lay still on the temple floor.

When Osho was going through his period of Tamas (inactive period) and living in the hostel of the Sagar University as a student. His hostel used to be an old army barracks and was surrounded by bushes and trees that were infested with snakes. There also, Osho has mentioned that a snake used to come and live under his bed. Osho used to say, "I never disturbed them and they never disturbed me."

OSHO AND HIS FAVORITE TREE

In 1960, Osho and Madan Kunwar Parakh met for the first time at a Jain festival in Wardha, in the northeast corner of Maharashtra in central India. He was invited there to give a talk and she read some of her poetry, along with other local poets. Osho instantly recognized her as his mother in a previous life and Madan also felt deep love and attraction, and that her intense, persistent longing to reconnect with her past-life son had been fulfilled. They used to behave with each other as a mother and son and had a very beautiful relationship. Later Madan took sannyas and became Ma Anandmayee. Osho wrote her hundreds of letters which were later published in two books Kranti Beej and Bhavna Ke Bhojpatron Par Osho.

Madan had great love for Osho and became his benefactor supplying him with many gifts for the furtherance of his work. When her husband bought her a car, Osho was then using a bicycle to go for his daily job at the University, Madan said to her husband how she could drive in a car while Osho was riding in a bicycle and insisted on him to first buy a car for Osho and then buy it for her. At that time Osho had a mere salary of 600 Rs which was not enough even for a scooter. When Osho started going to the University in a car it drew a lot of attention and jealousy especially from his seniors who used to come by bicycles and scooters. They were already jealous that Osho was so popular amongst the students and now to see him come in a brand-new car became unbearable for them.

Osho had a favorite tree in the university and used to park his bicycle under that tree. It was a tall and broad Gulmohar (check tree) tree that used to blossom hundreds of orange flowers in the season and provided a large shade. Osho had a very special relation with that tree and he used to hug it and greet it every day after coming to the University and before leaving in the evening.

Now he also started parking his car under the same tree while the rest of the campus parked in the specific parking lot. The bicycle was small, so nobody noticed but when he started parking the car under the tree, it gave an excuse to others to express their jealousy. They complained about it to the Vice Chancellor who called Osho and requested him not to park in the garden. Osho said to the Vice Chancellor, "I have a deep connection with the tree for many years and it makes me happy when I park under it. If I don't park under it, it will make the tree sad and I can't do that."

It created a lot of trouble and people started complaining that the rules should be equal for everyone and said that now they would also start parking wherever they liked. The VC had to again request Osho to park in the parking lot. Osho told the VC, "See, you are not understanding me. I have a very intimate connection with that tree and if I don't park under it, it will be very sad and I will also not feel good."

The world at large is very insensitive and it is foolish for us to expect this world to understand love and kindness. Today as I write these stories, I wonder how many of my readers will understand the subtlety of these feelings.

People kept on pressuring the VC and he finally gave strict instructions to Osho to park his car in the parking lot where everybody else parked. Osho has never compromised in his life and is a man of daring decisions. He said to the VC, "If I do not have even this much of freedom to share my love, I can not work in a place filled with barbaric people who cannot understand the language of the heart." He said if he was not allowed to park his car under the tree then he would not work at this place. And he finally handed over his resignation.

Osho was very popular amongst the students and when they came to know that he had to leave under such circumstances, the students went on a strike and said that they would not let the University function if Osho was not brought back. In those days Osho was already writing for different papers and was popular in the Hindi belt and amongst his students for his new ideas and vision. They loved him very much.

This created great turmoil in the university and the University administration had to finally give in. Osho was not ready to come back until he had the freedom to park under the tree. Then the VC called all the other professors and convinced them. He called Osho back and apologized to him and he was given a special privilege to park under the Gulmarg tree after which Osho rejoined the University.

By 1966 Osho was already very popular all over India and people were requesting him to resign from his job and start preaching full time. He had a meager salary of 600-700 a month and since 1964 only people were constantly telling him that they would themselves pay that much money to him as the University job was wasting his precious time. Osho wanted to keep his financial independence and had not agreed to them. Finally in 1966, Osho handed in his resignation from his 7 years of professorship.

When Osho left the University, a farewell ceremony was organized for him but after bidding farewell to the VC he rushed to his beloved tree. He hugged the tree and cried. For normal eyes, it must have looked crazy but it was pure love between an enlightened master and a tree that had received and understood it.

Later Osho spoke about that moment and said,

"I hugged the tree, and we remained together for a moment. The vice-chancellor rushed out, and came running to me saying, "Forgive me, just forgive me. I have never seen anybody hugging a tree with this much affection, but now I know how much everybody is missing. I have never seen anybody say goodbye or good morning to a tree, but you have not only taught me a lesson, it has really sunk in."

Until Osho was in Jabalpur he would once in a while go and meet his tree but once his travels became frequent, he could not go and meet his tree. Osho was soon to move to Bombay and maybe the tree had already sensed it. The same tree that used to blossom into an abundance of flowers slowly started to wither and stopped blooming at all.

After two months the VC called to inform Osho how the tree had become lifeless after Osho had gone.

"After two months the Vice Chancellor phoned me, just to inform me saying, "It is sad, and very strange, but the day you left, something happened to your tree" – it had now become my tree.

I said, "What has happened?"

He said, "It started dying. If you come now you will just see a dead tree, with no flowers or leaves. What has happened? That's why I phoned you."

"The next day in the early morning, before any of the idiots at the university were there, I went to see the tree. Yes, all its flowers were gone, and yet it was in season."

"All had gone – not only the flowers but the leaves too. There were just naked branches standing against the sky. I again hugged the tree and knew it was dead. At the first hug there was a response; at the second hug there was nobody to respond. The tree had left; only its body was standing there and may stand for years. Perhaps it is still standing, but it is just dead wood."

OSHO AND A DOG

Osho was conducting a meditation camp in Matheran, a hill station near Bombay when a dog fell in love with Osho and followed him everywhere for three days that Osho stayed there. He became his constant companion and would even sit in lectures silently listening to Osho and drinking his energy. When Osho was resting, he would quietly wait for him outside on the verandah. This dog showed a peculiar longing to be in Osho's energy and when Osho was returning to Bombay, the dog came to bid farewell with tears in its eyes. In His book, 'A bird on a Wing' Osho speaks about this incident and talks about the dog's longing to be freed.

" There are animals who are crying out to be freed from their forms.

It happened at a camp in Matheran. I was staying very far away from the campus ground. The first evening, when I was going to my bungalow, a dog followed – really a rare dog. Then the dog remained continuously. Three times I would go to conduct the camp, and three times I would return. It was half an hour's journey. Three times I was asleep, and he would sit just on the veranda. Even when I went to eat something, he never left me. For the whole camp this was his routine. He would follow me to the camp, and when others were meditating he would sit more silently, more deeply, than those who were attending the camp. And then he would go back with me.

The last day, when I left Matheran by train, he followed the train. He was running by the side of the train, and the guard took compassion on him and he took him in. Up to Neral he came. This train was a slow train, a toy train, coming from Matheran to Neral, traveling just seven miles in two hours, and the dog could follow. But from Neral it is a fast train; when I took the train from Neral to Bombay others were standing there on the platform weeping and crying, and the dog was also standing there in tears."

OSHO AND A BIRD

Osho came to Pune in 1974 and started speaking at the Chuang Tzu Auditorium from 1975. Before that Osho used to speak in the balcony of Lao Tzu house where a maximum of 30-40 people could fit in. In the early days there were not many people in the ashram but on Sundays people from Bombay used to come so the verandah used to get overcrowded and people used to sit on the stairs and wherever they got space. When it started getting crowded Osho asked for a hall to be built and the Chaungtzu auditorium was constructed. The auditorium was about 1000 sq feet and could accommodate about 500 people at maximum capacity.

With its surrounding greenery and probably some energy phenomena that we don't know of, Osho loved Chuang tzu and it was his favorite place to give lectures. Some of the most beautiful lectures of Osho were given at the Chuang Tzu auditorium as there used to be less people and the quality of his lecture used to be affected by it. I have always seen that amongst a small group of dedicated people Osho's lectures were always of better quality.

I was there at that time and witnessed a beautiful incident that happened around Osho. Osho used to come for morning lectures and evening darshan or sannyas. We saw that every morning when Osho came for lecture, a bird used to come and quietly sit on the branches of a shrub right in front of Osho and silently sit there until the lecture was over. We used to see it every day and in the evenings also it used to come and sit close to Osho and leave after the sannyas or when the darshan was over. We were all surprised to see this bird so loyally come and participate in both the lectures and the darshan. It was as though it understood what Osho was saying and had come to listen to him and drink his energy.

One stormy evening there was sannyas happening in the ashram and we all noticed that the shrub on which the bird used to sit regularly was empty and the bird had not come. It had become a regular visitor so everyone was missing it. The weather outsidc was very stormy as the winds howled and the sky poured heavily. It was around 8pm when the sannyas was over and the storm had become a little calm and the rain had stopped. Osho was just about to leave when suddenly the bird came flying and fell on Osho's feet. Apparently, the bird had tried to come but had been caught in the storm and couldn't make it. It was wounded all over and looked weak as it lay on Osho's feet.

Osho picked the bird in his hands with great love but the bird had already left its body at his feet. Osho became really sad and asked for it to be buried in his garden. In a similar incident a crow had left its body in Ramana's hands while Laxmi the cow had left her body in his laps. Osho told us to send her off with great celebration just like we would send a sannyasin. He said that she would move to a higher plane as she had left her body in a great thirst for liberation, he further said that sometimes the sensitivity of birds, animals and plants brings them closer to him than humans.

In the beginning when Osho came to Pune there were not many birds in Koregaon park, but in just a few years thousands of birds flocked to Pune. Birds from as far as Siberia started coming to Pune and some made it their permanent home. Before, birds used to come only in the spring but slowly they permanently moved to Koregaon and could be heard singing and chirping during Osho's lectures. They may not have understood Osho's words but they definitely understood his love better than humans and their arrival in Koregaon park only added to the spiritual oasis that it was. Today the whole of Koregaon park has hundreds of birds living there.

"THESE TREES ARE MY DISCIPLES"

Osho was always very sensitive to the plants around him and used to call the trees in and around the ashram his disciples. He said that all the trees in Koregaon park have silently drunk his energy. Ma Yog Mukta, the Greek heiress who gifted Osho his Lao Tzu house used to work in Osho's garden in Pune. In early 1974, when Bhagwan moved to Pune, she used to prune and trim the plants in the ashram and mostly the ones growing around Osho's pathway to make space for the master to walk through. It happened once that she had trimmed and pruned some plants and trees in the ashram. The next morning Osho called Laxmi and asked, "Has Mukta been pruning the plants in my garden?"

Laxmi called Mukta and inquired with her.

"Yes Bhagwan, I prune them once in a while." Replied Mukta.

"Last night all the plants came to me complaining about you, all of them were wounded. Some didn't have ears, some didn't have legs, some didn't have hands . They are all my disciples and when you misbehave with them, they come and complain with me. You hurt them when you prune and trim and they came to me and complained the whole night. I don't want to live in an arranged garden, I want to live in a forest."

"From now onwards, no one will prune or trim the plants in the ashram, it has to grow wild like a jungle." Said Osho and instructed everyone to let the garden in the ashram grow wild and natural.

As much as Osho loved the plants, the plants also responded to his love and were nourished by him. There was an innocent Maharashtrian gardener who was working in the Pune ashram from the early days. He used to tell me that whenever the plants in the pots were not growing properly or were not flourishing he used to put them on Osho's terrace, or hide them in his verandah where Osho used to eat or keep them somewhere near his room and every time it happened that just in a few days the plants would become healthy and start growing rapidly.

A SPIDER ON THE BACK

In the early days when Osho was traveling around India, he used to wear a white cotton lungi and a cotton shawl. Even in winter he only carried a shawl and covered himself with it. During one of the meditation retreats in Mt. Abu, Osho was giving a lecture when a spider started crawling over his body. Few people who were sitting behind Osho saw the spider and got alarmed by it.

Osho was totally engrossed in the lecture while the spider slowly crawled up his body. His shawl had fallen down while speaking and half his body was bare. Until the spider was moving on Osho's lungi people remained quiet but once the spider started moving towards his bare body one of the sannyasins sitting behind Osho on the stage got up to remove it. Without stopping his lecture and even turning back, Osho gracefully raised his hands and gestured to the sannyasin to sit down. The sannyasin sat down while the spider moved all over Osho's body and quietly crawled away.

There were many such incidents in Osho's life that reflected the amount of compassion and sensitivity he had in him not only towards living creatures but also non-living things. Even the simplest of acts had a great amount of grace, aesthetics and sensitivity. A simple act like wearing his slippers, or sitting on his chair, or holding a cup,

Osho did it with so much awareness and respect it seemed as if those objects were alive and breathing. His exceptional response towards life in general spoke tons about how an enlightened being lives and functions. Even in the most adverse of situations he remained equanimous and kept pouring his compassion on the world around him.

Billionaire Yogis of Patanjali

One fine morning in the autumn of 2019, after my meditation at Tapoban, I checked my phone, and to my surprise, saw a missed call at 5:00 am from Acharya Balkrishna of Patanjali Ayurved. Thinking it might be some emergency, I immediately called him back. A very jolly Balkrishnajee answered the phone.

He said he was on a personal retreat at Kedarnath, Uttarakhand, to regain energy and clarity, and his meditations were going very well. That particular morning, he was in deep meditation when he had the inspiration to work with me to spread spirituality in Nepal.

This feeling was mutual, and I felt that the spiritually-blessed land of Kedarnath had put this pious thought in his mind. Although I have known Balkrishnajee for decades, from that morning we have been spiritually connected more intimately, and have been trying to work together to spiritually uplift Nepal.

I have known Swami Ramdev and Acharya Balkrishna since their days of struggle. In 1995, the two had already opened Divya Yog Mandir at Haridwar, where they made various Ayurvedic products. Ramdevjee would deliver the products himself to his clients on his bicycle.

In the late 1990s, I had conducted a meditation camp in Haridwar where an elderly man who looked after the legal matters of the Divya Yog Mandir Trust had joined the camp. He had thoroughly enjoyed the camp and had taken sannyas. He said he wanted me to meet Swami Ramdev, Acharya Balkrishna and Acharya Karamveer who were busy running their small but noble venture. He took me to the Kripalu Bagh Ashram to show me how they made their Ayurvedic products, and that was when I first met Ramdevjee and Balkrishnajee. Acharya Karamveer later broke away from them, and began his own Ayurvedic endeavor.

Right from the early days, I have sensed in them a great zeal to help the masses, using the ancient sciences of Yoga and Ayurveda. Who would have guessed that within a decade they would be leading one of the biggest consumer goods companies of India.

I have been meeting them on a regular basis ever since those early days, and although they have amassed an empire, today they still have the same zeal and simplicity as they had when they were just starting out. They do not have any attachment to material things, even being in the midst of them.

In the 1960s, Osho had declared that the ancient concept of sannyas, which was based on renunciation of the material world, would not work in the twenty-first century. He said that the coming age belonged to Zorba the Buddha: a spiritual person who embraced material things, but remained detached. "Don't beg, but earn yourself, and share as much as possible," he told his neo-sannyasins, who did not have to renounce their materialistic pursuits, but rather add meditation and awareness to their daily lives. Although there have been hundreds of thousands of disciples of Osho, the term Zorba the Buddha fits these two yogis in Uttarakhand more than any of us.

The old concept of sannyas had created great yogis, but most of them did not make any material contribution to society. They preached renunciation. Consequently, even though some individuals were spiritually advanced, our society remained poor. Our best brains turned their backs on society, and collectively we began putting poverty on a higher pedestal than affluence. This led to the whole of South Asia being invaded either politically or culturally by Western countries that were more materialistic.

Osho presented a completely new concept of sannyas, where seekers were affluent both materially and spiritually. Swami Ramdev and Balkrishnajee are examples of the new man Osho spoke of. Both of them are renunciates at heart. They wear simple cotton clothes and don't own any personal property, however, their company, Patanjali India, creates more than 900 products and is worth billions of dollars.

Balkrishnajee is from a Nepali immigrant family. He met Ramdevjee while they were both studying at Khanpur Gurukul in Haryana. It astounds me that these two, with such humble backgrounds and no business schooling, achieved such great heights, and it surprises me even more that they still haven't lost their humility.

I remember an incident when Balkrishnajee and I had entered a temple together, and had to take off our shoes on entry.

When returning, somebody had to fetch Balkrishnajee's sandals, and Balkrishnajee said it was very easy to recognize his sandals, because they would be the cheapest ones around.

Right from their humble beginnings, Swami Ramdev was adamant that he would take yoga and pranayama to every Indian home. He realized that the best way to do this was through television. He started with a twenty-minute slot at 6:40 am on Sanskar TV. They had to actually buy the time slot with money they had borrowed, but the gamble paid off, and today, not only is Baba Ramdev a household name in India, but thanks to him, almost everyone with a television in India and Nepal, and many people around the world, know how to practice basic yoga asanas and pranayama, and are reaping the health benefits.

Swamijee's popularity also helped popularize their products, so they decided to go into large scale production, and opened their multibillion-dollar Patanjali Ayurved in January 2006. Their annual turnover has been growing astronomically each year since and is currently more than Rs 40,000 crore.

The main reasons for their success are their honesty, discipline and compassionate urge to help others. They wake up at around 3:00 am and begin their yoga and pranayama sessions at 4:00 am for the masses. While Ramdevjee focuses on conducting yoga retreats and dealing with the spiritual aspects of their organization, Balkrishnajee manages the business with his sharp yogic mindset. Employing more than 200,000 people directly, Balkrishnajee runs a tight ship. He told me that he himself conducts interviews with potential employees, and focuses not only on their competence, but also on their character, before hiring them. He is well known for holding meetings of less than ten minutes, making quick decisions and giving a lot of freedom to his department heads to run things their way. No wonder this Indian company has made the large Indian consumer market, which was previously dependent on multinational companies for household products, now proudly reliant on Indian-made products.

Patanjali Ayurved has changed the way people do retail business in India. Their main aim has been to provide the best quality products to the largest number of people at the cheapest price. While they don't compromise on quality, they maintain a low retail price for their products by adding five to ten percent to their cost price. They have done this by cutting out the middleman and having their own retail counters. Although initially retailers complained about the low profit margin, later they were happy to be making a lot of money. As the demand for Patanjali Ayurved products rose, sales began skyrocketing.

They began with a few churans and chawanprash (health supplements), but now they sell everything from self-care products and groceries to clothing and a wide variety of household products. Patanjali Ayurved Ltd currently has more than 47,000 retail counters, but that hasn't satisfied them. Their next venture is to have shopping malls all over India selling only Patanjali Ayurved products.

Another thing that amazes me about Ramdevjee and Balkrishnajee is that they have been able to maintain their friendship since their Gurukul days. Although Acharya Karamveer drifted away, the other two have remained together, and that has been the main ingredient of their success. It is difficult to maintain a friendship for so long, especially once you become rich and famous, but their humility, tremendous respect for each other and dedication to their mission of making Indians healthy by practicing yoga and pranayama has kept them together.

In 2013, Swami Ramdev and Acharya Balkrishna were gracious enough to allow us to conduct an Osho meditation camp on the Patanjali Yogpeeth premises in Haridwar. Thanks to them we were able to conduct one of the largest Osho gatherings with around 2000 participants. That was a feat that would not have been possible without their help.

Although they are on a tight schedule, I get the chance to meet them whenever I go to Haridwar. Balkrishnajee, being a Nepali, is forever concerned about the spiritual and economic condition of Nepal.

He tries to make it to Tapoban or to Osho Upaban, our commune in Pokhara, whenever he is in Nepal. He visited Tapoban last winter, although he was on the tightest of schedules, and was highly impressed by the way Tapoban had grown and was flourishing. His visit also uplifted the spirits of the residents of Tapoban.

I consider it my good fortune that I am in contact with these two rishis of the modern age. I feel proud that Ramdevjee has redefined what it means to wear the saffron robe. These monks of today are not renunciates or beggars, but are just as Osho had stated, right in the middle of the marketplace doing business, creating products, and making money not for their personal use, but for the greater good. While most Osho sannyasins are struggling to balance their material and spiritual life, these two from a traditional Hindu Gurukul background are ideal examples of Zorba the Buddha. I have only one humble request from them, that they add some sort of meditation in their teaching. Although we cannot doubt the sincerity of their practice, I have been doing meditation along with yoga and pranayama for decades and have seen the benefits meditation has on both the spiritual and mental wellbeing of seekers on any path. I have observed that yoga, pranayama, meditation and Ayurveda complement each other, and provide the complete package for physical, mental and spiritual well being. Ramdevjee and Balkrishnajee could add meditation to their teaching, and with their popularity and reach, help millions of people around the world to live a stress-free life.

Sipahi Ji Mandir

I am reminded of a beautiful incident that took place in the city of Muzaffarpur in India just a few decades ago. The Muzaffarpur railway station is a busy junction, and many trains pass through it. I have also been through the junction many times while traveling in India. Just beside the railway station is a famous Hanuman temple known by the name Sipahi temple. My maternal home is also close to Muzaafarpur and I did my schooling there staying with my maternal grandfather. I had heard about this temple and once when I was passing through Muzaffarpur I made a visit to this temple. It was a small temple dedicated to the Hindu God Hanuman with his small marble statue inside and when I went inside, I found the temple to be alive and with a very strong energy. It felt like Hanumanji himself was sitting inside in physical form.

Whenever a temple is created with great love and trust, the temple comes alive and is charged with spiritual energy. There are two ingredients needed to charge a temple, first is the love and trust behind the creation of the temple and second is the promise of the master or the deity for whom the temple is dedicated. If there is a promise, then even stone statues come alive.

We have three very small temples in Tapoban dedicated to Osho, Shivapuri Baba and Kabir and a temple dedicated to Buddha in our commune in Lumbini. There is no proper ritual that is followed in these temples like in other Hindu temples but the energy inside these temples is electrifying. People instantly feel a change in milieu when they enter these temples and spend hours meditating in these spaces. Any receptive person can feel the presence of the masters in these temples. Similarly, the Buddha and Osho temple at Asheesh Meditation center in Kathmandu are very small and can accommodate just a few people but both these temples are like a furnace of energy. This was all possible because there was love and trust behind the creation of these temples and they were all created through the inspiration and instruction of these masters. There is a promise behind them.

Another such temple that everyone should visit is the Mahankal temple in New Road, Kathmandu dedicated to Bhairav. It is not a very big temple, and the inner sanctum has one big statue of the Bhairav and space for just a few people. It is amidst the crowd of Kathmandu and is surrounded by the heavy Kathmandu traffic. It is not a picturesque location by any means but the energy inside the temple makes it one of the most powerful Tantrik temples in Kathmandu and is worshiped by devotees of both Hindus and Buddhist culture. For us meditators also it is a source of great spiritual energy. This is all possible because of the love and trust in the construction of the temple and the promise of the divine behind it.

The creation of the Sipahi Mandir also has a beautiful inspiration behind it. During British India, a sepoy used to guard the Government Treasury (State Bank) close to the Muzaffarpur Railway Station. He was a great devotee of Hanuman jee and used to worship and love the Hindu God Hanuman with great dedication. It is a common practice in India that every night railway coolies gather at railway stations and do kirtan and devotional chanting during leisure times with traditional musical instruments. The Muzaffarpur coolies also used to gather at nights for their daily kirtans. They used to gather around a small statue of Hanuman and sing devotional songs dedicated to him. Once the kirtan started, the sepoy who was a great Hanuman Bhakt could not stop himself and used to go and participate in the kirtans leaving his rifle at one remote corner of the bank. The Kirtans used to go on for hours before the sepoy returned to his duties.

Somehow people found out about these nightly escapades of the sepoy and complained about it to the Superintendent of Police who was a British officer. On hearing this the SP became furious and decided to visit the bank during the sepoy's duty hours and make an inspection himself. The sepoy's duty on that day was scheduled between 12 am to 2am in the morning and on that day also as soon as the kirtans started the sepoy left his rifle in one corner of the back and went for the kirtan. Just between the duty hours the SP's car arrived at the Bank to inspect the complaint made against the sepoy and as soon as he stepped down from his jeep, a loud voice came from the gates, "HALT!". The sepoy's voice was very loud and clear. As per the regular security protocols the same voice again asked the officer for the parol code. Once the SP gave the parol code the sepoy banged his boots and greeted the senior officer with a tight salute.

The SP who had not expected the sepoy to be at his duties was glad to see that the Bank was well guarded, and the sepoy was alertly present at the gates. He told the sepoy that someone had misinformed him, and he had come to inspect the Bank. He was clearly pleased with the sepoy and left.

As he was driving back, the officer could not believe what he saw. The same sepoy with garlands around his neck and orange tilak paste on his forehead was nonchalantly walking back intoxicated with his devotion and bliss. He had been lost in the kirtan for hours and was returning back to the Bank. When the sepoy saw the SP's jeep he was shocked and instantly greeted the senior officer. He had been caught and was really scared. The sepoy started apologizing, "I am really sorry sir, I love Hanumanjee and I was lost in the kirtan and neglected my duties. I made a great mistake and I am ready for my punishment."

The equally baffled SP replied, "What are you saying? I just met you at the gates and you were doing your duty very well." Both the officers were confused and couldn't comprehend what the other was saying.

The SP asked the sepoy to get in the jeep and returned back to the Bank. As soon as the Jeep arrived close to the bank, to their great surprise the same loud voice as that of the sepoy again stopped them, "HALT!" and asked for the parole code. Now both the officers were in great shock. The sepoy could not believe his ears, his own voice was asking them for the parole code.

Both the officers rushed to the gate and what they saw left them speechless. The gate was empty and a lone rifle stood there leaning against the wall.

The sepoy's eyes were filled with tears for he had understood the mystery. Everything became clear to him. He realized that Hanumanjee himself was guarding the bank for him while he was away immersed in kirtan. The sepoy instantly handed over his resignation with great apology to the SP and said, "The same Hanuman who came here in my form to save me will take care of me and feed my stomach." With the money from his pension and provident funds the sepoy built the small Hanuman temple and spent the rest of his life in devotion and love for Hanuman. The temple still stands today as a symbol of the beautiful relation between the Bhakt and the Bhagwan and is famous in Muzaffarpur as the Sipahi temple.

Yogi from Kanti Sarovar

In pursuit of sharing my master's message and meditation, I have traveled to many countries in the world. I have found that the thirst for spirituality and soul seeking is widespread among humans of every society, culture and country. In fact, looking at the rise in mental health, war terrors and violence, the need to spread meditation and spirituality in affluent and developed nations of this world seems even more urgent than it ever has been. However, from these travels, I have also come to a definite conclusion that deeper sadhana or soul seeking is only possible in a few countries on Earth. These countries are India, Nepal, Tibet and Bhutan. For thousands of years, moksha, or enlightenment, has been the ultimate goal of these cultures at large. It is this very undercurrent that weaves through the mass psyche of these nations.

For centuries, deep work has happened in the arena of consciousness in these lands, and great findings have been attained. In a way, the very soil of ether of these Himalayan nations are charged with spiritual vibrations that are conducive to meditation, and these lands are fertile for giving birth to Buddhas. It is not that these countries have not been victims of mad materialism, influenced by the West, but still there are thousands of yogis, hermits, enlightened masters, lamas and sannyasins who are living and meditating there and maintaining the god-inspiring vibrations of these nations.

Of these countries, India is the biggest hotchpotch for spirituality. There you can meet the greatest of men to the deadliest of thugs, all in the same garb of ochre robes. I have had many encounters with charismatic mystics who have inspired me for life, and have had brushes with charlatans who have taught me lessons I will never forget. One encounter was the meeting with a young Indian monk who left a deep impact upon me, but this time it did not happen in India or any of the above countries, but far away in the city of Moscow, the capital of Russia.

I have been visiting Russia for the past fifteen years facilitating meditation retreats and satsangs in various cities. I have visited almost every Russian city with a population of more than a million, and have facilitated many retreats, initiating thousands of people into Osho Neo-Sannyas. We have also opened about two dozen meditation centers. Russian people are very open and have a great thirst for Eastern mysticism and spirituality. The strong presence of the ISKCON movement has also made Russia a country frequented by gurus and therapists, so it is not uncommon to see a guru or sannyasin at the

Moscow airport. While many gurus and mystics visit Russia, many Russians visit Indian ashrams in Rishikesh, Haridwar and Mayapur.

Returning from Moscow after completing one of our retreats, I met a man at the airport who left a remarkable impression upon me. We were heading back home to Nepal via Delhi. Moscow airport is very busy and most of the time is crowded beyond its capacity. Sometimes it is even hard to find a seat in the waiting area, and people have to sit on the floor. I have also spent hours on the Moscow airport floor during many of my trips.

Russian friends had prepared some food for our journey, as most of the time it was difficult for us to get the food of our choice, especially while flying with Aeroflot. Whilc we were waiting for our flight, I went to buy two bottles of water from a nearby stall for me and Swami Arhat who was accompanying me. The water was very expensive like everything else at the airport.

I paid for the two bottles and was expecting to get my change. The man at the stall told me he did not have the change, and asked me to buy another bottle of water. It is hard to communicate in Russia as most people speak only Russian, so without haste I just took the three bottles. I came back to our waiting area carrying three bottles of water, one which I gave to Arhat, and another I kept for myself, the extra one I just placed beside us. That is when I saw an energetic young Indian sadhu, dressed in orange, who was also sitting in the waiting area.

All my life I have been fascinated by sannyasins, sages, monks and godmen. So, when I saw this young sannyasin in his late thirties sitting amongst us, I was intrigued. I noticed he was continuously staring at my extra bottle of water. I felt that he must be thirsty, so I asked him if he wanted it. He immediately said yes, and took the bottle of water. He must have been very thirsty because he finished the whole bottle of water within a few seconds. We were about to have our snacks, so I asked him if he was hungry and would like to share our food, to which he replied in the affirmative. We only had food for two people, nevertheless I shared our rotis and other food with him.

He was very hungry, but I saw that this young monk was very generous and would share everything with those sitting around him before eating. After finishing the snacks, I started talking to him, and when he told me he lived in the mountains above Kedarnath, I was thrilled beyond words. Whenever I am in the West, I get thirsty for energy. The West has all the comforts one could ask for, but what it lacks is spiritual nourishment. So, I am always counting my days to go home. I survive on pictures and videos of the Ganga, Kedarnath, Rishikesh, Gomukh, Gangotri and other areas in the Garhwal Himalayas, as they are abundantly charged with higher vibrations. The reader can read about my passion for the Ganga and the Garhwal Himalayas in other chapters in this book, as well.

Apart from that, from my teenage years I constantly romanticized running away to the Himalayas and meditating there. One thing or another always stopped me from taking this step, and I still have that 'What if?' in me - what if I had mustered some courage and followed my wish to be a wandering monk? So when the young sadhu said he was from that area, I felt instantly in tune with him and we decided to sit together on the plane during our five-and-a-half-hour flight. We asked the airline staff and were able to get three seats together. As we talked, I heard some very interesting stories from his life, which had a profound effect on me.

He told me he had left home as a renunciate at a very early age when his parents were forcing him to study and get married. He joined the Sivananda Ashram at Rishikesh, received initiation as a monk, and was working and living there. However, as he was of a rebellious nature, he could not fit into the system of the ashram, so he left. A senior monk who was kind towards him guided him to go to Kanti Sarovar, and asked him to meditate there.

Kanti Sarovar is a glacial lake a few kilometers from Kedarnath Temple in the Himalayas. In Sanskrit, 'kanti' means grace and 'sarovar' means lake. The legend goes that Shiva and Parvati lived on the banks of Kanti Sarovar, and would visit the many yogis living in Kedarnath. It is also believed that it was on the bank of this lake that Shiva explored the yogic sciences with his seven disciples, the Saptarishis, and that the first transmission of yoga happened from Shiva. Sadguru Jaggi Vasudev also talks of the spiritual significance of Kanti Sarovar as he had many spiritual experiences during his visits there. Due to the harsh mountain climate, and the inaccessibility of the area, living in Kanti Sarovar and meditating there is not at all easy. I had many questions to ask the young monk.

My first question was what did he eat up there? The jovial monk smiled and said that after going there, in no time, he had befriended the villagers around Kedarnath and they used to provide him with satu balls, which are dried balls made of different flours mixed with milk, jaggery and dried fruits. "I eat two to three satu balls in the morning, and again in the evening, and drink lots of water. That keeps me full and I remain in meditation throughout the day in my cave," the monk replied. There was no trace of complaint on the yogi's face about what looked to me like a harsh and austere life. In fact, he always had a radiance of joy and energy around him. He was so jovial that before long he had befriended everyone around us, and the air hostesses were also giving him lots of attention. He even did a bit of palm reading for them.

"After about fifteen days, the ration of my satu balls finishes and then I go down to Kedarnath. When I get there, the villagers feed me a wholesome Indian meal with chappatis, rice, daal and vegetables, and I really enjoy it. Then I collect my satu balls and go back to my cave," he added.

I was extremely impressed with the courage of this young sadhu living all alone in a cave in the high Himalayas without any company and under such adverse conditions away from human habitation.

I have heard many stories of the harsh realities in this terrain from those who have chosen to live in these abodes of the gods. Some sadhus and sadhvis who never descend, but stay in their caves through winter, have told me that sometimes it gets so cold that even the mouths of the caves become closed with ice, and one has to remain awake throughout the night making holes in it for oxygen to enter. A sadhvi from Tapovan, which lies above Gangotri, once told me that their whole life depends on matchsticks, and if by any chance they become damp, there is no way to light a fire, so they store them inside sacks of rice to keep them dry. She also said that once the routes are closed due to the snow, one has to wait for months before they see another human face.

The young sadhu was high with energy, and a great talker. He didn't keep quiet even for a minute, talking throughout the entire flight. During this conversation, he told me a story that helped me understand the higher synchronicity that functions in the Himalayas. Devoid of the vibrations of human thoughts, selfish ideas and ambitions, the mountains are a unique realm where higher vibrations get space to function. This is in stark contrast to the atmosphere on the densely-populated plains.

One day, the young sadhu was meditating in his cave as usual, but strangely, he couldn't meditate at all. He couldn't figure out what was disturbing him, but the usually calm and trained mind of his kept getting distracted, and he couldn't go into meditation. He tried very hard and made every effort, but nothing happened. This was a blow to the otherwise strong-willed monk. The situation intensified to such a degree that finally he became so frustrated, he decided to leave his cave forever, concluding that cave meditation was not for him anymore, and he should move somewhere else.

He had very few belongings which he packed up in a few

minutes, and then he started the descent. After walking for some time, he suddenly saw a human body lying face down in the snow in one of the glacier crevices. The sadhu rushed over to the person, and saw it was a foreigner. He immediately lifted the unconscious man, took him to Kedarnath, and had him treated with first aid, thereby saving the man's life. As the monk was rushing down with the body, it dawned on him why he was so much disturbed in his meditation that day. He had received the vibrations of what had occurred close to his cave and could not go into meditation as the foreigner needed his help. Something compelled him to leave his cave and find the trekker. The trekker was an adventurous guy who had set out on a trek alone and had slipped and fallen into the crevice.

People who meditate develop a higher sensitivity as their channels become purified and their mind becomes silent, and they are able to receive the vibrations of what is happening close to them or what is about to happen in the near future. Sometimes elevated souls can even receive vibrations in the form of visions or dreams about what is happening or about to happen not only close to them, but also thousands of miles away.

The foreigner was a German guy who felt highly obliged to the young sadhu for saving his life and invited him to his country for a tour. His German host arranged everything for his trip. After touring Europe, he was in transit in Russia while returning to India from Germany.

Then the sadhu told us about the synchronicity that had occurred between him and me. He said, "On this return trip, I lost all my money at the Moscow airport, and because of the language problem I was helpless. I was extremely thirsty and wanted to drink water but couldn't find free water anywhere." Moscow airport is very expensive and there are no free water fountains available. The water in Moscow city is highly polluted, so tap water is not safe to drink.

"I went to the washroom, and even though there were signs telling people not to drink from the tap, I was so thirsty I decided to drink it. But when the janitor saw me, he stopped me from drinking it," the monk went on, "So when I couldn't find water anywhere and I was very thirsty, I was collecting spit in my mouth and drinking that to quench my thirst, so when you came with a third bottle of water and offered it to me, I felt it was a godsend."

"I was so hungry and you also shared your food with me," he said with gratitude.

It is my experience in life that there is a higher rule that functions in this existence. Whenever someone is totally surrendered to the divine, the divine has to help that person. It is our own ego and plans that hinder this process, interfering with the bigger existential plan that is there for us. It needs great trust and surrender to allow this magic and the higher forces to function in our lives. The young sadhu was a wandering monk who totally surrendered to the divine plan, and that is why the divine had to intervene and send me as a medium to help him.

In my own life, I have witnessed hundreds of such incidents which have proven this phenomenon to me. Whenever I have used my mind, I have failed, and whenever I have surrendered and allowed the divine to function, I have succeeded. That is why this Christian prayer is very dear to me, and I recite it whenever I remember it, "O Lord, your grace is infinite. Thy will be done, my Lord, not mine!"

When we landed at the Delhi airport, out of gratitude, the sadhu offered me his small handbag which had been given to him by his German friend. I said I had my own luggage and did not need it, and asked him to keep it for himself as he had to carry his own clothes. But he insisted, asking me to keep it, and saying that he was carrying only two sets of ochre clothes, and did not need the bag. When I asked him how he was going to get back home, he said he had a friend in Delhi who lived about 15 km from the airport, and that he would help him get back to Kedarnath. When I enquired how he was planning to get to his friend's place, he said he was going to walk. He was not even sure of his friend's address in Delhi.

I asked him to come and spend the night with us at our Osho Center in Malviya Nagar as it was already one in the morning by the time we had landed. He did not have any luggage except for a small handbag, so we left him while we went to collect our luggage which took longer than usual. When we got back, he was no longer there. Just as we had met him suddenly amid the crowd at the Moscow airport, we lost him in the crowd at the Delhi airport. We searched for him, but he was nowhere in sight. Although we spent only a short time together, the jovial face of that young sadhu and his contagious joy and energy left a deep impression upon me and is still fresh in my memory today.

Mystical Life of Swami Rama

The owner of the Yak and Yeti Hotel in Nepal was a devotee of Swami Rama and an acquaintance of mine. He came from a famous and wealthy family. A group of lovers of Swami Rama called me to Yak and Yeti Hotel for tea. Since I was going to America, they suggested that I go visit Swami Rama in Pennsylvania and personally give a letter to him inviting him to Nepal. Since I was unable to afford the travel, they asked me to post the letter when I reached America. It was 1983, and the postal service in Nepal wasn't reliable letters used to take months

to deliver and even get lost many times. They asked me to drop this letter off in America when I reached to ensure its timely and guaranteed delivery. They told me that it would cost 25 cents for postage and asked me to speak to Swami Rama on the phone and gave me his number.

So came to be my first contact with Swami Rama when I called him from Rajneeshpuram in July 1983. I didn't know much about him before this. He picked up the phone himself. I told him that I was calling from Rajneeshpurum and that I was a disciple of Bhagwan Rajneesh. Swamiji said that since I had traveled this far to America, I should come to Pennsylvania to stay with him. I was reluctant to say yes, because I was short on money and said that I would send the letter by post, which he would receive in a day or two. I told him that the letter was an invitation by his Nepali devotees to come to Nepal. Sensing my hesitation, he said not to worry about money and that all would be taken care of in his Ashram. But at that time, even plane tickets to and back between Rajneeshpuram and Pennsylvania were difficult to afford for me. I did not have a budget for traveling and only had the resources to spend my time at Rajneeshpuram with my master. I was hesitant to say that to him, and I'm sure he would have sent tickets for my trip if I had asked. Swamiji said that Rajneeshji was a friend of his and that he respected him a lot. He asked me to meet him when he came to Nepal.

After a year, Swamiji came to Nepal, initially staying at Hotel Yak and Yeti and then moving to his Ashram in Banepa. His coming to Nepal was a big event, and everyone knew about it. The reason was that the King's sister, Princess Shova, hadn't had a son for many years. She went to America to find a medical solution. There Swami Rama gave her his blessings to have a son. And she did. He helped immensely in the delivery of the child, providing all kinds of logistic support. For this, the royal family of Nepal was joyous and extremely grateful to Swamiji.

From a previous visit to Nepal in 1981, his disciples had already purchased 1 acre of land for him in Banepa. Another 80 acres of land were promised to him by the government for his Himalayan health project. There was a hunt for design and engineering consultants for this multi-million dollar project, and many big consultancy firms lined up to be hired. When I arrived for the interview wearing Bhagwan's mala, I mentioned to Swamiji about our earlier interaction over the phone in the USA. He immediately said to his people, "Stop your search. I have found my consultant." He invited me to come to Banepa with him.

When I arrived there, he shared his dream with me. His grand plan was to build an integrated medical university that would include departments for Ayurveda, Homeopathy, and Allopathy, a hostel, a holistic health and wellness center, and a Yoga ashram spread in the beautiful lap of the Himalayas. It would be called the Vaidic University of Medical Science. He had already established a health center and school in Banepa. The nature of the terrain made this massive project a difficult but not impossible undertaking. He asked me to start the construction of a few rooms with attached bathrooms for his guests and devotees to stay at while the fundraising was completed.

During the ashram construction, Swamiji developed a great affection for me and after the engineering talk was over, we would spend hours discussing the Dharma and the similarity between his teachings and that of Osho. Swamiji enjoyed smoking and asked me to get him good-quality tobacco and hookah. He said that hookah was better than cigarettes as the tobacco smoke is filtered through the water. I said I would be glad to obtain this for him as my mother was also a hookah smoker. He was very happy to receive this gift. During this period, he asked me to join the Himalayan Institute and take care of his work in Japan. He wanted me to manage his affluent Ashram and many homes and properties there. I said that I couldn't accept his generous offer, as I was already doing my master's work in Nepal and couldn't leave Kathmandu for more than a few days.

Once, I arrived at Swamiji's hut at the Ashram and found him sitting alone: serene, facing the Himalayas in deep meditation. I did not approach further, not wanting to disturb him. Sensing my presence, he asked me to come to sit. I asked him, "Swamiji, were you in meditation?" His answer surprised me. He said, "No. I was with myself and enjoying myself."

The common thread between us that made me fall in love with Swami Rama was our love for the Himalayas and the Ganges. He would say that the Himalayas are his father and the Ganges his mother. I used to say the same ever since my childhood. He said that despite having lived in other countries, he wanted to leave his body in the presence of the Himalayas and the Ganges. When he did pass away from his body, he did so in Rishikesh, the perfect confluence of the two.

Due to events unknown, he had a falling out with the Royal Court and announced that he was dropping the project and leaving for America. This took me aback as we were on the verge of beginning a massive survey of the land to start the project. This project had the potential to transform the fortunes of the entire region. But unfortunately, this wasn't to be. Swamiji had a famous temper, and even the Royal family wasn't spared when they upset him. He said publicly, "Your royalty began through the blessing of a Rishi, Gorakhnath, and will also end by the curse of this Rishi. I will now return to Nepal only when your monarchy ends." And he left, eventually taking his project to Dehradun in India.

A few years later, when I was visiting Ma Madhu in Rishikesh, I learned that Swamiji was staying at his Ashram. The sight of his beautiful form enjoying himself on the banks of the Ganges was a sight to behold. He was delighted to see me calling out, "Arun is here! Arun is here. Come, come." We discussed the political situation of

Nepal at length, and he expressed grave concern about the prevailing state of affairs. He said that the monarchy was bound to end sooner or later. He said he would come back to Nepal when that happened. Then he enquired about my ashram work in Nepal. At the time, Tapoban wasn't built, and I was still doing Bhagwan's work from Asheesh and looking for land to build a commune. He immediately got papers from his office and signed them stating the handover of the Hansada Ashram in Banepa to his friend, Rajneesh, to start a commune. He said that the land was ideally located for an ashram and would be to the liking of his friend, Rajneeshji. I couldn't accept explaining I didn't have the capacity to get into a conflict with the Nepal royal family. The Banepa land that had been purchased by a yogi, Swami Rama, was eventually appropriately handed over to another yogi, Swami Satchitanand. True to his word Swamiji did come back to visit Nepal when the monarchy ended in 1990 on the invitation of then Prime Minister Krishna Prasad Bhattarai.

While Swamiji did not speak much, I learned a lot about him through the tales told to me by his devotees and his book "Living with the Himalayan Masters," a copy of which he personally gifted to me. When he went to America, he decided to do an astounding demonstration of his yogic mastery. He asked the doctors what their definition was of clinical death. Under medical observation, he voluntarily brought his heartbeat, blood circulation, and breathing to a halt. On demonstration, he asked the doctors to sign a certificate to declare him clinically dead.

His life is mostly of mystical dimension, and I'm going to share a few stories.

BIRTH THROUGH GRACE

His birth was through the Grace of his Guru. He came from a Garhwali Brahmin family. His parents had grown to old age without having a child. His father had an awakening and left home to become a sadhu, practicing in a cave of Chamundi Hills in Rishikesh. Bengali Baba was the family's Guru. On visiting the family home, the wife told Baba about the pain her husband had caused by leaving her. People thought that he was dead and had started treating her like a widow. She did not believe that her husband was dead and asked Baba to help. Out of his compassion, Baba promised to find the husband and bring him back. He found him in Rishikesh, scolded him for leaving his wife and family, and asked him to return immediately. On his return, husband and wife shared with Baba their sadness is getting so old and not having a child. Baba blessed them by saying that they would have a son of immense potential, but that boy would belong to him, and they should not get too attached and regard him as their own. Eventually, he was to become a student of Baba. Eventually, the boy was born, and Baba would periodically come to meet his young prodigy. His parents were getting on with their age and eventually passed away. Baba took the young boy away and raised him in the caves of the Himalayas, where he continued to live in various regions of the hallowed mountains till the age of 45.

SHANKARACHARYA OF KARVIRPITHAM

Once, he was meditating intensely in Amarkantak, on the banks of the Narmada. Many wild animals used to roam around him, but that didn't shake him from his meditative state. The Shankaracharya of Karvirpitham was looking for his spiritual successor and, on observing the young Yogi meditating, felt that his search had come to an end. He chose him as his successor and appointed him to the position of Shankaracharya. He held the esteemed post for a few years but had to leave, citing that the daily visits, duties, and obligatory rituals associated with the position were taking most of his time and causing a hindrance in the progress of his spiritual practice.

PARAM GURU'S SUMMON FROM TIBET

On the instructions of Bengali Baba, he was sent to Shantiniketan to further his education under Rabindranath Tagore. Swami Rama used to consider Rabindranath to be a Rishi and regarded him as his Guru too. He used to say that around the creative energy of Rabindranath, he would feel exactly the same way that he would around Bengali Baba. Around that time in Shantiniketan, he received a telegram from Bengali Baba asking him to come immediately. Fearing the imminent demise of his Guru, he rushed to Kalingpong. There Baba had instructions for him to travel to Tibet to meet their Param Guru.

Taking permission from Rabindranath, he and ten friends from Santiniketan who were curious to meet the Param Guru left for Tibet via Sikkim. This was before 1947, and traveling from Sikkim to Tibet was dangerous on the political level. The group was stopped by the British for inquiry. The British suspected them to be spies working for the revolutionary movement of the Indian National Congress. They even have some photos and letters of Nehru and Gandhi in the bags of a companion party that strengthened their suspicion. They were placed under house arrest at a guest house for a month in Gangtok. While the food and location were ideal for meditation, Swamiji's mission was to cross the border and meet his Param Guru in Tibet. He devised a plan. The gatekeeper at the guest house was Nepali; since Swamiji spoke Nepali, he was able to convince the gatekeeper to give him his torn overcoat. Covering himself in the torn overcoat and speaking the language, no one suspected him, and he was able to escape from the British.

The journey further through the mountains was arduous, to say the least. It took him two months to reach Lhasa on foot. The only food available was meat, which he didn't eat, and yak milk which was terrible to taste. I can only imagine his struggle and marvel at his will to push through this difficult terrain for two months only to meet his master.

On finally reaching the destination, his Param Guru revealed the reason for summoning him. The master wanted to teach him Parkaya Pravesh, or the way to leave one's own body and enter another. He spent many months training under his master to learn this secret skill. There is a story of a 90-year-old Sadhu who knew this skill. He had foreseen that the next day there was a young man who was to die from a snake bite. He waited on the ghat for the body to be brought for cremation. Before people could light the body on fire, it started raining, so they stopped. At that moment, the sadhu entered that youthful body and left his own, resuming his life and practicing again but now as a 25-year-old man! Such mastery was known by adept yogis. And this art of Parakaya Pravesh is what the Tibetan Master passed on to Swami Rama during his stay in Tibet.

THE MAGICAL KAMANDAL

There is another very miraculous incident I'd like to mention. After many years of training, his Guru told him that it was time to take the vows of renunciation. Swami Rama was quite fashionable and belonged to a wealthy family. All his associates were also quite well-to-do. As a renunciate, he was not allowed to own anything, and for the first time in his life, he had to even beg for his food. He went out to a home in Rishikesh and asked the man for alms. Seeing this strong youth begging, the man rebuked him and told him to stop begging and earn his living through hard work. This deeply wounded the ego of the young swami. He decided not to beg and went to the Triveni ghat by the Ganga, resolving to only drink the holy water of the Ganga from now on. He lived like this on the Triveni Ghat only on the Ganga water for 13 days! Then a miracle occurred. A hand appeared out of the Ganga, holding an object. It was Mother

Ganga herself. Young Rama asked what it was. The answer was that it was Kamandal. Whatever he desired to eat and in whatever quantity, this magical kamandal would make it appear. He could feed as many people as he wanted, and no matter how much food people left in his Kamandal, it would never fill up. His joy knew no bounds, and he was happily enjoying and sharing his newfound gift with a few other sadhus when his Guru found out about this. Bengali Baba said it was not the way of the Sadhu to live on supernatural miracles and that he should take only that which existence provides. Baba asked him to return the kamandal back to the Ganga with a heavy heart; he returned the gift back to the holy river.

TWO NAKED ASCETICS

Another time he was living in Ujjali, in Uttarkashi. There he would meditate and used to survive by eating cooked chickpeas with salt. In the area were two famous ascetics that used to live absolutely naked in the searing cold, bathing in the icy cold Ganga and eating whatever people gave. Swami Rama decided that he, too, should learn from these naked ascetics. On reaching their cave, he found both of them wrestling. He separated them and asked the reason for their quarrel. One of them said, "He stepped on my sleeping mat. What does he think of himself!" Seeing these ascetics fighting over such a petty reason convinced him that the path of the renunciate was not for him. It made him realize that despite renouncing worldly possessions, people were not ready to renounce their egos. His phase as a cave-dwelling monk came to a close, and he returned to the world as the fashionable Yogi that we came to know.

The other aspect of his life is rather obscure. In his book, he mentions having a son and having attended his marriage in Tikamgarh in Rajasthan. Nothing is known about his wife and marriage. There are also many controversial stories about him.

I recently visited his Ashram in Rishikesh after a long time. The Ashram is simple, clean, and beautifully located right next to the Ganga. His personal room is now well-preserved, and there is a wonderful meditation room right beneath it. I felt such a strong and sweet energy in the meditation room that I did not feel like leaving. Swamiji's presence is very tangible in that space. That room still calls to me. I have seen that every Yogi has his own style. While Swami Rama had an infamous temper and smoking habit, he also had many siddhis like Parkaya Pravesh and the ability to read others' thoughts and many others, which were quite normal for him. He was a fashionable yogi who led an affluent lifestyle, staying in the best hotels, riding in the best cars, and wearing the best watches. In some ways, his style was similar to Osho's. When I asked Bhagwan about Swami Rama, he said that Swami Rama was an accomplished yogi and he had left an enlightened soul.

Swami Anand Maitreya: Politics to Enlightenment

In 1984, Osho created a committee or a sansad of sannyasins in Rajneeshpuram which consisted of 21 Sambuddhas, 21 Bodhisattvas and 21 Mahasattvas. Swami Anand Maitreya's name was listed in the sambuddhas or the enlightened ones and he was also made the coordinator of the sansad. My name also came in the list of the Bodhisattvas. Osho said that when he would leave his body Swami Anand Maitreya would call the meeting of this sansad and the group would unanimously decide about how to take forward his movement. In Buddha's times Buddha had made Mahakashyap the head of a similar group of bhikkhus who would decide upon the future of the Buddha Dharma after Buddha left his body. Osho said that all decisions regarding his work should be made through unanimous agreement of all the members of the sansad. Osho wanted the number of this sansad to be 108 and if anybody died in the sansad, the new member should also be decided through unanimous decision by all the members. Swami Anand Maitreya was made the coordinator of the Sambuddhas, Vivek was the coordinator of the Mahasattvas and Teertha was the coordinator of the Bodhisattvas. Swami Anand Maitreya was the president of the whole sansad and the main coordinator and presided over the other coordinators.

It was instructed that immediately after Osho left his body, Swami Anand Maitreya would call the meeting of all the members and through which important decisions would be made. At that time there were rumors that Osho was soon going to leave his body so all the members had to give our address and phone numbers to Swami Anand Maitreya and were instructed to instantly report to Swami Maitreya if there was any change in our address or phone numbers.

Swami Anand Maitreya was a very simple man and dismissed this whole idea and said that he was not enlightened. He called Osho a rascal and said that he was playing a joke on him. When I met him a second time in Rajneeshpuram in 1985, he told me that he would never be able to call this meeting as he was very confident that he would leave his body before Osho. And that's exactly what happened, he left his body on July 17 1987, 3 years before Osho left his body in 1990.

I first met Swami Anand Maitreya in 1970 in January. We had invited Osho to speak at our University in Patna and he had accepted our invitation. Four of us had gone to receive Osho who was then known as Acharyashree at the railway station. Four of us included

Ram Chandrajee who was the head of the English department and later became the Vice Chancellor of the University, he was also hosting Acharyashree at his house, my friend from Kashmir, Swami Aatmo Vijay, a student from the University Toofan and I. The four of us received Acharyashree at the station and took him to Ram Chandrajee's house. We thought that he must have been tired from the whole night's journey and asked him to rest. Acharyashree told us that he was not tired and asked us to make the best use of his time in Patna. "I don't know if I will ever come back to Patna and my every minute is precious so organize as many programs as you can." He told us.

He asked me to first go and invite Mathura Prasad Mishra to come see him who was an Osho lover and a reputed politician of Bihar who had already been a member of the parliament three times. Mathura Prasad Mishra was the name of Maitreya Swami before he took sannyas and his house was in Rajendranagar which was very close to where Osho was staying. When I arrived at his house, he had just gotten up and was shaving his beard. That was my first encounter with Swami Anand Maitreya. I told him that Acharyashree had arrived and had called him. He offered me tea but since I had to rush back I politely declined his offer. Mathura Babu told me to go ahead and he would join us very soon after he had freshened up.

I could see that Mathura Babu had great love and respect for Osho and Osho also loved him dearly. For the three days that Osho was in Patna, we were always together until late night and this became the seed of our lifelong friendship as we grew close to each other through our common love for Osho.

I was a student and studying engineering in Patna and Maitreyajee was a reputed politician in Bihar and a former member of the parliament who had been many times offered Ministerial position and because of his popularity and seniority was also a probable candidate for the position of the Chief Minister of Bihar. In spite of his highbrow positions, Maitreyajee was a very simple and humble man and used to receive everyone with the same respect and love.

I used to often go to Maitreyajee's house whenever I wanted to talk about Osho or have a satsang. Maitreyajee was also a great connoisseur of tea like me and used to make tea himself whenever I visited him. I was surprised to see that we both drank the same brand of leaf tea, Happy Valley, and he used to brew it perfectly in a teapot just the way I liked it. Maitreyajee was a reputed parliamentarian and there were always some important guests visiting him at his house. But of all the people that I met at Maitryajee's house one person that I cannot forget was the great Hindi poet Ramdhari Singh Dinkar. He was a close friend of Maitreyajee and a great admirer of good tea. He used to come every evening to Maitreyajee's house, and I also visited him whenever I was free from college.

I was already a great fan of Dinkarjee's poetry and to experience its live recital through Dinkarjee himself was something else. With his tall personality, large expressive eyes and loud hand gestures he used to recite Rashmirathi, his epic poem on Karna from Mahabharat and transport us to the battleground of Kurukshetra where the great war of Mahbharat was fought. It was at Maitreyajee's house that I came close to Dinkarjee and became friends with him.

Osho came to Patna three times but I had not known him during the first time. The first time when Osho had come to Patna, Dinkarjee used to go this discourses and park his car at the back and listen to Osho from inside his car. He loved Osho very much but he had a very strange reason for not taking sannyas, he told me, "I would have also become a sannyasin of Rajneesh but in our Brahmin culture we don't touch the feet of those who are younger to us and since Rajneesh is younger to me and if I make him my guru I will have to touch his feet so I not take sannyas from him." In this way Dinkarjee's brahmin conditioning prevented him from becoming a disciple. Later his son Kedar Nath Singh came to Poona and took initiation from Osho and became his disciple.

Osho started initiating people into sannyas in 1970 during a meditation camp in Manali. He was speaking on Krishna and suddenly decided to initiate people into sannyas. Both Maitreya jee and I were not able to attend this camp. Bhagwan sent a letter and invited both of us to come to the meditation camp in Mount Abu in March and take sannyas. Kranti who was Osho's cousin and taking care of Osho then later told me that after making the decision to initiate people into sannyas Osho had first made a list of 50 names in his diary of those people who he wanted to make disciples and that my name and Swami Anand Maitreya's name was also listed on it.

Being initiated by an enlightened master also needs a great karmic virtue and because of my own karmic mistakes from the past, I had to suffer a great misfortune and despite making the decision to go to Mount Abu I missed my train by just a minute and could not go. Sometimes a delay of one minute has to be paid for by one's whole life. More than the situation, it was the fear of my own mind and my karmic bondages that pulled me down. All these things are very clear to me today. In his letter addressed to me Osho had said that he wanted to initiate me as his disciple and had also asked me to bring orange clothes. He had also said that he did only want to initiate me but he also wanted to take me into the deeper realms of spiritual heights. He also said in his letter that infinite possibilities are waiting for you. Maitreyajee had also received an invitation for the same camp and sannyas. But unfortunately, both of us missed it. If only I had done that 10 days retreat with him, I would not have had to go through countless unconscious mistakes and sufferings that came into my life after that and my spiritual journey would have completed a long time ago.

The next calling came for Bombay when Osho again invited us for sannyas. Osho was residing in the Woodland apartments in Bombay in those days and he had invited us. I missed it this time also while Mathura Babu decided to go but before leaving he told me, "I am not going to take sannyas. As a politician, my life is full of lies and hypocrisy and I don't feel that I deserve sannyas. I am only going because Bhagwan has called me." I had gone to the railway station to see him off.

After 7 days I received a letter from Mathura Babu. In the letter he had written, "Last night I met Bhagwan and he was asking about you after having read the letter you had sent to him through me." He further wrote, "Last night Mathura Babu died and Swami Anand Maitreya was born after Bhagwan initiated me into sannyas."

"I told Bhagwan that I was not qualified for sannyas and that my life was full of lies and conceit and as a politician I had to do many dramas." He had written in the letter. "When I told this to Bhagwan, he told me that since I was already doing so many small dramas why not do a bigger drama of sannyas and initiated me as Swami Anand Maitreya."

In his letter he told me that he would stay a few more days with Bhagwan in Bombay and come back to Patna. But that never happened. Maitreya jee never left Bhagwan and followed him wherever he went. He lived with Bhagwan in Bombay, Pune, Rajneeshpuram and again in Pune until he was in his body. He was a respected member of Parliament from the Congress party and had won the elections three times. He was also very close to the Nehru family so even after sannyas, many times he was invited back, and high positions were offered to him but he never looked back. The Maitreyajee that I had bid farewell at the railway station in Patna that morning only came back to his house in the form of ashes after he left his body in 1987 when his nephew brought back some of his holy remains and interred it into a samadhi at his house in Rajendra Nagar.

When Bhagwan had come to Nepal, Maitreyajee's nephew, niece and other members of the family had also come to Kathmandu. He did not have his own family as he had left his wife on the very first night of marriage after some quarrel between them. So, his friend's children who he used to call his nephew and niece were like his own and they all lived together in the same house. When they were in Kathmandu, he asked me to initiate them into sannyas but since Maitreya jee was more senior than me and I had seen him giving sannyas in Pune I requested him to do it. "Bhagwan has instructed you to give sannyas here in Nepal and it is your right so you give them sannyas. I will remain a witness." He politely declined and made me initiate his family members while he sat next to me.

I was not only close to Maitryajee but I was also close with his family members. I used to stay with them whenever I went to Patna and they used to also stay with me when they came to Kathmandu.

There are some beautiful and intimate moments that I have spent with Maitreyajee which will always remain fresh in my memory.

When Bhagwan was in the American jails, we used to have meetings at Rajyoga Meditation Center in Delhi for hours and discuss how to get Bhagwan back to India. Ma Yog Laxmi, Swami Om Prakash Saraswati, Swami Maitreya and I would sit for hours and discuss this. Those 12 days when Osho was in jail were the most challenging times for Osho disciples and I consider those days as the darkest days of my life. We were full of anger and always felt anxious and helpless. No one could eat or sleep properly during those 12 days.

We tried to reach out to the then Prime Minister of India, Rajiv Gandhi but due to the lack of proper contact and resources we could not reach him. Those who had some power and could help us were not interested. Then we decided to reach out to the Indian President Gyani Zail Singh through Vinod Khanna or Swami Vinod Bharati.

Vinod was also a Punjabi and a famous Indian actor so when we sent our request to meet the President it was instantly approved.

We had to give names of those going to the president so we discussed it amongst ourselves and decided on Swami Om Prakash Saraswati, Swami Vinod Bharati, Swami Anand Maitreya and I. The day of the appointment came but Vinod had to cancel at the last minute as he had to fly to Bombay to attend the funeral of Sanjeev Kumar. Sanjeev was one of the veteran actors who had helped Vinod in the earlier days, and he considered him as his guru in the acting profession. I tried very hard to convince Vinod to attend the meeting with us and go after that but to no avail. At that time I could not understand how one could go to the funeral of an actor when your own spiritual guru was in jail and it was crucial for him to be there as he was the only one popular and influential amongst us. I was very hurt by what Vinod did.

In Vinod's place we finally decided to take Swami Anand Atul, the son of Swami Om Prakash Bharati who was running the Rajyoga meditation center. The President was a jolly man and apparently Swami Maitreya's presence became the ice breaker as they were both parliamentarians from the same time and knew each other very well. The President also reminded Maitreyajee that their quarters were next to each other and that they were neighbors. The President had given us an hour time for the meeting but for half an hour Maitryajee and Gyani Zail Zingh kept talking about their old days and I started feeling anxious as slowly the clock was moving ahead. Maitreya jee in his simplicity went on with the conversation. I had to finally interrupt and remind them the real purpose of our meeting and requested the President to intervene in freeing Osho from the American jails.

Gyani Zail Singh said, "I listen to Osho's lectures and when I look at him, I see grace dripping from his face. I had his lecture tapes on Guru Nanak but someone took it from me and never returned it back."

I told him that I would send the cassettes to him and joked, "How can things be safe in India when even the President's items are stolen like that."

He laughed at the joke and asked if we had a center in Delhi. When we told him that there was a center in Safdarjung called Rajyoga, he instantly asked us why we hadn't invited him until now.

Nobody was prepared for this so everyone remained quiet, so I replied spontaneously, "Our center is very small to invite you, Your Excellency, we have purchased land in Delhi and are soon building a bigger commune. We want to invite you there to inaugurate the Commune."

Swami Om Prakash Saraswati had purchased land on the outskirts of Delhi and was planning to open a commune. However, I was later rebuked for acting in the moment, "Who gave you the authority to speak about the commune?" Someone told me after we came out.

The President was a man of instant action who made his secretary call the Indian Consular Deb Mukherjee in San Francisco as it was close to Portland where Osho had been arrested. He asked the Consular to personally go on his behalf and call on Bhagwan and ask him what help the Indian government could provide him. I had told the president that Osho was being mistreated in the American jails and was being treated very cruelly like a serious criminal for a minor immigration violation. So the President also told Deb Mukherjee to tell the American authorities that Osho was a celebrated writer and had millions of admirers in India including the President himself and he should be treated respectfully. This was the main reason why Bhagwan was released the same day after the visit of Deb Mukherjee. When the American government saw that the Indian President was concerned and took personal interest in Osho they became cautious that this issue might affect the Indo-American relations and had to expedite Osho's release.

At that time in Rajyoga I got to witness the simplicity and innocence of Maitreyajee and how much he had evolved around Bhagwan. He had a very sweet presence and humility in him. Like some of the other senior sannyasins he was provided food and accommodation at Rajyoga during that time in Delhi but he had no money or other possessions. He had a habit of smoking and sometimes he did not even have the money for his cigarettes and he would innocently ask money from sannyasins to buy cigarette. This I saw in Pune as well. People in Delhi and other sannyasins would criticize him and say, "He lived with Bhagwan for so long and still needs cigarettes and asks for money." I found it to be very narrow-minded of people to see it that way. I thought it was Maitreya jee's greatness that a man of such stature was living without any money and had no complex in him and could ask for money with a childlike ease. He was a very simple man and had no trace of hypocrisy in him.

Later when Bhagwan came to Nepal, Maitreya jee also came along with him. By then a coterie of a few dubious individuals had already surrounded Bhagwan and in Kathmandu it became even more clear to me about their heinous intentions regarding Bhagwan's life. I openly voiced my opinion to Bhagwan and also in public. When I told this to Maitreya jee he totally dismissed my suspicions and said that Bhagwan had chosen them to be around him and he could not be wrong. It took many years before Maitreya jee realized the truth behind what I was saying.

After Bhagwan came back to Bombay after his world tour Maitreya jee was already back in Pune and was staying in the ashram. Bhagwan was staying at Sumila, a private bungalow in Juhu that belonged to a sannyasin Swami Suraj Prakash who was facing many oppositions from his family members as they had to give up their personal space and move to the lower floor leaving the whole upper floor for Bhagwan. His son, daughter-in-law and his wife were all against it as it had been months since Bhagwan was staying in their Bungalow and Suraj Prakash jee was withstanding them all alone and keeping Bhagwan in Sumila. Many sannyasins requested Bhagwan to return to Pune as everything was according to his needs and comfort in the ashram but Bhagwan was also adamant that he would not go back. Bhagwan did not want to go back to Pune as it was his habit of not returning to the place that he had left once.

Bhagwan asked the sannyasins to look for a property in or around Bombay itself where he could settle. Property in Bombay was very expensive so he asked them to at least buy a house where he could stay in Bombay and that the rest would slowly grow around him after he was settled.

A meeting was held in which Neelam who was then Bhagwan's Indian secretary called all the prominent sannyasins and conveyed Bhagwan's wish. She said that at least 2 crores was needed to buy a house worthy of Bhagwan in Bombay and that we should all go to our respective cities and collect whatever donations we could collect. The coterie that had tagged along with Bhagwan since USA had already taken control of the money and did not want to give the money and always showed some problem or the other saying that transferring the money was not possible even though a huge amount had been collected after the sale of all the Rolls Royces, buses and planes and other sellable items of Rajneeshpuram. I had experienced the same problem from them when Bhagwan asked me to buy the Fishtail Lodge in Pokhara in Nepal or the other properties that were then available in Nepal.

Neelam asked me to go to Nepal and collect the money. I told her that Nepal was a poor country and I also did not have the money as I had finished my savings in making the second storey of my house as Bhagwan had told me that he would love to stay in my home instead of the hotel and that he might come back to Nepal which never happened. I told Neelam that I would rather go to Bihar as I grew up and did my studies there and was more familiar with the place. Swami Yog Chinmaya was then sent to Nepal instead of me. I then requested Neelam to also send Maitreyajee with me as people knew him in Bihar and it would be easier to collect the money jointly. When the proposal was taken to Maitreyajee, he was reluctant and said that he was old now and could not travel and as he was also the editor of the Rajneesh Times and he needed to publish the magazine in time. Finally, he agreed to go and the ashram provided us plane tickets adhering to Maitreyajee's health and old age.

I spent some very beautiful moments with Maitreyajee on this trip which I will always cherish in my memory. While we were waiting for the plane at the Bombay airport he shared with me some very interesting incidents from his life which amazed me.

He told me, "When I was in Rajneeshpuram I used to take long walks with my cane after my breakfast in the morning. One day as I was walking alone, I met an Indian man wearing a white kurta and dhoti. I had never seen the man before and was surprised to see him in that attire as everybody was a short term or long term resident in Rajneeshpuram and in those days it was compulsory to wear the shades of the sun. There were no Indian visitors or guests in Rajneeshpuram that wore dhoti and kurta.

When we came across each other he greeted me and I also greeted him back. As I was still surprised to see him there I asked him where he lived and he told me that he lived in Rajneeshpuram itself. I had never seen him before. He joined me for my walk and we shared a good conversation in Hindi. But just when I was about to reach my apartment where there were other people, he suddenly vanished into thin air."

I was immensely surprised at this incident and later came to know that Swami Dev Peter who was the caretaker of Bhagwan's

Rolls Royces and one Ma who was one of Bhagwan's household staffs had also met a similar Indian man in white who used to converse with them in English and later would disappear in the company of other people. When all these three incidents were taken to Bhagwan, Bhagwan told us not to be scared and said that we were not the only ones who were living in Rajneeshpuram. Many evolved souls from all over the world had come there as it was easier for them to meditate and grow spiritually in Bhagwan's presence. He told us that we were lucky just to even see them and get their darshan and that if we met them again we should talk with them and not be scared." Maitreya jee told me that he met that man a few times again during his walks.

Bihar was not a very rich state and collecting money in Bihar was not easy. We stayed at Maitreyajee's house in Patna and held different meetings with sannyasins there. We were able to collect around 2 lakhs in Patna after which Maitreyajee had to return back to Pune to meet the deadline of the Rajneesh Times. He said to me, "Arun now I have to go back to Pune because if I am late with the Rajneesh Times issue, the management will kick me out."

After Maitreyajee left I along with my other friend Swami Samarth traveled to other districts of Bihar. We went to Jamshedpur, Ranchi, Jharkhand among other places and were able to collect about 5 lakh rupees. In those days it was a great amount. A large amount of money was collected from Gujarat through Swami Satya Vedant and Punjab through Swami Anand Swabhav and also through Bombay. However a house was never purchased in Bombay and we don't know what happened to the 77 lakhs rupees collected from all over India which we had given to the same coterie of people and the management that surrounded Bhagwan at that time.

Maitreyajee told me about another similar encounter that he had in Pune. After Bhagwan's discourses, as per his usual habit Maitreyajee used to go for walks with his cane. One time he met a man by the burning ghats who asked him for a cigarette. After smoking with him, the man then asked Maitreyajee for some money. When Maitreyajee told him that he was a sannyasin at Bhagwan's ashram and did not have any money, the man then revealed his identity. "I am already dead and was burnt here in the burning ghats. I have taken this form to contact you." He told Maitreyajee and showed a house across the river and said that his family lived there and that he was in great pain seeing their suffering as they did not even have money for food.

Maitreyajee told him that he would arrange some money and bring it in a few days and give it to him when he came for his regular walk. The ghost told him not to give it to him but to take it to the house and give it to his family members and gave the address of the house. Maitreyajee collected some money from friends and later took it to the house. Maitreyajee told me how the soul is affected by the family members and is haunted with attachment even after leaving the body. He told me that he had never shared these incidents with anybody as no one would believe him. He said that even he did not believe in these things until he became a witness of it in his own life.

There is another incident from Maitreyajee's life that left a great impression upon me. Maitreyajee had given all his property in Bihar to his nephew and had contributed all his savings to Bhagwan's work and was living the life of a sadhu with no possessions. One time when he was cleaning his drawers he found an old passbook which showed that he had 10,000 Rs saved in a post office in Begusarai where he had his ancestral house. In those days people used to keep their money at the post office as banks were not very popular. The post office used to give 4% interest and I also had an account when I was doing my engineering in Bihar.

Maitreyajee's innocence, non-possessiveness and his surrender towards Bhagwan was unparalleled. It was a few years before he left his body that he asked for an appointment to meet Bhagwan in

Bombay. In that meeting he went to Bhagwan with the cheque of 10,000 Rs and said, "Bhagwan I have given all my property to my nephew and whatever I had I put it in your work. Now I have found this 10,000 Rs in my name and I feel very burdened with it. Please accept this money and unburden me. I came empty handed and want to go empty handed."

Bhagwan was very happy to hear this from Maitreyajee and accepted his cheque and gave it to Neelam. During bidding farewell to Maitreya Jee after his death, Bhagwan spoke about this incident and said, "Just before I came back to Poona, Maitreya told me in Bombay, "I have got ten thousand rupees in a post office deposit in Begusarai, Bihar; that's all I have, but now I will not need it." Certainly, he was becoming aware that his time of departure was coming closer. And he transferred the money to Neelam for the ashram. He died without anything, any possessions." This incident was symbolic of how Maitreyajee had surrendered his all to his master and is a very poignant moment that carries a subtle message and if looked upon keenly can give us great insights.

As fate would have it, my last meeting with Maitreya jee was on the same night he left his body. It was 1987 and Bhagwan had already moved back to Pune. Bhagwan had given me the work to assist Narendra Swami in the publication department and Yogini and I were staying at the house of Sohan Ma and Bafnajee in Pune. That night we met Maitreya Swami at the Premji restaurant near the ashram, Bafnajee had taken us there for a Gujarati dinner while Swami Satish had brought Maitreyajee from the Pune ashram. We had our dinner while Satish and Maitreyajee had some juice and snacks.

Maitreyajee and I were the only two in the ashram who used to read the newspaper and Bhagwan used to taunt us saying, "I have two politicians in my ashram." Maitreya jee knew about my love for books and he said, "I know you love reading and I have just finished reading a book by Pupul Jayakar on Krishnamurti." I instantly asked to borrow the book and he said, "I knew you would ask for it so you come to my room tomorrow after Bhagwan's lecture and take it from me." Then he also said, "But in the book, Pupul has talked and praised Indira Gandhi more than Krishnamurti because she was Indira's secretary."

We chatted and joked for hours and stayed in the restaurant till midnight. Maitreyajee was exceptionally radiant that day and we kept pulling his leg asking him why he was glowing so much and what was the secret to his youth. "You have been eating too much of sweets tonight." He jokingly answered.

In his last days Maitreyajee was very loving and kind to me.

When we were in Bihar in 1986 to collect the money for Bhagwan's house, Maitreyajee and I had a small argument as he told in the meeting what I had said in Kathmandu to Bhagwan that some of the western people around him were going to kill him. Maitreyajee openly said that he did not believe in it and that Bhagwan himself had chosen those westerners. I had told Maitreyajee that I had nothing against anybody and was only saying this out of my devotion and love for my master. This had created a difference between the two of us.

I still remember when I had first met him during that visit in 1987 at the gates in Pune ashram he rushed to me and hugged me with great love. I used to always greet him with a Pranam and he used to respond back but this time I was surprised to see him receive me with so much affection. He said in hindi, "Aapto bade chupe rustam nikle Swamijee, apne bare mai kuch bataya hi nahi.Aapko kaun pehchanega" (You never told about yourself and have been hiding it all. Who can recognize you here?) He kept saying this everytime we met and on that last night also he called me Chupa Rustam, "This Swami is not an ordinary man, he is not what he shows, he has been hiding it all from us." I will never know what he knew about me but I came to know that now he had also sensed the danger around Bhagwan and had come to know about the conspiracy going on around him which I had told him in Kathmandu.

After midnight we dropped Maitreyajee at the ashram gates in our car and went back to Bafnajee's house.

Next morning, we woke up late so missed Dynamic Meditation and went straight to Bhagwan's lecture. I did not see Mitreyajee in the lecture that morning and that day strangely Bhagwan who used to speak for 90 mins only spoke for 45 minutes and left. I noticed that he was not in a good mood. We had our breakfast and then went to the Laotzu house around 11 to get the book that Maitreyajee had promised me the earlier night. He used to live in a very small room in Bhagwan's house so we always needed a special permission to go inside. The gatekeeper would first call Maitreyajee and then if he got the permission then we could go inside.

That morning the Punjabi Swami Gurudayal Singh who was famous for his uproarious laughter was guarding the gates of Laotzu house. When I approached him, I told him that Maitreyajee had called me and I was there to get a book from him. Gurudayal Singh looked at me and exclaimed, "You don't know? Maitreyajee has already left his body."

I was shocked at what I heard. We were with Maitreyajee till midnight, and he was absolutely healthy and glowing exceptionally that night. It was impossible for us to believe that he had already left his body in the night.

The new coterie around Bhagwan had somehow made everyone who had been residing in Bhagwan's house to leave the Lao Tzu house. All the Indian sannyasins, his caretakers like Vivek, Shunyo and others who had been around him all their lives were made to leave the Lao Tzu house with some excuse or the other. Maitreyajee was one of the remaining people in the Lao Tzu house from the old group and he told us that the management had been constantly pestering him to leave the Lao Tzu house saying that his room was too small and that they would provide him a better room in Krishna House with attached bathroom. Everytime Maitreyajee had denied their offer and had said that there was a lot of energy in Bhagwan's house and he was happy living next to him.

Maitreya jee had a habit of eating Isabgol (Indian laxative made of husk) and drinking warm milk before bed which used to be left in a thermos outside his room. That night also he must have drank the milk and went to bed after we dropped him off. We will never know if it was a normal death or if there was any foul play in Maitreyajee's death as no post mortem was carried out.

His body was later brought to the Buddha hall where we celebrated him. Bhagwan also came and blessed him before he was taken to the burning ghats and given a celebrative farewell. Bhagwan spoke of him and said that he had died an enlightened man and again reminded everyone that he had made him the president of the Sambuddhas or the enlightened ones in Rajneeshpuram. He spoke about his ordinariness and simplicity and how he had not accepted when Bhagwan had declared him enlightened.

Although later Bhagwan had called it a joke, this time Bhagwan again reconfirmed it. He said "Sometime in 1984 Maitreya became enlightened, but he had chosen to remain silent, so he remained silent. He did not even tell me what had happened to him. But the day it happened I called a small meeting of a few sannyasins in Rancho Rajneesh in America. I declared that there were going to be three special committees: one of mahasattvas, the great beings who were destined to become enlightened in this very life; the second of sambuddhas, who have already become enlightened; and the third of bodhisattvas, who will also become enlightened ... but perhaps they will take a little longer than the other two categories, but certainly before their death...."

Bidding him farewell Bhagwan said, "This evening is special, because one of us has moved from the world of mortals to the world of immortals. He will not be born again. He has attained to the freedom and the liberation we have been talking about."

Bhagwan asked for a samadhi to be built for him in the gardens next to the Lao Tzu House. Afterwards Maitreyajee's ashes were brought to the ashram and interred into a marble samadhi while a portion of it was taken by his nephew and interred into a samadhi at his house in Rajendra Nagar in Patna.

Maitreyajee was an ideal disciple and his devotion and trust in the master remained unwavering throughout his life. Osho used to say that Maitreyajee never missed an opportunity to meditate and by and by became gradually absent and eventually dissolved totally into the master. His was a life of trust, grace and simplicity. Today during every celebration, meditation and satsangs in which we talk about Osho with deep love, Osho comes alive and along with him a subtle presence can be felt of his leela sahacharis who accompany him wherever he goes and among them is forever present our beloved Swami Anand Maitreya.

Clairvoyant Woman From Hyderabad

Bhagwan was a pragmatic master who always made sure that what he was teaching was practical and based on factual ground. He always wanted to bring us to the present moment using the science of meditation techniques that he had designed for us. Even while explaining the most otherworldly phenomenon he would try his best to give a logical explanation that could be understood by today's modern minds. It is not that Bhagwan totally denied the mystical dimensions of spirituality, in fact there have been very few masters in history like

Bhagwan who have attained and explored all dimensions of the spiritual world as he has. Just by sitting in his presence one could feel that the Bhagwan we saw, heard and understood was just a small fragment of his huge persona, the major part of it remained hidden in the wombs of the mystical.

However, whenever Bhagwan was questioned about the otherworldly, the mystical, he would immediately hammer us and ask us to come back to reality, to the present moment. It was only on rare occasions that he would discuss or lecture about such subjects. Most of the time he called it our esoteric bullshit. Whenever I have asked him about such subjects or told him about my experiences he asked me to keep it to myself and not share it with others. Firstly, because most of the time people would not believe in it and secondly, even if someone believed it because it was not their own experience it would only create an unnecessary fantasy and expectation in them.

So, whatever such experiences I share in my books or my lectures, I only share it with the permission of my master. Most of it remains a secret and I cannot talk about it openly. Bhagwan asked me to keep a diary of such incidents so I have maintained this since 1974 and these diaries are my greatest treasure and guide me even today.

During 1987 a lady sannyasin from Hyderabad became a witness to similar extraordinary phenomena which also helped me understand the nature and spectrum of Bhagwan's work.

One thing I noticed about Bhagwan was that although he was very open and lenient about other duties and works at the ashram, there were a few things whose authority he only kept within himself. One such thing was choosing people who could give sannyas on his behalf. After April 10, 1981 Bhagwan stopped giving shaktipaths and sannyas and assigned this duty to his close disciples. Giving sannyas was a very special and sacred part of Bhagwan's work and I noticed that Bhagwan was very particular about it. For foreigners he had assigned Swami Teertha and for Indian's he had first assigned Ma Yog Laxmi who denied it saying that people would start worshiping her as the guru and she was not interested in it. These sannyasins were sincere and seasoned meditators and had lived very close to Osho.

In Pune II Ma Neelam was Osho's Indian secretary while Hasya was his western secretary. Ma Neelam had an Indian secretary called Swami Manu who had been recently dismissed because of some shortcomings during his work. Being Neelam's secretary also came with a lot of power and responsibility, it was almost like being the third authority in the ashram after Bhagwan and his secretary. When Manu was dismissed, Neelam asked Bhagwan who she should choose as her next secretary. Bhagwan asked her to give that responsibility to me. I was greatly surprised when Neelam told me that I was supposed to help her as her secretary. I think Neelam was also equally surprised by Bhagwan's decision.

I had to assist Neelam in handling the Indian faction of Bhagwan's work. This meant answering letters, meeting people, listening to people's queries and complaints, assigning work and facilities to sannyasins and conveying them to Neelam who would later convey it to Bhagwan. Neelam was always busy and was not really interested in meeting sannyasins and listening to them every day. She had instructed me how I was to answer letters and only to bring them to her if it was really important or if they needed to be reported to Bhagwan.

During this time a Ma from Hyderabad came to meet me at my office in Krishna house the same day I was appointed. She came from a very humble background and her husband was a tempo driver. She had two daughters and there was nothing very significant about her, she was like any other normal Indian sannyasin. But what she told me next completely changed my opinion about her. She reported to me that Bhagwan used to appear to her in Hyderabad and he used to have conversations with her, answer her questions and even instruct her. Many times she had tried to report these incidents to Neelam or to the western authorities close to Bhagwan but had always been ridiculed and dismissed as esoteric bullshit. Apparently after constant dismissal and being made fun of she had decided to keep it to her shelf. When she told me the reason why she had come to Pune this time it totally blew my mind.

She told me that Bhagwan had appeared to her in Hyderabad last evening and had said to her, "Come to Pune. Now I have kept a man in the ashram that will listen to you and will understand you as well."

Being with Bhagwan, I have had my own share of experiences that could not be comprehended by the mind. So I could understand and relate to her. Many a times in my life I had contacted Bhagwan and he had guided me beyond the laws of the physical realm and I totally trusted this poor lady and knew that these phenomena were possible with our master. I told her that as I was busy with my other work at that moment I would love to meet her during lunch time and talk to her in detail about her experiences. We ate our lunch together and I listened intently to all her experiences with Bhagwan.

When I later reported about her to Neelam she just dismissed everything and said that the woman was a liar and I should not listen to her. She always talks esoteric bullshit. It is very difficult for those who have not had such experiences to understand it when others tell it. This was why Bhagwan always asked us to avoid esoteric gossips.

During those days Swami Narendra Bodhisattva was initiating the Indian disciples . Maitreya Swami had also been given this authority but since he had already left his body it was only Narendra Swami who was facilitating the sannyas in those days. Bhagwan had sent him outside Pune for a few months regarding some work so there was no one to initiate the Indians. Neelam went to Bhagwan to ask him who was supposed to give sannyas in the absence of Narendra. Bhagwan told Neelam, "Ask Arun to initiate the Indians."

Now this time, Ma Neelam was totally shocked. I was a nobody in Pune and the new management around Bhagwan, comprising of Jayesh and his team did not even like me. Nobody expected that Bhagwan would ask me to facilitate the sannyas inside the Pune ashram. I used to facilitate sannyas back home as a center leader but being chosen in Pune where there were many senior sannyasins and those who had more special positions than me was a completely different thing. I was also shocked when Neelam told me about it.

For me the sannyas initiation ceremony is a very pure and special event and I have always held great respect for it. It is the time when a person opens and surrenders himself to Bhagwan who accepts them as his disciple. Even though sannyas is facilitated by a medium, the medium does nothing in it other than being totally absent for the master to function through him. So it is an affair between the master and the disciple and the medium is nothing more than a postman or a bridge. I have always had my own style of facilitating the sannyas ceremony, even then I used to play sanskrit sutras followed by Bhagwans kirtan and short discourses and other music. During sannyas celebration there is always a strong transcendental energy and Bhagwan's presence can be felt very strongly. In those days when I facilitated the sannyas, there used to be few Indians who came to be initiated but many westerns would also come and join the celebrations and the number of people kept on increasing in every ceremony.

The Ma from Hyderabad was a clairvoyant seer and she could see much more than what met the eyes. These things usually happen to simple and innocent people who don't have a cunning mind. She used to be present during our sannyas celebrations in Pune and later one day when she told me what she used to see, it further strengthened my understanding of Bhagwan's work. She told me that during every sannyas celebration she used to see Bhagwan standing behind and he would put his hands on the head of the medium who was facilitating it throughout the initiation. She told me that it didn't matter who was the medium but Bhagwan was present in every sannyas celebration. Then she told me what she used to see in the ceremonies that I facilitated.

She told me, "In other sannyas celebrations I have seen Bhagwan come and put his hands on the medium's head but during your sannyas Bhagwan comes and then he totally enters into your body."

At that time I was stunned to hear what she said but slowly in all these years it has become clear to me that what she was saying was absolutely true. If a disciple is ready and surrendered, a master can use his body for his work. The more absent a disciple's ego is, the stronger is the presence of the master. This ancient method is called Parkaya Pravesh in Sanskrit. In all these years many people have seen Bhagwan during sannyas and have reported to me and Bhagwan has also confirmed it when I asked him about it.

Ramakrishna, the Advent of Kali and the Panchavati Spirit

Born in the village of Kamarkupur in India's Bengal, Ramakrishna Paramhansa was an enlightened master who lived in the last century and whose life was full of many mystical events. Appointed by Rani Rashmoni as the priest to the Kali Temple, Ramakrishna Paramhansa was a rebellious man who did not follow any traditional methods or norms and worshiped the deity as his heart guided.

The appointment of Ramakrishna as the priest of the Kali temple also happened through unconventional ways.

A religious woman named Rani Rashmoni, who was a low-caste woman married into an aristocratic family, was preparing for a pilgrimage to Banaras with a hundred boats full of goods to donate there. The night before she left, she saw Goddess Kali in a dream. "Instead of going to Banaras and making donations there, build a temple for me on the bank of the Ganga River. There I shall receive your offering daily," said Kali. So she built a beautiful Kali temple at Dakshineswar, Kolkata, which is known today as Dakshineswar Kali Temple.

Traditionally, a priest of any Hindu temple needs to be a Brahmin, but since the temple was built and owned by a low-caste woman, no Brahmin was ready to be the priest at Dakshineswar. In the end, out of poverty, Ramakrishna's older brother, Ramkumar, became the priest of the temple. After the initial rituals of consecrating the Kali statue, he and Ramakrishna lived at Dakshineswar, and after some time, Ramakrishna replaced his brother as the priest of the temple.

Very few people know about this but the same Rani Rashmoni was later born as Osho's disciple Ma Yog Laxmi in this life. She was one of Osho's most devoted disciples and served him as his secretary and spearheaded his ashram and his work during Pune I before Osho left for America. Later Laxmi became enlightened and died as a fully liberated soul.

Ramakrishna was a man of a pure heart and innocence and his devotion for Kali was unwavering. His longing to realize the divine was so strong that it's vibrations can still be felt in the Dakshineshwar temple in Kolkata today. As the divine yearning burnt his heart he would cry for hours and with every passing day as the sun would start setting he would rub his head until it bled on the stone stairs of the temple and wail like a child that another day had passed without god realization. Even today there are curves on the stone steps where Ramkrishna had rubbed his head in a frenzy of vairagya and devotion.

THE ADVENT OF KALI

The advent of Kali and how she came alive for Ramakrishna is a story of great miracle and how the impossible was made possible through a devotee's true longing.

While worshiping Kali one day, Ramkrishna had a strong feeling that if Kali is real then she should show herself to him. She had already appeared before a few Bengali devotees and Ramkrishna had heard about it. He was overtaken by this feeling and started to cry. His prayers intensified. At one point, the intensity was so great that he took a sword which was hanging on the wall of the temple, and said to the statue of Kali, "If you don't show yourself today then I will slash my own throat." And when he actually was about to do it, Kali appeared and held his hands and stopped him from doing so. This is how he had his first darshan with Kali. That mysterious event changed Ramakrishna's life, as the statue of Kali that was just stone for everyone else, came alive for Ramakrishna. It was no more a statue, but the goddess herself. After that day, Kali and Ramakrishna had a relationship like that of a mother and a son. Whenever in trouble, Ramakrishna would go into the temple and ask for direction from Kali, just like a son would from his mother.

The temple still exists, and millions go there and pay homage to the goddess. I also went to the temple many times and hoped that the statue would come alive for me. When we see, we only see a beautiful statue, but for Ramakrishna, she was Durga Bhawani fully manifested. Ramakrishna didn't have to go anywhere to look for a master; masters would arrive looking for him. Later Kali sent Bhairavi and Totapuri to guide Ramakrishna.

THE PANCHAVATI SPIRIT

Another incident that happened in Ramakrishna's life is very interesting as it throws light over the existence of the otherworldly.

Just next to the Kali Temple in Dakshineswar was a secluded grove of trees which provided a beautiful space for meditation. As the grove was made of five trees it was called the Panchavati. Ramkrishna used to spend hours meditating and doing sadhana in that grove and it was very dear to Ramakrishna. It was at this place that he had innumerable spiritual experiences during his sadhana.

In those times the land of the grove did not belong to the temple. There was a British rule in India so it belonged to the British government. As it was right on the bank of the Ganges, the British chose the spot as a perfect site for gunpowder factory and decided to build it there. When Ramakrishna came to know of this, he was in great pain and started crying unstoppably under one of the trees in Panchavati. It was the same place where he had learnt Vedanta from Totapuri Baba and Tantra from Bahiravi, they had both stayed in Panchavati and that place was very dear to Ramakrishna.

Suddenly a spirit in a human form descended from one of the trees and asked Ramakrishna why he was crying so much. Ramkrishna had seen the spirit before also and had told others about it. The spirit used to talk and guide Ramakrishna. Few other people had also seen it before. Ramakrishna shared the reason of his sadness and said, "This was my only place for sadhana where I could meditate in solitude and now they are going to build a factory here."

To this the spirit replied, "Don't worry, we will not let this happen. You stay assured no one will build anything here."

Ramakrishna was like a child and instantly stopped crying and started dancing in joy. When others saw him and asked why he was dancing, he said, "The spirit in Panchavati has assured me that they will not let the factory be built there. Now my place of sadhana will not be destroyed."

Later Rani Rasmani filed a case against the construction of the factory which went on for a few years and later the High Court decided in favor of the Rani. More than hundred years have passed today and Panchavati is still there in Dakshineswar and is vibrant with the energy of Ramakrishna and many other enlightened beings that lived in that grove.

RAMLALA COMES TO LIFE..

Another incident that took place in Ramkrishna's life is worth mentioning here and is one of the most affecting episodes of Sri Ramakrsihna's life. It was probably in the year 1864 that the wandering monk Jatadhari came to Dakshineswar. Ramlala or 'Child Rama' was his favorite deity and he used to worship and carry the diety's statue everywhere. After staying in Dakshineswar for some time, when Jatadhari was leaving, the statue of Ramlala came to life and refused to go along with him. It kept pestering Jatadhari until he finally decided to leave the deity to Ramakrishna. The deity was alive for Ramakrishna and he used to converse with it and treat it like a child. Speaking of this, Ramakrishna said, "I saw Ramala vividly as I see you all -now dancing gracefully before me, now springing on my back, or insisting on being taken up in my arms. One day I was going to bathe. Ramlala insisted on accompanying me. I took him with me. But he would not come out of the water, nor did he heed any remonstrances. Then I got angry, and pressing him under the water said, "Now play in it as much as you like." Ah, I saw him struggling for breath. Then repenting of my act I took him up in my arms.'

'Another incident pained me greatly, and I wept bitterly for it. Ramlala insisted on having something which I could not supply. To divert him, I gave him some parched rice not well husked. As he was chewing them, I found his tender tongue was scratched. The sight was too much for me. I took him on my lap and cried out: "Mother Kaushalya used to feed you with cream or butter with the greatest care and I was so thoughtless as to give you this coarse stuff!"

Today the same statue is still in Dakshineswar temple but it doesn't talk or move like it did for Ramakrishna. It was Ramakrishna's innocence and purity that channeled his devotional human sentiment and brought the statue of Ramalala to life.

Osho's Cosmic Form

Bhagwan's parents named him Rajneesh Chandra Mohan Jain as a child. Later he shortened his name and started using only the name, Rajneesh. While he was a professor in Jabalpur, he started giving discourses and conducting camps. In India, both a professor or professor as well as a knowledgeable spiritual master is referred to as Archarya. So, when he started giving discourses and publishing articles and books, people started referring to him as Acharya Rajneesh. This was the name he was known by till he started giving Sannyas in September 1970.

When I met him in 1969, we used to call him Acharya Ji or Acharya Shree. Before that, many people, including me and others who had been connected with Bhagwan from earlier, had been requesting him to initiate us as disciples, but he would never accept. When I requested him, he asked me to simply follow his teachings that suited me and to continue my sadhana. But he did not wish to accept this responsibility of being Master and that he and I should both remain free and independent. He would help in his capacity, but he did not have the desire to initiate others, take their entire responsibility and become their Guru.

But in 1970, in Manali, while he was giving the discourse series "Krishna Meri Drishti Mein," maybe through some play of the divine, something came over Bhagwan, and he changed his mind. It feels similar to the story of Buddha, where the Gods came down from their realm to request Buddha to initiate people and form a sangha to share what he had realized for the benefit of all beings. Similarly, I feel that many Buddhas of the past must have requested Bhagwan to do the same and take on the responsibility of being a Master. Later, Bhagwan disclosed that Gurdjieff, Ramkrishna, and Buddha had handed over their unenlightened past life disciples to be guided through me.

In the early days, people used to say that Acharya Rajneesh was Krishnamurti of the Hindi language because Krishnamurti also used to refuse to initiate anyone. But during the Manali camp, all that changed as Osho initiated 14 people, thus beginning the Neo-Sannyas movement.

He immediately stopped traveling after that, confining himself to a flat in Woodland apartments in Bombay. Before that, he used to travel extensively wherever requested. He referred to that period as his 'Rajas' or extensive action period. Even if one person requested him to come anywhere, he would travel to give a discourse or conduct a camp.

During this Rajas period, he gave me the dates 19th to 21st

March 1970 for Kathmandu. I was unable to arrange the money to make that happen and missed out on this benediction. I feel like that was the biggest loss for me, my family, and the whole of Nepal. I still deeply regret being unable to make that happen. But he had allocated me this time for a Nepal camp. The plans for his travel and camps used to be made a long time in advance. Once he started giving Sannyas, he canceled all his discourses and said he would stop traveling. He would stay in one place henceforth because Bhagwan said now he has to work on many people he has initiated and given deeksha. He said that he is responsible for their spiritual growth, and when they need him, he has to be present for them in many ways. Therefore, traveling has to be stopped completely. He was only interested in those who were committed and ready to transform their lives completely.

From September 1970, Osho confined himself for this purpose in Woodland apartments. He would conduct only two 10-day camps in Mount Abu in a year. One sometime between Jan to March and one in October/November, depending on weather and logistics. He had asked me to come for the very first camp because deeksha had started by that time. Due to misfortune, I missed the train and was unable to attend that camp. I have talked about this incident in my book, "In Wonder With Osho."

When a lot of people started gathering around Acharyaji, he devised a way to dispel the crowds. He asked us, disciples, to suggest a new name for him. He wanted to filter out the people who were unnecessarily hanging around him. These were people who were non-meditators, wouldn't attend camps, and wanted to only engage in conversations and intellectual gossip. They only wanted to be associated with Osho. Famous Indian writers, poets, artists, businessmen, intellectuals, bureaucrats, and high-ranking officers would line up at his apartment in Woodlands to meet him. This left him with no time. So he decided to come up with this device for a name change. People came up with many suggestions. Someone suggested "Jagatguru Rajneesh," another was "Sadguru Rajneesh," and another was "108 Brahmarishi," and numerous others. I feel he already had something in his mind. Then Swami Yog Chinmaya suggested that just as Raman Maharishi was called Bhagwan Raman and Ramakrishna was called Bhagwan Ramakrishna by their disciples; we would like to call you by the name Bhagwan Rajneesh. Acharyaji chose the name, Bhagwan Rajneesh.

Many people were offended by this name change to Bhagwan and started criticizing him. Even his long-time host in Patna, Ramchandra Babu, was upset by this. People asked how he could call himself Bhawan or God while he was a human. A lot of people, including half of Bollywood, started leaving Bhagwan at this point. Much later, Bhagwan explained how he used this name change as a device to remove these insincere people who were taking up space and time that would be better spent on sincere seekers who could surrender their ego and accept him as their Guru.

In our culture, a master has always been considered equivalent to God as they recited in the famous shloka,

"Guru Brahma, Guru Vishnu, Guru Devo Maheshwara;
Guru Sakshat Param Brahma, Tasmai Shri Guravay Namah"

Meaning we bow to the one that shows the path of light. Thus, as a realized soul, Guru is the embodiment of Param Brahma, the ultimate Godhead.

Osho said that he could only transform those who were ready to walk with him by accepting him as their Guru, and the long line of egotists that had gathered should fall away. He also said that he would drop this name, too, when the utility of this device was over. In 1989, the year before he left his body, he dropped the name Bhawan and took the name Osho. For about 20 years, he used the name Bhagwan to keep away egotists who were put off by his name. Only those who could see him deeply as their Master would come to him. So many of my friends in Nepal also who used to read his books and were admirers left Osho saying that "Acharyaji has become very egoistic and started calling himself Bhagwan, so I won't read him." In this way, a space for sincere seekers was created around Osho.

During this time, he was conducting camps in Mount Abu and was speaking on the Upanishads and the Gita. In January 1973, he was speaking on the 11th chapter of the Gita during his discourse series "Gita Darshan." This chapter is referred to as the "Vishwaroop Darshan Yoga," in which Lord Krishna shows his Vishwaroop or Cosmic form. Here Osho described how Arjuna had requested Lord Krishna to show his Vishwaroop. Arjuna knew that he could not see this form through normal eyes. Thus, he requested Lord Krishna to allow him the divine vision to be able to see his true form. Osho says that an enlightened being has the gift of this Divine Vision to see the universe in this dimension. Arjuna wasn't enlightened, but he was a complete devotee of Lord Krishna. So, Krishna said that because Arjuna was so dear to him and was so devoted to him, he would allow him the divine vision to see his Vishwaroop. When Arjuna saw Krishna's cosmic form, he got frightened. He saw how all Kauravs and many Pandav warriors had died, and they had been absorbed in Krishna's Mahakal form. This form of Krishna included all life as well as death and destruction.

Seeing Arjuna so scared, Krishna told Arjuna that the enemies he had to kill in the war were already dead at another place in existence. At some point, these people will have to die. Time will take their lives. If Arjuna doesn't do his allotted task, existence will find someone else who will. Therefore, he should simply become a medium of existence to do its work. He showed Arjuna how all these people were already dead in the mouth of his Mahakal form. I would request the dear reader to read the 11th chapter of the Gita for a better description of Krishna's enormous Vishwaroop. It's an incredible chapter. It is a must-read for devotees, especially with Bhagwan's wonderful commentary.

During this time, many who were filled with doubts about Bhagwan would also come to his discourses. Since Sannyas had started only three years before, the total number of sannyasis was small, probably between two to four thousand. And at the camps, there were a few hundred attendees, out of which the non-sanyasis outnumbered the sannyasis as it wasn't possible for everyone to attend the camps. Many of the non-sannyasis used to leave in the middle of the discourse. This used to cause a lot of pain to Bhagwan, which I feel as well when people start leaving in the middle of Sannyas. Once, Bhagwan got so upset that he told the audience not to bother attending the discourse if they didn't have the patience to stay till the end. Only those who could sit till the end of the discourse should stay, and he wasn't interested in any others. He had been compelled to speak such harsh words.

Amidst so many doubters, the question used to arise very often, "Are you Bhagwan?", "If Krishna, Mahavira, and Buddha didn't refer to themselves as Bhagwan, then why do you call yourself Bhagwan? Weren't they enlightened masters? We called them Bhagwan later, but they themselves never referred to themselves as Bhagwan." Such wayward questions would always get asked. Then a man asked Osho," If you are really Bhagwan, can you not show us your Vishwaroop like Krishna did to Arjun?"

When many such similar questions got accumulated, Bhagwan decided to answer them all at once. He told the audience that they had a wrong view and understanding that enlightened beings like Krishna, Rama, and Buddha did not refer to themselves as Bhagwan. Krishna said "Sarva-dharmān parityajya mām eka⊠ śara⊠a⊠ vraja". Here, Krishna asked Arjun to leave all dharmas, leave all thoughts and come take refuge in him, and Krishna would set him free. If someone reads these words, they would assume Krishna to be a supreme narcissist and egoist who's asking someone to surrender to him in return for the promise of moksha. Bhagwan said that reading these words from the egoistic mind could only lead to the wrong conclusion that Krishna was egoistic. He further explained that while he himself is God, he knows that everyone else is God too. The only difference is that since he has realized, he is an awakened God, while everyone else is a sleeping God. "The day you wake up, you too will see that you are all gods."

So on the day, this man asked if Bhagwan could show him his Vishwaroop by presenting him with Divine Vision like Krishna gave to Arjun, we saw a very strange version of Bhagwan. He said with complete confidence that today he was ready to show his Vishwaroop. He asked everyone who wanted to see his Vishwaroop to get ready and that he was prepared to show them his Cosmic form. He then said that to be able to see this form, it was necessary for them to have trust and devotion as Arjuna had toward Krishna.

This vision of enlightened beings can also be received through complete surrender. Meera was able to see Krishna and his form despite a gap of 4500 years between them because of her unconditional surrender. "So if you have trust, devotion, and surrender like Arjuna and Meera, then I am ready to show you my Vishwaroop at this very moment." He asked those who thought they were ready to come on stage. The audience was taken aback.

There are many characters in the Mahabharata that were more knowledgeable and spiritually evolved than Arjun, like Dronacharya and Bhishma Pitamaha, but they too were unable to see this form of Krishna because they did not have total trust and were not surrendered in their heart towards Krishna the way Arjuna was. Only Arjuna had complete faith that Krishna was Bhagwan.

Those who were present for this discourse got to witness a

unique version of a 'Rudra' or roaring Bhagwan. Many fortunate ones who had complete faith in their Master got to have a vision of his Divine Brilliance.

Bhagwan once said that a person would either die or go mad if they were to see a Vishwaroop. I'd like to recount an incident where such a thing occurred. This happened to a friend of mine who was staying in Pune at the time. He really wished to see Bhagwan's Vishwaroop. One night he decided to sleep on the hotel rooftop because of the summer heat. At midnight, He saw Bhagwan walking with a kamandal in a Rishi form with his feet on the ground and his head higher than the top of the hotel. The hotel was five stories tall! This man was a good friend and a sannyasi initiated by Bhagwan himself, but after this vision of Bhagwan, his psychological state was never the same. Even though my friend didn't see his complete form, where the whole world is being absorbed in his mouth in the Mahakal form as Arjuna did, this 60-feet tall Kamadal-bearing Rishi form vision of Bhagwan was enough to disturb his psychological state, and his behavior was never again what we would consider normal.

Bhagwan said that unless we are well prepared, we can die seeing this Vishwaroop. He has talked similarly about enlightenment as well; that unless we are prepared, the person will have to leave the body within twenty-four hours. Only if you are completely prepared should you ever wish to get enlightened. Indeed, it is a blessing and a safeguard from existence that it protects us from such instances. Because if we were to see a Vishwaroop or if enlightenment happens to you without being ready, the nervous system would not be able to bear such a massive phenomenon.

Rupaidiha Incident

I have seen how Bhagwan helps his sannyasins in many mysterious ways, and I'd like to recount one such incident. Once, a sannyasi came up to me at Tapoban and started thanking me for changing his life. I couldn't understand as I had never met this man before. So, I asked him to tell me more.

He said that he had a huge fight with his family and had left home to live his life as a renunciate. He wanted to cross the border to India and reach the Rupaidiha border on the Nepal side. According to him, he saw me at the border on a carriage, and I asked him to sit on the tanga. I took him along across the border and started buying some stuff. Then I asked him about what had happened at home, and he explained about his fight at home and that he had left his family.

He said I proceeded to explain to him how he would face many problems in the outside world and that, as a mala-wearing Osho sannyasi, he was not likely to be accepted at any ashram. All these ashrams belonged to a particular creed, and they would ask him to drop his mala to be accepted. That would lead to the breaking of his connection to Osho. It wouldn't be viable for him to live according to himself as all ashrams have their own ways, and disputes could arise anywhere. I further advised him how this wasn't Bhagwan's way for his sannyasis and that he should return to Nepal. I bought myself something and gave him something to eat as well. Then I dropped him back across the border at Nepalgunj on the carriage. I supposedly had an Airport project going on in Nepalgunj at the time, and I had to go back to work. But before leaving, I reiterated how he should not pursue this idea of running away any further as no ashram would accept an Osho Sannyasi and that this process would only upset both himself and his family, and that it would only end in tears for everyone. Therefore he should return home.

When he recounted this story at Tapoban, he thanked me for giving him the right guidance and reconciling him with his family. I told him that no thanks was necessary as I really didn't remember being in Rupaidiha at that time! He insisted that it was indeed me that was on the carriage and again recounted the details of our trip across the border and the advice that I gave him to return home to the mountain region above Nepalgunj. Since it surely wasn't me at Rupaidiha, it is my understanding that Bhagwan must have taken my form to help this man instead of taking his own form, as this would have seemed implausible. Later I confirmed with Bhagwan that it really was him that had saved this man from a certain ruin of his life and his family.

Dilip Kumar Roy and Manifestation of Krishna

There are many other such incidents in the lives of devotees when mere statues have come alive and have transformed into forms of the divine itself. Until ultimate liberation a devotee's mind also plays many games and is not always filled with trust and devotion. There are peaks and valleys in a devotee's life and during times of doubts and darkness, the divine has to manifest itself through extraordinary ways to reassure the devotee of its existence and to nudge them towards light.

Sri Dilip Kumar Roy was the disciple of Sri Aurobindo and a contemporary Indian yogi, renowned musician, philosopher and a great scholar of his times. He was also the guru of visionary poetess and mystic Indira Devi and a class fellow of the great leader Subash Chandra Bose. Having graduated from the esteemed Cambridge University, Dilip Kumar Roy was a man of great achievements. His musical talent was appreciated not only in India by the likes of Rabindra Nath Tagore but also by great international figures like Romain Rolland and Bertrand Rusell. Sri Aurobindo cherished him and called him his friend and son. However, all of this was not enough to give solace to Dilip's spiritually seeking heart and his longing to realize Krishna. Time and again, in his book Pilgrims of the Stars, co-written by him and Indira Devi, he expresses his times of despair and frustration seeking for a sign of divine presence.

During a similar incident of despair Dilip Kumar Roy expresses his longing to experience divine grace. After Indira Devi came into his life, Dilip had witnessed miracles after miracles happen in Indira's life while he was lurking in the dark specially after the passing away of his Gurudev Sri Aurobindo. Troubled by his doubts and frustration in his failure to attain the divine grace, Dilip longed for a sign that could prove him of Krishna's presence in his life.

Nine months after Aurobindo's passing Dilip's frustration had reached its crescendo and he was in great pain. It was midnight and Dilip was meditating on his verandah. He prayed with tears in his eyes, "If you are, indeed, a Redeemer of the derelict, do not let me peter out like this in deep frustration after more than twenty years of yoga – away from my home, my friends, my relations and everything men cherish. Now that my Gurudev, my best beloved, is no more, I implore you, Lord, to come in person to my rescue. My Gurudev saved me in some of the darkest crises of my life, assuring me again and again that he would lead me to your feet; but since he cannot guide me anymore, it is up to you now to come and give me a sign that you are still there to care for me. . ."

A friend had given a figure of Sri Krishna and Mira etched on a glass slab which could be lit by a bulb attached to it. Dilip had placed this figure on a pedestal in the prayer room and used to switch it off before going to bed. That night also he had switched it off and taken out the plug before retiring to his bedroom.

As he was praying in great despair, he heard a soft but clear voice: "Go and See: He has lit the bulb."

Dilip rushed to the prayer room and to his great amazement saw that the three-pronged plug which he had himself plugged out earlier had been plugged in and the figure was lit and was alive with light. There was nobody present in the prayer room. Dilip could not believe his eyes and called Indira to witness this miracle. Indira was overwhelmed with tears and they sang the lord's name for an hour before retiring back to their rooms.

Dilip had a very strong mind, and the lurking doubt again sprang in him. He doubted himself if he had inadvertently left the plug in and had forgotten about it.To test the incident this time he left the plug in and came back to his room. He was still unconvinced and could not dismiss his doubts. Haunted by his delirium he prayed again in great unhappiness, "If the Lord himself had put it in, he might as well take it out and convince me of his intervention."

To his great surprise again the same voice rebuked him, "Doubting still? Go. The plug has been taken out."

He rushed to the prayer room with Indira and to his thrilling delight the plug had been taken out and the figures were now completely invisible in the darkness. Dilip Kumar Roy's speculating mind had to finally surrender and succumb to divine intervention and was replaced with trust and faith in the presence of his Lord.

Mirabai—Merged into Krishna

Mirabai was a 16th century mystic poetess and a devotee of Sri Krishna. Her whole life is an ideal example of devotion and trust. I have written about her in my previous book Lone Seeker Many Masters and the many incidents that happened in her life. The poignant climax to Mira's life is the ultimate peak of Bhakti and the best example of the merger of a devotee and the divine. There is no better account in human history that can express how the impossible can also be made possible through love and devotion. In the first discourse of his lecture series 'Pad Ghungroo Bandh' Osho has also confirmed about this incident and has spoken about it with great love and reverence to Mira. Every seeker should listen to this series and approach it with an open heart and great subtlety to experience the magic of Mirabai.

After leaving the palace, Mirabai went to Vrindavan and lived under the guidance of her guru Sanatan Goswami. After her guru left his body Mira went to Dwarka where Krishna had spent last days of his life and started living in the Ranchor Das temple worshipping her beloved Lord Krishna. When Mira's husband died, his second brother Vikramjit ascended the throne and banished Mira from the kingdom of Chittore after harrassing her and making many failed attempts on her life because of her ascetic lifestyle which he thought was a disgrace to the royalty. When Vikramjit died, he was replaced by his brother Udai Singh. Udai Singh was urged by the people to bring Mira back to Mewar, and being a man of kindness Udai Singh realized the atrocities made upon Mira and felt that the unjust behavior made upon Mira was a great disgrace upon his dynasty and decided to respectfully bring her back to Mewar from Dwarka.

Udai Singh sent many messages and invited Mira back to the palace, he sent many messengers and delegations to bring Mira back but to no avail. Finally he sent a large delegation of holy persons headed by the chief royal priest to bring Mira back to Mewar. He ordered them not to come back without Mira and asked them to go into hunger strike and camp outside the temple until she decided to come back. He ordered them that even if they had to give their lives to bring her back they shouldn't think twice.

When the delegation arrived in Dwarka, they made many requests and appealed to Mira to return with them. Dwarka was the land of Mira's beloved and she wanted to spend the rest of her life there in worship and devotion singing and dancing to her Lord's name.

There was no other place in the world for her. Mira again declined Udai Singh's appeal. The delegation camped outside the Ranchor Das temple and went on a hunger strike.

As the days passed by, Mira was in a great dilemma. The men would die of hunger if she didn't go with them. Mira finally said, "I will go with you but let me first ask permission from my beloved." She went into the Ranchor Das temple and never came out. It is said that when the men went inside the temple to look for her the temple was empty and Mira could not be found anywhere and only a small piece of Mira's sari was hanging from the mouth of the statue of Krishna.

Similar incident happened in the life of Chaitanya Maha Prabhu also, the great devotee of Krishna who is believed to have been merged with the idol of Jagannath Puri at the Jagannath temple in Puri, Orissa. His body was never discovered and the incident of his passing away always remained shrouded in mystery.

Osho beautifully speaks of this incident and calls it the ultimate merger of the devotee and the beloved. Speaking of this incident Osho says, "Mira must have prayed to her beloved – either you come with me or take me with you. And Krishna dissolved her within him."

Mira had dedicated her whole life to Krishna and it was now Krishna's turn to prove his love for her. This incident was the final climax of Mira's life of devotion when all her prayers were answered and she entered into Mahasamadhi and merged with her beloved.

In these lines from his epic poem, 'Savitri', Sri Aurobindo subtly speaks of how the impossible is made possible and how the miraculous manifests in the mundane through a heartfelt prayer-

"A prayer, a master act, a king idea
Can link a man's strength to a transcendent Force,
Then miracle is made the common rule."

Esoteric Events from the Life of Indira Devi

In my previous book 'Lone Seeker Many Masters' I wrote about Ma Indira Devi, the daughter disciple of Dilip Kumar Roy and the daughter disciple of Sri Aurobindo. To me she was a guiding light in the darkest hours of my life when my guru had left his body. Her consolation and firm guidance had comforted my distressed heart in those dire times. I can never forget the love, guidance and blessings that she bestowed upon me as though I was her own son. Her blessings are with me even today and have played a pivotal role in the expression of Tapoban's devotional side.

Ma's whole life was a musical grandeur of mysticism and miracles. She became the medium of Krishna's beloved Mira and through automatic writing revived all of Mira's songs that we sing today. Just like that of Mira, Ma's life is also a great example of how the divine can be attained through the path of devotion, surrender and love. In these modern times when logic and rationale rule every explanation and event Ma's life was the perfect example of the existence of that which lives beyond the boundaries of factual tangibility and what meets the eyes. Ma Indira Devi was a personification of utmost purity, through arduous sadhana and devotion she had attained to the ultimate and had purified every channel in her body. This was the reason why she was highly sensitive and the center of many mystical incidents that took place through her and around her.

Apart from the advent of Mira there are many other mystical incidents that took place in the life of Indira Devi that are worth mentioning here.

ONE WITH PLANTS AND ANIMALS

Like all elevated beings Indira Devi was also highly sensitive towards the pain of others around her. She was extremely empathetic and could feel other's pain as if her own. Around September of 1956, on a normal afternoon Indira Devi had gone out to drink coffee with her guru Dadajee and his friend. After the coffee Dadajee and his friend were walking on the promenade while Indira was waiting in the car. As she looked out of the window, she saw a half-starved dog go up to the café and look logingly at the bread, only to be driven away by the counter man who brandished a stick. Immediately , Indira experienced the most terrible pain of hunger in her stomach. It was as if this hunger were ganwing at her inside. She had never dreamed that hunger could be so unbearable. Without thinking she quickly got out of the car and bought a couple of buns which she gave the dog. As soon as it ate the buns she felt her normal self again.

The second time, Indira was standing near her window watching a man plough his field opposite the ashram. Suddenly he took a thick stick and hit the bullock hard on his back. Indira screamed out in pain as though someone had struck her. When she picked up her sari, Dada and other inmates of the ashram saw that there was a round, black bruise on her thigh. This bruise caused her severe pain for some days.

The third time involved a bougainvillea plant in the ashram garden. Between two red plants there was an orange flowering bush. The orange color clashed with the red and Indira asked her brother disciple who was in charge of the graden to remove the orange plant. That night when she was meditating Indira saw the trunk of the orange blossoms part in two, revealing a young boy standing within, in orange robes. He said to her, "Why do you want to destroy me, mother? I am still young."

Thereafter Indira instructed the brother disciple in charge and forbade anyone to cut any branch from the trees or to uproot any plant without asking her.

Another afternoon while meditating Indira saw some little boys and girls in green dancing happily around the mango grove in the ashram. Suddenly, there was blood on the grass and two little boys shouted : "Ma they are cutting our arms!" Indira jumped up and ran downstairs . She was deeply moved and was sobbing, and there she saw the gardener cutting down branches from the mango trees. The brother disciple had forgotten to issue her instructions.

Indira was a sensitive soul and these trees and flowers and plants spoke to her through their vibrations.

YOGIC FEATS AND MIRACLES

Indira used to go into deep bhava samadhi specially during Kirtan sessions sung by Dadaji. She would be immersed in ecstasy as tears rolled down her cheeks. She would be lost in devotion for Krishna and had no awareness of time and space. Just like Ramkrishna Paramhansa she would have these spontaneous samadhis and people around her had to support and take care of her. Many miracles used to happen around her, whenever in deep samadhi her body used to emanate a strong yet soothing fragrance of sandalwood and after that whatever or whoever she touched would also emit the same fragrance.

On a similar occasion Indira was with her 11 year old son Premal and a retired brigadier general, Srikant, listening to Dadajee sing a song that was dictated by Indira in one of her samadhis. Indira went into a half trance of ecstasy and said to Dadajee, "Dada shall we have prasad?"

She went down to the garden and asked her son Premal to get some mud for her. Premal took some mud and put it in her palms. Indira started swaying in Bhava-Samadhi and then put the mud into Srikant's hand which was no more mud. The mud had transformed into granulated sugar. Then she poured the remaining prasad into Dadajee's hands. Then again as if this wasn't already enough, she again folded her hands and, upon reopening them, produced more prasad and this time out of nothing at all.

On another occasion in 1960, Indira's younger sister and disciple Kanta underwent a major surgery during which a serious medical blunder occurred. Indira used to have visions and could sense if somebody was in danger. Indira had seen a black shadow over her sister and had invited her to come to Pune for the surgery.

Coming back to her senses after the surgery, Kanta developed severe pain and had a high fever of 102.8. The doctors consoled her for a few days saying it was just the after effects of the surgery. When the fever did not go down for 3 days, it was eventually found that the doctors had inadvertently left a gauze plug inside and two inches of it was protruding outside. It was a major blunder and an operation had to be immediately done to remove the gauze. The next morning Indira and Dadajee arrived at the hospital in which they were informed about what had happened. The doctor examined Kanta and scheduled an operation in the late morning.

As soon as she met Indira, Kanta started crying and said, "Ma, they've killed me."

Indira consoled her and asked the doctor to reschedule the operation to the afternoon. Then she asked everyone to leave the room and not to disturb them.

When they were alone, Indira said to Kanta, "Forget everyone. Think of the Lord alone and surrender yourself to him."

Kanta asked Indira, "Ma, will I be all right?" She replied, "He knows best, His will be done." Indira held Kanta's hand and asked her to remember Him.

Here is Kanta's account of what happened next.

"I was still very frightened. As she kept holding my hand, I closed my eyes and vividly felt as though she was conveying something to me by her touch. Gradually as my being relaxed it was permeated with peace. When I opened my eyes, it was twelve noon. My body was no longer burning with fever and the pain was much diminished. It was only then that Ma let go of my hand and went out to call the doctor. She duly arrived with her retinue to reexamine me. What was their amazement to find that the gauze had entirely disappeared! They searched everywhere for it but in vain. In the end they agreed that it was, indeed, a miracle.

When Ma came back to the ashram her temperature had risen to 102.8 and she continued to run a fever for three days."

BLACK MAGIC

In the beginning years of Indira Devi's spiritual life after she had met her guru Dada jee and had spent some time at the Sri Aurobindo ashram, a series of events took place in her life that involved a sinister individual who tried to take control over Indira Devi through black magic.

A certain Swami D summoned Indira to meet him at a royal palace where he was a guest of the Maharaja. Being summoned by the so called sadhu was looked upon as a great privilege and Indira was forced by a family member to go see him through whom the sadhu had sent the message.

The Swami was an exceptionally beautiful looking man with long white beard who at his very first meeting with Indira asked her to join him and help him in his supposedly spiritual endeavors to attain samadhi and what he called his 'big spiritual manifestation.' He already had a great insight into Indira's special personality and her mystical powers and tried to convince her to join him.

During the very first meeting Indira felt a strong repulsion towards the energy of the man and politely denied his offer saying that she was not interested in any sadhu and that she already had her own guru. An exchange between the two individuals in the very first meeting is very interesting.

"Shall I tell you what you are thinking? You want someone to enter the room so that you can go away, but you are wrong - you will never be able to get away from me," said the Sadhu reading Indira's thoughts.

Indira looked up at him and as luck would have it his thoughts came as clearly to her as if she were reading an open book. "You yourself are thinking that since I can't be caught by threats you must be gentle with me," returned Indira.

Indira politely denied his offer to join her for meditation and somehow escaped what had become a suffocating atmosphere for her.

After that the Swami sent many messages to Indira but she was adamant. A week later Indira suddenly started to develop a severe pain in her chest and developed a fever. Indira's appetite was lost, and her health kept declining. A few nights later Indira saw her mother who had died about twenty years earlier. She walked up to Indira and told her in a gentle but firm voice, "Don't take anything that is not prepared in your presence."

Indira wrote a letter about this to Dadajee who forwarded it to Sri Aurobindo. Sri Aurobindo immediately wrote back to Dada and told him that if Indira did not come to the ashram immediately she would die and that a dark force was working on her.

Dada came to Indira's house to take her to the ashram. There he took her personal maid aside and asked her if she was putting something in Indira's tea? The maid broke down and confessed that upon the instructions of an elder member in the family she had been mixing a powder in Indira's morning cup of tea which was supposed to cure her asthma. Later it was found that Swami D had convinced the family member that Indira brought all luck and prosperity in the household and she should be anyhow stopped from going away to Aurobindo's ashram. He had given the powder and had instructed it to be mixed in her cup of tea which would make her a little sick but stop her from going away.

Indira left for Pondicherry on a stretcher. She could hardly walk or eat but she flew in that weak state and reached the ashram.

The sinister Swami could not be so easily sidestepped. He started torturing Indira. One night when Indira awakened from her meditation, she saw two bloodshot eyes and then a hand clutched her just below the neck. The voice hissed, "You can't get away. You'll die if you don't come."

She had black painful bruises on her chest the next day of a thumb and three fingers. This recurred for a few more nights when it eventually started bleeding at the place where Indira was clutched.

Indira had had enough with the Swami and decided to go back and confront him. Sri Aurobindo advised against it and asked her to not leave the ashram at any cost. He told her that even the idea to leave and confront him was being put into her by the Swami D. Sri Aurobindo provided her all the spiritual support and asked her to remain fearless no matter what as fear would help the black forces the Swami was using upon her.

Sri Aurobindo wrote to her, " The physical pain and suffering inflicted by him is hard to bear, but you must try to remain firm in spite of it until his power to touch you diminishes and comes to nothing. Be courageous and push the obsession of him away from you; it is through the nervous being and some pressure of his force upon it which he has been able to establish that he makes you suffer. Try to be calm and steady there; then it will be easier to remain firm. Be sure that the Mother's help and mine will always be with you. Call for it whenever you need it."

One day when Indira was in the bathroom, suddenly, without warning, the door opened and what appears to be Dada entered the room. Indira became cautious as Dada would never enter like that. The form called her name when she instantly drew back from it and spontaneously exclaimed: "Jai Guru Dada, Jai Guru."

At once the spell broke and the form turned indistinct and hazy and she saw that it was none other than Swami D. Before he vanished, he gave Indira a vicious push so that she fell against the bathtub.

Later it was revealed to Indira in her meditation that the man's evil influence on her would cease with the next full moon. And it happened accordingly. A disciple of the Swami wrote to them, "Swami got a paralytic stroke and died in great agony; he left instructions to cremate Indira's photograph which he had bought in Mussoorie from a photographer."

Indira Devi's life was full of ups and downs, and she went

through many testing times that only purified her more and paved her way towards her beloved Krishna through whom she eventually attained her ultimate liberation. Anybody who is interested to immerse in this experience of Ma's romantic affair with the divine should definitely read her books, 'Pilgrims of the Stars', 'Flute calls still', Miracles Do Still Happen', and 'Fragrant Memories' among others and visit her ashram and samadhi in the Hari Krishna Mandir in the Model Colony of Shivajinagar in Pune where her absent presence still overflows through every corner of this hallowed space.

The Resurrection of Sri Yukteshwar Giri

Paramhansha Yogananda's Autobiography of a Yogi is one of my favorite books as it is one of the rare authentic accounts of the mysterious events encountered by a yogi during his life of seeking. Paramhansa Yogananda relates the tale of how a young boy's quest is heeded by the unknown forces of the universe before and after he finds his Guru. I have bought dozens of copies of this book and distributed it to many friends and acquaintances in the hope that it might spark the fire within them. Because if Autobiography of a Yogi, which I consider

one of the highest spiritual tales, cannot spark the spiritual fire within you, then what will?

My own life has also been blessed by countless mystical events, and I have tried to tell my own experiences in all honesty in this book. And if you have also traveled in the spiritual path with zeal, you will be able to relate to these tales that are in risk of being labeled mere fantasy. And I have revealed as much as it has been allowed by my Master, Osho, just as the Paramhansa has told his tale, revealing just as much as his Guru, Sri Yukteswar Giri has allowed him to.

THE MATERIALIZATION OF A PALACE IN THE HIMALAYAS

A mystifying event beyond our wildest imagination happened during the initiation of Sri Lahari Mahashaya, Sri Yukteshwar Giri's Guru.

Lahari Mahashaya worked as an accountant at the Military Engineering Department at Danapur, Bihar. One morning the office manager summoned Lahari Mahashaya and told him that he was being transferred to a newly opened military branch at Ranikhet, on the foot of the Nandadevi Mountain in Almora district.

The year was 1861 and traveling on horse and buggy, it took Lahari Mahashaya thirty days to complete the 500 kilometer journey through the Himalayan mountains and reach the secluded Ranikhet.

Once he was settled in Ranikhet, Lahari Mahashaya, finding that he had very little office work in his new station, used to spend his days roaming in the magnificent Himalayan hills. Having heard a rumor that a band of Himalayan yogis resided in the caves in that area, Lahari Mahashaya felt a strong desire to meet them.

One day while he was exploring the Drongiri Mountain a little uphill from his station, he heard someone calling his name up from the mountain. He kept walking up even if it was getting dark and he reached a small clearing dotted with little caves.

On one of the rocky ledges stood a radiating young saint who looked uncannily similar to him.

Welcoming him to one of the caves, he said, "Lahari you have come! It was I who called you."

Inside the cave, the saint pointed to a neatly folded blanket and kamandal and said, "Lahari, do you recognize that?"

Lahari Mahashaya, perplexed by the happenings said that he needed to return back to his station as he had to be at my office in the morning.

The mysterious young yogi said, "The office was created for you and not you for the office!"

He then explained to Lahari Mahashaya that it was he, Mahavatar Babaji who had arranged for his transfer to Ranikhet. In fact the military base was made there just so that he could come there.

He then told him that he was his guru from his past life and he had spend his days here in that same cave. After this he touched Lahari Mahashaya's forehead and in a flash of light, all his memories of his past lives flashed before him.

Once he recognized his Guru and the meaning behind his transfer to Ranikhet from Danapur. He overcame with emotions and bowed down to his eternal Master.

Babaji then gave him a pot full of oil and told him to drink it as Lahari Mahashaya needed purification. He drank the oil and lied down.

After a while Lahari Mahashaya was woken up by one of Babaji's disciples who told him it was time for his initiation. He pointed to a shiny object on a clearing nearby where there was nothing previously.

When Lahari Mahashaya asked what that was, his Gurubhai

said that as it was Lahari Mahashaya's wish in his past life to experience what it felt like to live in a palace, Babaji had created a palace made of gold, diamonds and other jewels out of his spiritual powers so that he could experience it. He told him to get ready as his initiation into Kriya Yoga was going to happen inside the newly created palace. He lead him through a forest pathway and into the palace that was beautiful beyond Lahari Mahashaya's imagination.

Fragrance of incense and fresh flowers wafted through the hallway and devotees were either singing devotional songs or were siting silently for the ceremony.

That is when Babaji who was sitting at the center beckoned Lahari Mahashaya to sit beside him and created a ceremonial pier out of thin air. He then proceeded with the ceremony. Lahari Mahashaya had one of the grandest initiation in yogic history and he was greatly thankful to his master that the only desire that was blocking him from final emancipation was also fulfilled.

After the ceremony was over, Lahari Mahashaya walked out of the palace with his his Guru only to find that the palace had disappeared into thin air.

YUKTESHWOR GIRI WHO IS IN CALCUTTA APPEARS IN SERAMPORE

One morning during their college days, Paramhansha Yogananda and his roommate at the Panthi Boarding house, Dijen Babu, were getting ready to go receive their Guru, Sri Yukteshwar Giri from the train station. The Guru had send them a postcard previously stating that he would be arriving by the nine o' clock train.

Just as they were about to leave for the station, Paramhansha received a telepathic instruction from his Guru stating that he was not on the nine o' clock train as he was late and that they should not come to receive him until further instructed.

The Paramhansha told this to his friend Dijen but instead of believing him, Dijen said that he believed on the Master's written words rather than Yogananda's intuition. He left for the station alone.

Paramhansha Yogananda on the other hand, remained in his room and waited there meditatively. After a while he started to see a flash of light in the other side of the room that turned into the form of Sri Yukteshwar.

The young Yogananda couldn't believe what he was seeing.

"I have been summoned by the Devine to give you this experience," Said Yukteshwar Giri. "You are not seeing a vision, rather what you are seeing is my flesh and blood form. You know know that the physical form can manifest as well as disappear according to divine will. I am coming in the ten o' clock train so you can receive me then."

After saying this, Yukteshwar Giri's form started to disappear. His feet disappeared first and slowly his whole body disappeared as if a scroll was being rolled up.

The young Yogananda couldn't believe what just happened. Gathering himself together after the shock that he had just received, he was about to leave for the station when Dijen Babu came back from the station, frustrated.

"Sri Yukteshwar did not come in the nine o' clock train, nor did he come on the nine thirty train," he said.

"He is arriving in the ten o' clock train, so lets hurry!" said Yogananda.

Dijen Babu was not in the mood to go back but Yogananda said that he was sure that Sri Yukteshwar would come on this train and had to drag him out of their hostel room.

When they reached the station, the train had just arrived and they saw Sri Yukteshwar walking towards them. Yogananda noticed that his Guru was wearing the same clothes that he was wearing when he saw him in his room.

"I sent the message to you too," said Yukteshwar Giri to Dijen babu. "But you were not ready to receive it yet."

HOW PARAMHANSHA YOGANANDA RECEIVED HIS UNIVERSITY DEGREE.

The young Yogananda spent most of his college days in his Guru, Shri Yukteshwar Giri's ashram. Rather than his formal college education, Yogananda was more interested in learning from his Guru and doing the various duties in his Guru's ashram.

When his final exams approached, Yogananda was tormented by the demands of his teachers and begged to his Master to drop out of his college.

"If you drop out, your parents will think that it you were unable to graduate because you spend so much time in the ashram. You will have to appear and you will get help, don't worry," Sri Yukteshwar told his disciple.

Yogananda attended extra coaching classes to learn the chapters that he had missed out but he still was not confident. He also got help from one of his classmates who was very good in studies. Once the exams arrived, Yogananda felt that there was no way that he would pass his exams.

When Sri Yukteshwar asked him how prepared he was, he started to cry and said that there was no reason to go and appear in the exams as he was sure to fail.

Upon hearing this, Yogananda's Guru said to him, "Either the sun and moon will change their places in the sky or you will pass your exam, so go and appear in your exam."

Reluctantly Yogananda appeared in his final exams and although he felt that he could pass all the other subjects he was sure that he would fail his English exam. But he heard from one of his friends that the pass marks of English had been reduced to 33 from 36 that year. 33

was what Yogananda had thought he would get in English. When the results came, Yogananda was surprised to find out that he had passed.

When he hurriedly went to his Guru to share the good news, Yukteshwar Giri laughed and said, "God found it easier to pass you than to change the places of the sun and the moon."

Not only was Paramhansha Yogananda freed from the turmoil of college education for ever but his farther also thanked Yukteshwor Giri for making sure that he graduated college.

SRI YUKTESHWAR COMES BACK FROM DEATH

In the 43rd chapter of the book, Autobiography of a Yogi, Paramhansa Yogananda reveals one of the most mysterious phenomena in all spiritual literature. For some, the event of the resurrection of Sri Yukteswar may seem made up, but for those with an open mind to the tremendous possibilities of the spiritual realm, this incident can be a telescopic peak into the astral and causal worlds that lie beyond the material world that we experience with our five senses.

The incident that happened on the afternoon of June 19, 1936, at the third floor of the Regent Hotel, Bombay, has been etched in my mind forever. The Paramhansa was in deep meditation when suddenly the unthinkable happened. The room was engulfed with the most intense light, and Sri Yukteswar Giri, the beloved Guru of Paramhansa, who had left his body around three months ago, appeared in his full physical form to the utter astonishment of his disciple.

Sri Yukteswar remained in his bodily form for quite a while and related to the Paramhansa about Hiranyaloka, a heavenly realm in the astral world where the most advanced beings are born. Sri Yukteswar said that he was born there as a Guru to help the highest of the astral beings to rid their astral karmas to enter the even higher casual world, a world beyond even the subtlest of forms. A world consisting only of ideas where the nearly illumined beings resided.

The Paramhansha was not Sri Yukteshwar's only disciple for whom he appeared after his death.

One of Sri Yukteshwar's disciple was an aged women whom everyone called Maa. She lived close to Sri Yukteshwar's ashram in Puri. A week after Shree Yukteshwar left his body, she came to the ashram and asked to meet her Master.

When told that the Master has passed away a week ago she couldn't believe it.

"How can he be dead! I just met him this morning at ten o' clock when he passed by my house in his usual walk. I talked with him for several minutes before he left," she said.

THE UNEXPECTED MEETING

Between 2005 and 2010 I conducted several meditation retreats on a ferry in West Bengal through the Sundarban Delta and Ganga Sagar. I always visit the Belurmath and Dakshineshwor temples whenever I am in Kolkata. During my stay in the city, I also visit the Yogananda Ashram in Dakshineshor and Swami Yogananda's house at 4, Garpar Road, where he was born. I have met some of Swamiji's family members including the son of his brother Sananda Lal Ghosh and the granddaughter of his younger brother Ananta.

At the 4, Garpar Road House we were greeted by Mr. Hare Krishna Ghosh, the son of Sananda and nephew of Swamiji. Mr. Ghosh was taking care of the house in those days. He was a rather amicable person. We talked in length about Swamiji. I told him I was an admirer of Swamiji and had written several articles on him and spoken about him in national radio and television. He was kind enough to allow us to meditate in the small attic room where Swamiji attained enlightenment. It was empty except for a small altar with Swamiji's picture and a shelf with a few photos and relics. Swamiji has written in detail about his stay in that house in Autobiography of A

Yogi. The room was still vibrating with his strong presence. Sitting in that tiny room for half an hour I was absorbed into deep meditation.

After the meditation, Mr. Ghosh showed us around the place. Swamiji had presented a lot of things to him - a tea set, Swamiji's

clothes and many of his rare pictures. Mr. Ghosh was showing me a photo album and both of us were totally absorbed in the photos. He told me that Swamiji and Indian poet, Rabindra Nath Tagore, came from the same ancestral root. When we were busy peering at the family tree, from the corner of my eyes I noticed a bright orange robe fluttering behind Mr. Ghosh. I thought perhaps it was someone from the house. Mr. Ghosh was talking in a deep sonorous Bengali accent. The night was silent and cool and the master's presence was very palpable. I was blissed out.

We spent a long time leafing through the pictures. And the robe kept fluttering in the background. Suddenly, I was seized by this intense desire to look at the person who was wearing the robe. I looked up and what I saw left me dumbfounded! Swami Yogananda himself was looking at me and smiling. He stood that way for the next few seconds and disappeared into thin air, just like that.

I left Swamiji's house in a very meditative state and went to my room that I was renting at the ISCON guest house. That night I slept feeling very blessed due to the event that had occurred earlier.

In the middle of the night, I woke up as I felt a warm hand on my forehead. Blissful energy was emanating from the hand. I opened my eyes and saw the hand and as a reflex I grabbed it with my own hand.

Suddenly the hand disappeared. I got up and looked around but saw no one. I then realized that I had been blessed by a Master as the energy around me and within me had completely changed. I then sat in meditation for a long time and I was transported to a state full of blessings and bliss. It is my trust that Swami Yoganand himself had come to bless me that night.

Although I had felt a deep connection with Paramhansha Yogananda ever since I first read Autobiography of a Yogi, after that night, the connection became much deeper and became permanently established.

Astral Yogi in my Room

The Siddhartha block where I reside today at Tapoban has developed into a three storied house with many rooms, kitchens, meeting halls, Osho's archive room, the International Office and the Publication office. In the beginning it was just a two storied house with two guest rooms on the ground floor and my quarters on the upper floor. My floor had a small living room where I used to receive guests and a small corridor kitchen adjoining my bedroom.

My bedroom was also my meditation room where I kept Osho's chair and his robe that he had given to me as a gift when he came to Nepal and to Pune 2 respectively. Today the same room has become Osho's archive room and houses His robe, chair, His letters, His ashes or holy remains, his hair, nails, his sock and two of his handkerchiefs along with some gifts that Osho had given me personally. When I was living in that room many spiritual experiences happened to me in there out of which most of them I am not allowed to share but there is one incident that I would like to mention here which left me baffled and awestruck.

Many a times when I go in deep meditation I have felt the presence of other beings sitting around me. Osho always assured me not to be scared as all these beings had also come to meditate or help me. Sometimes evolved beings also look for places or people who can help them evolve faster in meditation. These kind of incidents are always happening in all charged Buddhafields.

On that fateful night I had finished my evening meditation and had gone to bed after dinner. I was fast asleep when suddenly in the middle of the night I woke up with a strange feeling, it felt like there was a strong presence in the room. The room was softly lit by the moonlight that had entered the room through my windows. I have never liked curtains or blinds so my bedroom windows are always uncovered. I always have a small meditation corner in my room usually against a wall with a cushion and a back support cushion. As I kept feeling this presence in the room, I sat up and looked down from the bed and lo and behold I saw a monk meditating with closed eyes in lotus posture, sitting on my cushion. He was in deep meditation. I was speechless at what I saw and could not comprehend anything for a moment. All the doors and windows were locked from inside and it was not possible for anybody to enter. When we wake up just from our sleep, our conscious mind is not very active and we can see things beyond the physical dimension. I looked at him for sometime but as

I came to my senses and my conscious mind started thinking the man instantly vanished.

The sight of that man meditating is still very vivid in my memory. He looked like a great monk in deep meditation. During my contact, Osho later confirmed to me that there was nothing to be scared and he was an evolved soul who had come to meditate in a charged space. These kind of incidents still happen in Tapoban specially in the night when many non-physical beings come to meditate in this charged Buddhafield.

Asheesh—The Mystical Ashram

When we look into the history of places which have strong buddhafields, and where temples and ashrams have been built, we always find a great spiritual legacy hidden in their wombs. Usually, we find that such places hold a glorious history of some spiritual work or events that have happened there over a period of time. The vibrations of these events remain alive, but in a dormant form, until the day similar works of inner seeking and growth begin there again, after which they are strengthened and multiplied a

thousandfold. Meditation happens very easily in such places. In fact, every such place on Earth waits for the right person to come and start the work that is commensurate with the great history that it holds.

Live temples and ashrams can only be created at such spots, and inner growth can take roots and flourish amid such conducive vibrations. When the place is right, it takes a very short time for the temples and ashrams to grow, and thousands of seekers are drawn to them within just a few years. All of this happens because of the supporting energy that safeguards and nourishes the ashram, temple or buddhafield, and acts like a magnet drawing seekers from all over the world. There are two types of energies in the world: one is supportive, and the other, destructive. When we choose the wrong place to occupy, sometimes things become very difficult and there ends up being conflicts, problems and eventually the closing of such places. That is why it is very important to choose a location that supports meditation and inner growth, before building an ashram, meditation center or temple.

Anyone with a certain level of spiritual maturity can sense these vibrations, and some people also have clairvoyance by which they can look into the past and actually see what events have occurred at such places.

When we first arrived at Tapoban, it was a wild jungle where one had to hold on to shrubs just to climb down the steep hills. I had come here on an office picnic, and the only flat land available was the land where we built the meditation hall and the top of the hillock where Osho's samadhi is located today. That is where we decided to have our picnic. While my friends were eating and drinking, I was drawn to the only tree that stood there in the middle of this area, and I began meditating under it. I was immediately immersed in deep meditation.

Before Osho left Nepal and went on his world tour, he had

asked me to open a commune in Nepal and had given me certain parameters for the area on which it was to be built. We had been looking for land for years but had not been able to find the right place. There was always something missing whenever we tried to match it with Osho's parameters. While meditating under that tree, it suddenly dawned on me that our search had ended and this was the place where the future Osho commune would be built. It was 1990, and Osho had just left his body.

We eventually purchased the land and slowly the commune began taking shape. Many evolved souls, mystics, lamas and gurus also started visiting Tapoban, and they gave me hints about the place after staying here or meditating here. Some told me that the rounded hillock on which we had created the Osho Samadhi was a very sacred place and asked us to pay special attention in preserving its sanctity. Some clairvoyants in their meditation saw hundreds of Buddhist monks meditating there, while some even had the darshan of great masters at the samadhi. At the time we purchased the land, the local villagers used to worship the tree on the hillock and asked us to preserve the tree in its totality, not even breaking off a leaf. This was a village deity belief. Slowly, as my meditation advanced, I also started getting visions and guidance about the significance of the place.

One day, it was revealed to me in my meditation that Nagarjuna, a great master of Buddhism and the founder of the Madhyamaka Karika, or the Middle-Path in Buddhism, had come to Nepal at the advanced age of eighty and had meditated for thirty years in this very forest where Tapoban is located today. After many years of sadhana, he had attained enlightenment under a tree here, and the tree at the Osho Samadhi today is the offspring of that original tree. After attaining enlightenment, Nagarjuna went back to Nalanda, but his twelve disciples who had come with him, remained in this forest meditating. When they left their bodies, their bodies were buried in the earthen stupa on which the Osho Samadhi stands today. This was later confirmed by my master and many other mystics I came in contact with. This place had waited for 2,000 years for us to come and make a temple of meditation here.

Likewise, other energy centers or temples that hold a spiritual history have been built at places similar to Tapoban. When I had the inspiration to build the Shivapuri Baba temple at Tapoban beside the Osho Samadhi, I faced much opposition from my architects and trustees as it was not in accord with the master plan. However, despite all the hindrances and opposition, something compelled me to build the first temple of Shivapuri Baba there, and it has become the heart of Tapoban. As soon as you enter the temple, you are immersed in a volume of energy there, and feel an instant connection with Shivapuri Baba. Recently, a Kabir temple has also been built at Tapoban under similar circumstances. The place was used as a dumping site for metal and other construction waste at the ashram, but with spontaneity and divine intervention, a beautiful temple dedicated to Kabir was built there, and from the very first day it was highly charged with strong vibrations. Both of these places have a great spiritual history and significance which I cannot yet reveal here, but it was through the invitation of the vibrations present there and the wish of the masters themselves that these temples were created in their names.

The Buddha Temple at our Osho commune, Osho Jetban, in Lumbini, is another masterpiece of energy. Now I have come to understand that the temple was not built for the commune, but the commune was built there so the temple could come into existence. In the formative stage of Jetban, friends had already paid for a different parcel of land in Lumbini for the commune, and it had been easier to acquire than the final one as it belonged to a single person. But when I saw the land, I could not get in tune with that place; something was missing there. Later, we had to sell that land. But when we arrived at the land where Jetban stands today, I felt an instant harmony. It was not easy to acquire though, as there were many owners.

I still remember the meeting under the mango tree, which was the only tree on the whole property, when I sat with all the villagers and explained to them how the commune would help the whole village, and convinced them to sell it to us. Miraculously, all the villagers were convinced, and the owners each decided to sell their land to us. Today, under the same mango tree, there is a beautiful marble statue of Buddha, and just behind it is the big Buddha Temple that houses a large marble statue. The whole commune site is now lush with trees and gardens. I have been to many Buddha temples of great importance, including the places where Buddha was born, became enlightened, gave his first sermon, left his body and stayed the longest, but nowhere do I feel the strong energy that I feel at our new temple in Lumbini. There is an esoteric secret behind it; it was not that we had chosen the land, but it was the land which had chosen us. The place has been a witness to a great incident in the past, and so has a highly-charged energy, which is why the commune has grown so beautifully upon it. I am not allowed to speak in detail on such things, but when time matures, I am sure there will be revelations to many more meditators.

The Indian mystic, Sri Aurobindo, has a similar story in his life. In the very early days of moving to Pondicherry with four disciples, Sri Aurobindo was living in a rented house of meager condition. Of its two rooms, one was for Aurobindo, while the four disciples lived in the other room. The amenities were so scanty that the group even had to share the same towel. Aurobindo would use it after having a shower, then the other four would use it before washing and drying it for Aurobindo to use the next day. A candle cost one paise, and two candles were required every day. As Aurobindo had a habit of reading at night, one was given to him, while the other was used in the kitchen, and afterwards by the other four. Aurobindo came from an affluent Bengali family and was given the best education available at the time. While living in England, he came eleventh out of 250 candidates in the famous ICS exams, however, after his arrest as a political revolutionary and spending one year in Alipore jail, Kolkata, his life transformed. He became more spiritually inclined after his conversations with Swami Vivekananda and Lord Krishna, who appeared in physical form in the jail to guide him. In order to avoid further arrests, he was guided by higher beings to go and live outside British India in Pondicherry, and spend his life meditating. However, after moving to Pondicherry, his financial situation became very tight, and a point came when it seemed they could no longer survive there.

Aurobindo's peril is well articulated in the lines of a letter he wrote to a friend, asking for money, "I must ask you to procure for me by will power, or any other power in heaven or on Earth, fifty rupees at least as a loan." He further writes, "The situation just now is that we have four annas or so in hand. No doubt, God will provide, but he has contracted a bad habit of waiting until the last moment." A yogi like Aurobindo would never ask others to use spiritual power, especially to acquire money, so it can be understood how dire a situation he must have been in. But all his problems came to an end with divine intervention.

In his meditation, Aurobindo had a vision of Rishi Agastya, one of the seven hermits of the Vedic culture, who guided him to go and establish his ashram at the same spot where Rishi Agastya had lived, meditated and had his ashram 15,000 years ago. According to ancient tradition, Rishi Agastya went to the south to spread Vedic lore, having been sent there by Shiva, and had established his ashram in Pondicherry. The rishi told Sri Aurobindo that if he went and meditated at that spot and established his ashram there, all his problems including his financial difficulties would be solved, and it would be easier for him to continue his sadhana. So the first temple of Aurobindo was established there, and he started practicing his sadhana. Soon the French Mirra, who later became Mother, came to Pondicherry and joined Aurobindo. She began taking care of everything including the administration and finances and became instrumental in materializing Aurobindo's dream. Today, Sri Aurobindo Ashram is affluent, with its own industries, school and township, and has become a modern-day spiritual city and a center for spiritual learning. It occupies half of Pondicherry.

The reason I am telling these stories is to emphasize how important it is to choose the right place. When the place is right, any kind of work will flourish there, but sometimes there are places on Earth where negativity exists in a more concentrated form. I have known of some such places that are very life-opposing, and where multiple suicides have taken place. There are many haunted houses in the world, also, where whoever goes to live is compelled to commit suicide, and in which many people have taken their lives. It is very difficult to do spiritual work among such vibrations. It is our great luck and the grace of higher blessings that we have always been provided with places that are helpful for meditation.

Asheesh Meditation Centre in Kathmandu is another place that holds a great spiritual importance and has a sweet spiritual past of its own. The secret of Asheesh was revealed to me by Osho many years ago, and I have also seen it in my own meditation and visions. It has been confirmed by many mystics, but I have kept it to myself until today because I was not allowed to speak of it. I am close to eighty years now, and we all have a limited time here on this physical plane. My master has now given me permission to reveal this secret so that the coming generations can understand the significance of this place and preserve it for future generations as a spiritual center.

My father was a simple and honest government officer and served as private secretary to four prime ministers of the country between Bikram Sambat 2008 and 2014. Later, he also became Bada Hakim, or the Chief District Officer, and his salary was increased to 450 rupees. In spite of his highbrow positions, my father only had the money to purchase land in Kathmandu once, when he found a cheap deal of 1,527 sqm for just 1,800 rupees. It was the land beside the Tri-Chandra College, and was owned by a farming woman. My father had paid the money, and only the formal transfer of the property remained.

In those days, my father was secretary to Prime Minister Matrika Prasad Koirala who was fond of Indian food. He used to come to our place to eat as my mother was a very good cook. When my father told the PM about the land he had purchased, he scolded my father, "Who builds a house in a shit pond like that? It is farm land and people are always shitting there. If you want to build a house, buy something in Baneshwor. It's a good residential area."

My father immediately went to the farmer and asked her to return the money. She said that as she had already bought a buffalo out of it, she would pay us back in daily rations of milk. Existence had other plans for us, and Matrika Babu was only a medium in the picture. If that land had been acquired, my father would never have purchased the land where Asheesh is today. The farm land later became prime real estate, and we bought a very small fragment of it for millions of rupees. Today, Osho Bhawan, the building that houses my BDA office, is located on that land.

After my father retired from his government job, he started an import and export business. In just a few years, he was able to earn more money than he had earnt in his whole life with his high-position government job. Then he was able to purchase the land in Tahachal where Asheesh is located today. The land is about 2,550 sqm and is located right behind the Soaltee Oberoi's compound where Osho stayed for forty-five days when he visited Nepal in 1986. Tahachal then was situated on the outskirts of Kathmandu and had a very sparse population when we bought the land. Now it has been transformed into an upmarket suburb, with huge bungalows and apartment buildings.

Situated at the base of the hill on which stands the great Buddhist stupa, Swayambhu, which is believed to be one of the main sources of Kathmandu's spiritual energy, Tahachal is connected with many mystical and esoteric myths, mostly relating to the great naags, or serpent gods, that are believed to reside there. Strangely, a large black snake has lived at Asheesh since the early days and can sometimes be spotted slithering around the temple garden.

Neo-Sannyas had already started in 1970, and despite Osho's invitation, I had missed it due to my past bad karmas. When I went to take sannyas with him in 1972, he was staying at the Woodlands apartments in Bombay. Osho declined my request and told me that as I was already in the last year of my engineering degree, I should complete that first. Then he asked me if I had a house in Kathmandu. I told him that we only had land, but not a house. He gave me two conditions that I had to fulfill: one, complete my engineering studies, and two, build a small house. Only then would he initiate me. I told him my father's business had already folded, and we did not have the money to build the house. He said to first build a small house, and only then come back.

It took me two years to fulfill his conditions. We built a small single-storey house with just two bedrooms and a kitchen, and immediately after the house-warming celebration, I went to Osho to take sannyas. He was very happy when I told him I had built a house, and he gave me sannyas. I had finished my duty of fulfilling his conditions, and now I just wanted to stay with him. I was in absolute bliss living around him, and although I was already married, I forgot about everything at home, and kept extending my stay at the ashram. When a telegram arrived to announce the death of my grandfather, I couldn't even identify with it.

When Laxmi reported this to Osho, he called me and asked me to go back. I told him I did not want to go back and was in immense bliss in Pune. He said I had to go back to open a meditation center in Nepal, at my house. When I said there was no space, he asked me to open the center in my bedroom, and put a board outside the house with the name of the center on it. Really, I did not want to go back, so I told him I was not financially sound enough to run a center, and my room was very small. Furthermore, it would be futile, as nobody knew him in Nepal, and no one was interested in meditation and would ever come to the center.

Osho instantly rebuked me, "You don't know about Kathmandu's spiritual potential. One day, it will become my spiritual headquarters. I am asking you to put your energy into it, and you have a very bad habit of putting your mind to it. Just do what I ask you to do and stop using your head." He forcefully put a certificate in my hands, on which was written in his handwriting "Asheesh Rajneesh Meditation Centre". Reluctantly I accepted the certificate after Osho hammered me with his zen stick.

So I went back to Kathmandu, put up a board outside on the wall, and started the meditation center in my room. My father was very angry as the house was very small, and after I went to the office each day, my parents would throw the board away. If someone came to enquire about the center, they would say there was no center at the house. With all these struggles, somehow Asheesh Rajneesh Meditation Centre came into existence.

Today, the same one-storey house is a two-storey bungalow with a beautiful garden and a huge terrace. The ground floor houses the meditation hall, and the other rooms are used by the sannyasin family that runs the center. The upper floor is usually kept closed, except on special celebration days, and still has the room and a bathroom that were made specifically for Osho. The garden is well maintained and has two beautiful temples for Buddha and Osho, the Osho temple being the first in the world dedicated to the master.

In the forty-eight years since its inception, Asheesh has grown a very powerful buddhafield, and remains the source of inspiration for all the Osho communes and centers in Nepal. As soon as one enters the gates of Asheesh, a seasoned meditator can feel the denseness of the blanket of energy that surrounds Asheesh. It's like entering a completely different dimension. The energy that is there at Osho's temple, Osho's room and the meditation hall is sometimes even stronger than what can be felt at Tapoban.

Many mystical events happened at Asheesh even before the house was built. Before my father's business had collapsed, he had a plan for a bigger house, and had already laid the footings for it. Our neighbor, Mr Sharma, was a builder, and his wife was a simple innocent lady. Before the construction started, she recounted to me that every night she used to see a beautiful lady dressed in a red sari walk on the footings of the house. She explained that the lady was very radiant and beautiful and looked like a devi, or goddess. Mrs Sharma used to see her from her windows. At the time, we did not pay much attention to this, but many years later, I realized the significance of this phenomenon, and also came to know who the lady was.

Both of my parents had political connections, and many leaders, ministers and prime ministers used to visit them at our home. After turning it into a meditation center, I had even removed the sofas that my father had put in my room so there was no place where my parents could receive their guests. Later, when I earned some money, we added a big living room and a small room next to it. My room was becoming smaller every day for the growing number of people who were coming for meditation, so one day when my father had gone to Janakpur, I instantly captured the bigger room by shifting my bed there, and I moved the furniture of the living room into my now old bedroom. My father became very angry with me when he came back, but it was all worth it, as now I had a bigger space for meditation.

When we were constructing the big room, a large black snake used to come and rest at the same spot where we have placed Osho's chair today. The construction workers used to get scared and wanted to kill the snake. There is a commitment in our family not to kill snakes, so we instructed the workers to put it on a long stick and leave it outside in the garden. But the next day, the snake would come again and rest at the same place. Many years later, in my meditation, I had a vision of a man who came and asked me if I recognized him. When I said that I did not, he said he lived with me in the same house. I laughed and said, "I live here with my parents, nobody else lives here." To this, he laughed and replied, "I was living here even before your parents came to this place."

When I asked him who he was, he replied, "I am Naag Raj, king of the serpents."

When I recounted this to Osho, he said, "That's very good, much good will happen." He also instructed me not to disturb the snake, and every Monday, put out some milk for it near the place where it stays. To this day, Naag Raj still lives behind the Buddha temple and can sometimes be seen roaming around the gardens of Asheesh.

Once, it was the day of Diwali, and everyone in Kathmandu was getting ready to celebrate this festival of lights. At Asheesh, my mother was also preparing for the evening worship. Suddenly, my father's friend, Mr Shrestha, who had held high positions in the government, like my father, came through the gates with a friend. Mr Shrestha had an inclination towards Osho, and sometimes would come for meditation. As soon as he entered, he exclaimed, "I was pulled by something to your center today, and I want to meditate. I had a big fight with my family when I was leaving the house. Now teach us some meditation." He was from a well-known Newar family in Kathmandu, and Diwali is a big festival, so I could understand his family being angry when he simply left during the festival. When I began teaching them Kundalini, my mother exclaimed, "What madness is this? You have to become a guru on the day of Diwali, too!"

The other man who accompanied Mr Shrestha was Chief of Nepal Electricity and had no interest in meditation. He said he would not meditate, so we sat him on a sofa in the meditation hall and started doing Kundalini. It was a very good session and both of us went into deep meditation. After an hour when we opened our eyes, we saw that the other man had fallen down and was on the floor, and it looked like he was in a deep trance. He was very frightened and his whole body was shivering. I got a little scared seeing his condition, so we helped him back onto the sofa and asked my mother for some warm milk. After drinking some milk, he finally came back to his senses. We asked him what had happened to him, to which he replied, "I was not interested in meditating, so I was looking at you guys. In the second stage, both of you were dancing, and then suddenly I saw Lord Vishnu also dancing with the two of you. I was fully awake, and I saw three of you dancing. He was looking at me and smiling. After some time, I couldn't tolerate this sight any more, and fainted." It was very difficult for us to get him to leave the ashram, as he kept shivering and shaking with fear.

When I was at Asheesh, I used to experiment with all kinds

of paranormal and esoteric methods. Sometimes I would contact different mystics by different methods and talk to them. When we contacted the mystic PKjee, invoking him at Asheesh, he also said it was a very pure place, and he felt very good when he came there. He said, "Your guru comes here every night and touches your forehead and gives you energy." This phenomenon I had experienced many times when I suddenly woke up and felt somebody's hand on my forehead. On one occasion when I was half asleep, I even caught hold of a hand touching my forehead, but as soon as I opened my eyes, it disappeared. But I still remember the feeling and the touch of holding that hand. PKjee also said, "When your master comes, he doesn't come alone, he is accompanied by many other elevated souls who come here and bless you and this place."

During the period 1974 to 1981, I had all kinds of mystical experiences and visions at Asheesh. I could see incidents that were going to happen, way ahead of time. Once, I saw a vision of a red army crossing the Himalayas and entering a country. I thought the Chinese were going to attack Nepal, and I even told this to my father and the then secretary of the king, Ranjan Raj Khanal, who used to come to Asheesh. He was a disciple of Shivapuri Baba, and a seasoned meditator himself. He was aware of my visions and also trusted them.

He became wary, and asked me, "Did you really see it?" But apparently, I had wrongly decoded my vision; a day later, the Russian Army, which is also a red army, crossed the Himalayas and captured Afghanistan.

It is believed in the East that you cannot see an enlightened master or an elevated soul in your dreams until they themselves wish to come and give you a message.

I always had a question about one incident involving Swami Vivekananda and his guru, Swami Ramakrishna Paramahamsa. When an inquisitive Vivekananda asked Ramakrishna if he had seen

God, Ramakrishna not only said yes, but also asked Vivekananda if he wanted to see God now. Vivekananda was baffled by this unexpected question, and had no answer at all. Ramakrishna, who was sitting on the bed, put his foot on Vivekananda's chest. Vivekananda instantly went into a deep satori. I was always curious, and kept asking how could just a touch give Vivekananda a glimpse of samadhi. One night when I was sleeping at Asheesh, Ramakrishna appeared in my dream and touched my forehead, and instantly I, also, went into a deep satori. Although I was asleep, I went into a real satori which lasted for some time.

On a similar occasion at Asheesh, I saw a vision during my meditation in which someone had planted a bomb under a bridge in a conspiracy to kill the then king, King Birendra, who was on a trip abroad at the time, and was soon to return. I even saw the location where the bomb was planted, and the face of the person who was the mastermind behind the conspiracy. The man was a political figure who I instantly recognized. King Birendra was a good leader and I had great affection for him, and I was very worried because in those days, all my visions used to come true. I told Osho about the vision, and he said not to get involved. I said that Birendra was a very good human, and pleaded with him to help the king. Osho listened to my plea, and said, "On the day of his arrival, you have a holiday and just meditate near my chair. I will try to help."

When the day came, I did as Osho had instructed. Somehow, the king's intelligence department was given a tip-off about the potential attack, and to everyone's surprise, at the last moment, the route of the royal carcade was changed and a completely unlikely route was used to transport the king to the palace.

Whenever a big accident was going to happen, I would see it beforehand in a vision. And every time an accident did happen somewhere, I saw many souls with wounded bodies coming to

Asheesh crying for help. I got very disturbed and scared by this, and when I consulted Osho about it, he said not to be scared and just pray for those departed souls. "They come asking for your help." These are just a few mystical incidents that I experienced when I was living at Asheesh, but there are many more esoteric incidents that happened there which I am not allowed to share here.

By 1981, my little house of two bedrooms, a hall and a kitchen was being swarmed by Rajneeshies. On Saturdays, there were more than a hundred people coming for satsang and then being served prasad and tea by my mother. It was not a big house, but we had a large front porch and garden where we were able to somehow accommodate all our visitors. But the visitors were increasing in numbers. Not only was it getting cramped, but also my parents who were living there were annoyed by the crowd and felt invaded. The house had just two bedrooms, one for my parents and one for my sister. The living room, which was larger than the other rooms, had been changed into my bedroom cum meditation hall and the center's office, so my parents had to receive all their guests in their bedroom or on the front porch, which was not a very pleasant experience for them.

Until 1981, my parents had been tolerant, but, as they say that every seven years a cycle is complete and a big change comes, soon we were to experience a big change in them. My parents were not regular meditators and they felt left out from the laughter and celebration of the other sannyasins. Osho sannyasins are usually very juicy and like to talk, laugh and make jokes. Many sannyasins used to hang out in the garden or on the porch after the meditations, and stay long-lost in their conversation and gossip. Sometimes we would start talking about Osho, and hours would pass without anyone moving. My family felt they had no private space and they had to tolerate and suffer because of me. They were pressuring me either to reduce the crowd or to take the center elsewhere.

At the same time, there was a group of Nepali sannyasins who were jealous of me and did not like me receiving so much attention from the VIPs who came to the ashram. They were making many complaints, one of which was that they did not feel free at the center as it was in somebody's private house. They believed the center should be moved from my house to another location. My parents, who had a traditional mindset, did not like the carefree and wild ways of sannyasins, and they also started to support the move. It was a push and pull situation where my parents wanted to push the center out of our house, and the sannyasins wanted to pull it out from there.

On June 1, 1981, while I was working in Hetauda, I received news from Kathmandu that after a small verbal conflict with my parents, a few sannyasins had moved the Asheesh Rajneesh Meditation Centre to another location. These sannyasins were always provoking my parents who were already in a vulnerable situation, and they just needed a reason to relocate Asheesh.

They had acquired a house for rent in Pulchowk for just 1,000 rupees a month and had immediately moved the ashram to that rented house. Later, I discovered that the reason for the cheap rent was because the house was haunted, and nobody wanted to stay there.

As coincidence would have it, the same day Asheesh was moved, I heard news from Pune that shocked me even more. That very day, Osho had left Pune for the USA.

Later, when Osho came to know of the center's move, he was not at all happy about it having been moved away from Tahachal. He told me I had to move the center back to my house, and that it should remain on the same property. He insisted I do it as soon as possible.

For various reasons, I was not able to move the center back for five and a half years. By 1987, I had made some money working at the BDA, and was able to add one more storey to our house. The plan was to move my parents upstairs, and have the whole ground floor for the meditation center. Asheesh had already been moved closer to Tahachal, and was now at Soalteemode. We had planned to move the center back to Asheesh as soon as the construction work was finished. On January 3, I had a strange dream. In the dream, Osho ordered me to move Asheesh back to Tahachal immediately. I told him the construction was not finished, and my family was still living there. Osho replied, "Do it immediately!" The next day, Swami Anand Ramesh came running to Asheesh, asking me, "What are you about to do?" He had also had a dream in which some other master told him I was going to do something important, and asked him to help me.

Somehow, we managed to pack everything from the center into a cart and took it all to my home in Tahachal. My father was very angry with us, and asked us what this madness was all about, and why I couldn't wait a few days. My sister's house was also under construction behind our house, and she said she would move into it as soon as it was completed and asked us to wait until then. I could not tell them I had a strict instruction from my master to move on that very day, because they would not have understood. The discussion turned into huge chaos, after which my father and sister remained angry with me for a very long time.

We had moved the center back to Tahachal on January 4, 1987, and what later came as an enormous surprise was the news I received that Osho had finally returned to the Pune ashram, after his stay in Bombay, on the very same day. The day Asheesh was moved from Tahachal, Osho went to America, and the very day Osho moved back into the Pune ashram, Asheesh returned to Tahachal. It is a spiritual mystery why these two events coincided exactly, and shows an uncanny connection between Osho and Asheesh.

There were many times when my parents wanted to sell

the property. They were constantly pestering me, and after a hard struggle, I would give up and take their proposal to Osho. Osho would immediately dismiss these proposals. He always insisted that the house should never be sold, and Asheesh should always remain at that Tahachal house. After Tapoban came into existence, my father argued, "Now that you guys have a big ashram, we should use the whole house for our own purpose." When I asked Osho during my contact with him, he reiterated, "Your family can do whatever they want on the upper floor, but the center will always remain on the ground floor."

Many mystical phenomena have taken place at Asheesh, and every evening as the night advances, and especially after midnight, one can feel a strong current of energy in the garden, the meditation hall and around the temples. It almost feels like there are some other people there, and it is a very heavy presence. Sometimes it almost gets scary. I have experienced that there is a gathering of non-physical elevated souls every night at Asheesh, and any sensitive person can feel it.

Just few months ago, Osho finally gave me permission to reveal the secret connection between him and Asheesh, and why he doesn't want it to be moved from there. As I am now in the advanced stage of my life, Osho wants it that even after I leave my body, Asheesh should always remain on the same land, and someday, even if a new building is constructed, the ground floor should always remain the meditation center. He also gave clear instructions that the two temples should always remain where they are, and never be removed or relocated.

Osho's last two lives were in Tibet. One was 700 years ago and the other was about 900 years ago. Publicly, Osho has only spoken about his last life which was 700 years ago, and has kept everything else a secret. Osho revealed to me that his life before these two lives was in Nepal where he was a meditator and was doing his sadhana living with a few disciples. The place where he was living and doing his sadhana was exactly where Asheesh is located today.

In 1981, I also had a vision in which I saw that he was living in a small hut in the exact spot where Osho's temple has been created. Back then, the temple was not there, and when I asked my master about it, he confirmed it was the exact spot where he lived and instructed me to build a temple there. Today, as I come closer to my departure from this plane, I am compelled to reveal what I have kept secret for so many years so that sannyasins understand the significance of this energy space and preserve it in its purest form for the coming generations.

Asheesh was like my mystery school where I grew as a meditator, met many remarkable mystics and had some of the most esoteric experiences of my life, which my mind cannot comprehend even today. Although Asheesh is housed on a property my family purchased, I am fully aware that it doesn't belong to me, and it was indeed a great blessing and grace that my family could partake in this great existential phenomenon of creating a place like Asheesh.

Asheesh literally means 'blessing', and it was my master's great compassion and blessing that he allowed me to live here and serve this energy space. As per the instructions of my master, I want Asheesh to always remain on the ground floor of my Tahachal house. My family members can use the upper floor, and if ever the house is demolished and a new structure built, the ground floor should always be dedicated to the meditation center. This will bring great fortune and blessings to my family members. The two temples of Buddha and Osho are also there for a reason and should never be demolished.

Asheesh belongs to every soul that wants to enter the deeper realms of self-seeking. It belongs to every seeker who wants to go through the arduous task of self-transformation. It belongs to every lover of Osho who wants to come closer to him and get a taste of his enlightened consciousness. It gives me great joy to see that today it is being run by a family of devoted Osho sannyasins, and regular meditation has taken place there every day for the last forty-eight years, with satsangs conducted every Wednesday. As the foundation stone of Osho's movement in Nepal, Asheesh has played and always will play a significant role in spreading Osho's vision of meditation. I am fully assured that one day it will be recognized as a pilgrimage destination for Osho lovers, and thousands will come from all over the world to experience its beautiful energy.

OSHO BOOKS

So far Osho Tapoban has published 181 books. Out of that 88 Books in English published by Osho Tapoban

BOOKS IN ENGLISH

1. Meditation: the First &Last Freedom
2. In Search of the Miraculous
3. Meditation the Art of Ecstasy
4. Tantra the Supreme Understanding
5. I am the Gate
6. The Silent Explosion
7. Books I Have Loved
8. The Psychology of Esoteric
9. From Sex to Superconsciousness
10. My Way the Way of the White Cloud
11. The Dhammapada-Vol-1
12. Come Follow Me-Vol-1
13. Communism-Zen Fire en Wind
14. Why I am Not Against Sex
15. The New Man-The Only Hope for the Future
16. A New Vision of Women's Liberation
17. The Golden Future
18. Seriousness is a Disease
19. Life, Love, Laughter
20. Love Makes You Real
21. Money Can't Buy Love
22. Silence is the Only Answer
23. Sex Money &Power
24. Priest &Politicians: Mafia of the Soul
25. I Teach Religiousness Not Religion
26. Tantra Spirituality &Sex
27. The Tantra Experience
28. The Alchemy of Gratitude
29. Mysteries Behind Sannyas &Mala(New Compilation)
30. Vigyan Bhairav Tantra (The Book Of The Secrets) Vol-1
31. Vigyan Bhairav Tantra (The Book of the Secrets) Vol-2
32. Vigyan Bhairav Tantra (The Book of the Secrets) Vol-3
33. Vigyan Bhairav Tantra (The Book of the Secrets) Vol-4
34. Vigyan Bhairav Tantra (The Book of the Secrets) Vol-5
35. Vigyan Bhairav Tantra (The Book of the Secrets) 112 Techniques
36. The Heart Sutra

37. The Diamond Sutra
38. The Alpha &the Omega Vol-1
39. The Discipline of Transcendence Vol-1
40. Mysteries of Meditation
41. Love, Relationship &Marriage
42. Beware of Socialism
43. Satsang (Communion With the Master)
44. Nothing Fails Like Success
45. From Misery to Happiness
46. Revolution in Education
47. Sex: A Quantum Leap From Sin to Fun
48. Orgasm is Always Nonsexual
49. Death-The Greatest Fiction
50. The Rebel—The Salt of the Very Earth
51. Beyond the Frontiers of the Mind
52. The Revolution
53. The Great Challenge
54. The Secrets of Seven Chakras &Kundalini Energy
55. Ten Non Commandments
56. The Book of Wisdom
57. Neither Easy Nor Difficult, Be Simple
58. So Much To Do, So Little Time
59. Silence: The Magical Door to Eternity
60. Reincarnation, Karma & Destiny
61. Laughter: The Best Medicine Part-I
62. Laughter: The Best Medicine Part-II
63. Love &Freedom
64. Osho on Basic Human Rights
65. Parenting & Children
66. Walking on Your Own Path
67. India My Love

SMALL BOOKS IN ENGLISH

68. Who is Osho? Why He Visited this Planet?
69. Unknown Life of Osho &Jesus
70. Flight of the Alone to the Alone
71. How Meditation Really Works?
72. How to Get Help From Advanced Soul?
73. Sex—Quotations From Osho
74. Awareness—Quotations From Osho
75. Creativity—Quotations From Osho

76. Sexuality is Ugly Not Sex
77. Take the Risk to be True
78. Life is a Mystery
79. Roots of Suffering
80. Don't be a Lawyer; Be a Lover
81. Maturity & Aging
82. Vegetarianism
83. Essentials of Neo-Sannyas

BOOK BY SWAMI ANAD ARUN
84. Lone Seeker, Many Masters
85. In Wonder With Osho
86. Panchasheel
87. Encounter with the Mystics

SPECIAL EDITION
87. Art of Enlightenment (HD- Colorful)
88. Art of Enlightenment (PB- Economic Ed.)

ओशो पुस्तकें

अब तक ओशो तपोवन द्वारा 181 पुस्तकें प्रकाशित की गई हैं।
इनमें से 93 पुस्तकें हिन्दी में प्रकाशित हुई हैं।

हिन्दी में पुस्तकें
१. जिन खोजा तिन पाइयां
२. ध्यानयोग प्रथम और अंतिम मुक्ति
३. गीता दर्शन-भाग एक (अध्याय एक और दो)
४. गीता दर्शन-अध्याय तीन
५. गीता दर्शन-अध्याय चार
६. गीता दर्शन-अध्याय पांच
७. गीता दर्शन-अध्याय छ
८. गीता दर्शन-अध्याय सात
९. गीता दर्शन-अध्याय आठ
१०. गीता दर्शन-अध्याय नौ
११. गीता दर्शन-अध्याय दस
१२. गीता दर्शन-अध्याय ग्यारह
१३. गीता दर्शन-अध्याय बारह
१४. गीता दर्शन-अध्याय तेरह
१५. गीता दर्शन-अध्याय चौदह

१६. गीता दर्शन-अध्याय पंद्रह
१७. गीता दर्शन-अध्याय सोलह
१८. गीता दर्शन-अध्याय सत्ररह
१९. गीता दर्शन-अध्याय अठारह
२०-३२. एस धम्मो सनंतनो : भाग-१-१२
३३. शिव सूत्र
३४. अष्टावक्र महागीता-भाग एक
३५. अष्टावक्र महागीता-भाग दो
३६. अष्टावक्र महागीता-भाग तीन
३७. अष्टावक्र महागीता-भाग चार
३८. अष्टावक्र महागीता-भाग पांच
३९. अष्टावक्र महागीता-भाग छ
४०. शिक्षा में क्रांति
४१. ध्यान विज्ञान
४२. संभोग से समाधी की ओर
४३. समाजवाद से सावधान
४४. गहरे पानी पैठ
४५. साधना पथ
४६. सर्वसार उपनिषद
४७. एक ओंकार सतनाम
४८. अंतर्यात्रा
४९. व्यस्त जीवन में ईश्वर की खोज
५०. ध्यान एक वैज्ञानिक दृष्टि
५१. ज्योतिष अद्वैत का विज्ञान
५२. नारी और क्रान्ति
५३. मैंने राम रतन धन पायो
५४. संन्यास और माला के रहस्य
५५. विज्ञान भैरव तंत्र
५६. स्वप्न का मनोविज्ञान
५७. नारद भक्ति सूत्र
५८. हंसना एक महाऔषधी
५९. एक ही दुःसंग, मन का संग
६०. बुद्धत्व के सूत्र
६१. कठोपनिषद
६२. निर्वाण उपनिषद
६३. कैवल्य उपनिषद
६४. केनोउपनिषद
६५. ईशावास्योपनिषद
६६. मैं मृत्यु सिखाता हूं
६७. मन से मुक्ति मोक्ष है

हिन्दी में पुस्तिकाएं

६८. मेडिकेसन से मेडिटेसन
६९. मन के पार
७०. मन का महाभारत
७१. गरीबी और समाजवाद
७२. प्रेम और विवाह
७३. जनसंख्या विस्फोट
७४. संसार ही मोक्ष बन जाए
७५. युवक और यौन
७६. यौन—जीवन उर्जा का आयाम
७७. आज की राजनीति
७८. क्रांति की वैज्ञानिक प्रक्रिया
७९. विष से भरी महत्वाकांक्षा
८०. प्रगतिशिल कौन
८१. काम से राम तक
८२. ध्यान के रहस्य
८३. शाकाहार—सुसंस्कृत व्यक्तियों का आहार
८४. बिन गुरु नहीं ठौर
८५. दुख हमारा आयोजन,
आनन्द हमारी नियति
८६. नव-संन्यास के आधार-सूत्र

स्वामी आनन्द अरुण द्वारा रचित

८७. पंचशील (संवर्धित संस्करण)
८८. संतो के संग

नेपाली में प्रकाशित ५ पुस्तकें
स्वामी आनन्द अरुण द्वारा
नेपाली में रचित साहित्य

८९. संत दर्शन
९०. अंतरयात्रा
९१. संत गाथा
९२. अचम्म जो मैले देखें
९३. पंचशील

BOOKS BY SWAMI ANAND ARUN

IN ENGLISH

IN NEPALI

IN HINDI

FORTHCOMING

Latest arrival in Nepali

स्वामी आनन्द अरुणका नयाँ पुस्तक

ओशोसँग बिताएका अविस्मरणीय क्षणहरुको सँगालो

अचम्म जो मैले देखेँ

स्वामी आनन्द अरुण द्वारा रचित हिन्दी में
नवीन प्रकाशन

संतो के संग

बोधिसत्त्व
स्वामी आनन्द अरुण

आध्यात्मिक जगत की उच्च चेतनाओं के साथ सत्संग और उनकी कृपा का जीवंत और हृदयस्पर्शी वर्णण।

Books are available in all leading book stores in Nepal and Osho centres around the world.

For details:
OSHO TAPOBAN, Nagarjuna Hills, Kathmandu, Nepal
Ph: +977- 9847807082(viber/WhatApp), +977-1-5112012/13
Email: otpublication@gmail.com, www.tapoban.com
facebook.com/swamianandarun, facebook.com/oshotapoban1

OSHO TAPOBAN COMMUNE AND OTHER KEY COMMUNES AROUND THE WORLD AFFILIATED TO OSHO TAPOBAN

OSHO TAPOBAN

An International Commune & Forest Retreat Centre
Nagarjuna Hills, Kathmandu, Nepal, Ph: +977- 9847807082, (viber/whatsup), +977-1-5112012/13 Email: otpublication@gmail.com, www.tapoban.com, facebook.com/swamianandarun, facebook.com/oshotapoban1

OSHO UPABAN SPIRITUAL VILLAGE

Dobilla, Pokhara 17, +977-61-692030, 9846025478,
yoganandswami@gmail.com, www.oshoupaban.com

OSHO JETBAN SPIRITUAL VILLAGE
Mahelbari, Lumbini Ph: +977-71-580046
jetbancommune@gmail.com, www.oshojetban.com

OSHO TATHAGAT ASHRAM
Banganga, Kapilvastu Ph: +977-9857010123
oshotathagatcommune@gmail.com

OSHO VENUBAN COMMUNE

Gumdi-6, Dhading

Ph: +977-10692237, 9741006494

OSHO PALPA ASHRAM

Prabhas, Palpa

Contact: +977 9867295339 (Viber)

OSHO NIRVANA ASHRAM
San Diego, CA
(760) 407-6746

OSHO KAIVALYA DHAM
1564 FM 1310, Denison TX 75020
Tel: (469) 712 OSHO, (214) 395 6857

OSHO
OSHO
NEVER BORN NEVER DIED

Meditation
at Indoor Osho Samadhi

Evening Satsang at Meditation Hall

Sannyas at Osho Tapoban

Satsang at Kabir Mandir

21-day OSHO INTENSIVE TRANSFORMATION MEDITATION RETREAT at Tapoban

1st Week Shuddi:
1-7 of every english month Osho No-Mind therapy to cleanse the mind.

2nd week Sadhana:
9-15 of every english month Osho Intensive Meditation camp for inner transformation.

3rd Week Shunyata:
17-23 of every english month Osho Neo-Vipassana to go beyond the body and the mind.

(6 meditation session everyday including morning yoga and evening silence at Nirvana Grove)

*You can also participate in only 1 week of the any 3 weeks of the package. For details and booking contact us at
Ph: +977- 9847807082 (viber/whatsup), +977-1-5112012/13
email: osho.tapoban@gmail.com
web: www.tapoban.com